Repairing Attachment Injuries in Close Relationships

This book is an essential guide for those who have experienced an attachment injury in an important relationship and are struggling to process their hurt and betrayal or to imagine rebuilding the trust in this precious bond.

Dr Clare Rosoman guides readers on a path towards healing and recovery, informed by attachment science and emotionally focused therapy. Viewing close relationships as attachment bonds, this book examines betrayal and how these painful events can create an "attachment injury," which redefines the relationship bond as insecure. It offers strategies for healing relationships and restoring security in connection, and looks at many different types of attachment injuries including those that can happen in monogamous or non-monogamous relationships. As Rosoman suggests, relationships can emerge even stronger after being rocked by broken trust.

This book is a vital resource for therapists looking to facilitate healing and growth in their clients in individual, couple, or family therapy, as well as for individuals seeking an encouraging self-help resource.

Clare Rosoman, D.Psych., is a clinical psychologist in Brisbane, Australia. She is the author of *An Emotionally Focused Guide to Relationship Loss: Life After Love* and co-author of *An Emotionally Focused Workbook for Relationship Loss: Healing Heartbreak Session by Session.*

"Love hurts, and it also heals. Whether you have been hurtful, or hurt, or some combination of both, Dr Clare Rosoman once again beautifully translates the wisdom of attachment science, offering readers a guide from injury to repair, into ongoing growth, and resilience. This book is a must read for anyone wishing to understand why love hurts, and the roadmap for healing."

Dr T. Leanne Campbell, ICEEFT Certified Trainer in Emotionally Focused Therapy (EFT); co-author with Dr Sue Johnson of the first text on EFT as applied to individuals, *A Primer for Emotionally Focused Individual Therapy (EFIT): Cultivating Fitness and Growth in Every Client (Routledge, 2022)*; co-author of *Becoming an Emotionally Focused Therapist: The Workbook (Routledge, 2022)*

"In *Repairing Attachment Injuries in Close Relationships: An Emotionally Focused Guide to Moving Beyond Betrayal* Dr Rosoman undertakes the brave task of guiding readers on a self-help journey through the pain and repair of broken trust in their most important attachment relationships. Utilizing a process, shown to be effective in a therapeutic context, Rosoman provides practical tools that equip readers with personal and relational agency for navigating a path towards healing. Rosoman's dedication and enthusiasm to offer tangible support and comfort to readers shattered by a wide range of relational ruptures shines a beacon of hope through every page. The book is a treasure of unshakeable hope for the repair of shattered trust in familial, friendship, and romantic bonds, and for growing through grieving, where wounds are beyond repair."

Lorrie Brubacher, author of *Stepping into Emotionally Focused Therapy: Key Ingredients of Change (2nd ed.) and Workouts for Stepping into Emotionally Focused Therapy: Exercises to Strengthen Your Practice*; Trainer and Director of the Carolina Center for Emotionally Focused Therapy; adjunct, UNC Greensboro

"This is Clare's quintessential book. As a seasoned author, and blending science and humanness, Clare's writing offers her readers honest reflections of what is needed to repair a love relationship, a lovely invitation to heal, and many clear glimpses into the science behind what makes healing from a rupture in trust possible. Give yourself the gift of this book. You will feel seen, heard, and understood as you make your way through these pages.

You will gain clarity and depth about yourself and your relationship that will serve you for decades to come."

Kathryn Rheem, Ed.D., LMFT, ICEEFT Certified Trainer, Supervisor & Therapist. Co-author: *An Emotionally Focused Workbook for Relationship Loss: Healing Heartbreak Session By Session (2023) and Becoming an Emotionally Focused Therapist: The Workbook* (2nd) (2022)

"Clare Rosoman has done it again! She has captured both the emotional anguish and process of healing relationship wounds in a highly relatable, inclusive book. You will appreciate Dr Rosoman's clarity in demystifying relationship ruptures and offering step-by-step tools to guide partners in repairing these hurts. A must have book where she walks alongside you with deep care, empathy, and encouragement to keep going so you can mend and revitalize your most precious relationships."

Veronica Kallos-Lilly, Ph.D., Certified EFT Trainer & Therapist, and contributing author of *An Emotionally Focused Workbook for Couples* and *Becoming an Emotionally Focused Therapist*

"In *Repairing Attachment Injuries in Close Relationships*, Clare Rosoman offers individuals, couples, and families a clear guide for dealing with attachment injuries – those events that betray the bond in a relationship. The pain that can come with attachment injuries can linger and become a source of corrosion in a relationship if not tended to. The breadth of material Clare covers is thorough, grounded in clinical experience and research, and, most importantly, is accessible for people to work on healing relationships that matter to them most. With a grounding in attachment theory and emotion, the clear path that Clare lays out for recovery offers hope for healing where hope may not seem possible. This clear pathway to a healing that offers specifics for both the person who was injured and the person who may have caused harm, makes it possible for those who have been through an attachment injury to understand how they can recover together, and ultimately, improve their relationship. Clare lays out the ideas clearly and offers exercises and tasks that allows for self-pacing, provides concrete ways for each person to communicate how they are dealing with each step in recovery, and strategies for staying on task throughout the process. For anyone who has been through an attachment injury, this book is a must for all who were involved!"

Dr Robert Allan, *School of Psychology, University of Roehampton*

Repairing Attachment Injuries in Close Relationships

An Emotionally Focused Guide to Moving Beyond Betrayal

Clare Rosoman

Routledge
Taylor & Francis Group
NEW YORK AND LONDON

Designed cover image: Clare Rosoman

First published 2025
by Routledge
605 Third Avenue, New York, NY 10158

and by Routledge
4 Park Square, Milton Park, Abingdon, Oxon, OX14 4RN

Routledge is an imprint of the Taylor & Francis Group, an informa business

© 2025 Clare Rosoman

The right of Clare Rosoman to be identified as author of this work has
been asserted in accordance with sections 77 and 78 of the Copyright,
Designs and Patents Act 1988.

ISBN: 978-1-032-73879-6 (hbk)
ISBN: 978-1-032-73876-5 (pbk)
ISBN: 978-1-003-46649-9 (ebk)

DOI: 10.4324/9781003466499

Typeset in Sabon
by codeMantra

Access the Support Material: www.routledge.com/9781032738765

Support Material
This book contains supplementary material, which can be photocopied
from the back of the book. This material is also available for free digital
download online. Please visit www.routledge.com/9781032738765 and
click on the link that says Support Material. A link to the supplementary
material will appear.

Contents

About the Author

Clare Rosoman is a clinical psychologist and ICEEFT certified trainer in emotionally focused therapy (EFT) from Brisbane, Australia. She is the Director of the Brisbane Centre for EFT, where she teaches EFT to therapists, and of a psychology practice named the Brisbane Centre for Attachment and Relationships. Clare has spoken nationally and internationally on attachment, relationships, and EFT. She believes in the power of attachment and connection for all people, in all relationships, regardless of culture, structure, or identity. Clare is happiest when helping people to build secure connections and when inspiring other therapists in their work. Clare is the author of two resource books for therapists and the self-help book named *An Emotionally Focused Guide to Relationship Loss: Life After Love*. Along with Dr Kathryn D. Rheem, Clare is the co-author of *An Emotionally Focused Workbook for Relationship Loss: Healing Heartbreak Session by Session*. Clare is continually motivated by the power of EFT, grateful to Dr Sue Johnson for her vision, and remains committed to sharing this most amazing model of therapy with the world.

Acknowledgements

I would like to acknowledge Dr Susan Johnson for her outstanding contribution to the adult attachment literature and for her pioneering work in developing emotionally focused therapy (EFT). Sue created a revolution in relationship and couple therapy, centring emotion and attachment in how we shape and maintain loving bonds. She gave us a roadmap to connect with the EFT model, which profoundly influenced the field of relationship therapy and positively impacted people all over the world. Through her development of the Attachment Injury Resolution Model, Sue provided us with a clear path to the restoration of loving bonds, providing fragile hope for shattered ties. I am so grateful to have learned from Sue and to have been inspired by her throughout my career. She has left us with a remarkable legacy to uphold.

I would also like to acknowledge my family for their unwavering support and, especially my husband, Nicholas, for his belief (and proofreading) throughout yet another all-consuming project. Creating in this way would never be possible without this wonderful encouragement and fortification. I am truly grateful for the special humans in my life.

Importantly, I would like to acknowledge the collective wisdom of the special people who share their pain and their love and allow me to see into their hearts when they enter my therapy space. This book is an assembly of learnings built over time, enabled by the openness and generosity of the wonderful humans I have been lucky enough to walk beside. I hope that your hardship and bravery is honoured in this book and lives on to assist others.

Foreword

When I first met Dr Clare Rosoman, I knew she was a special kind of psychologist and relationship expert. She was so clear-minded and competent, but warm too. She spoke the truth, gently, clearly, warmly, and I knew I had to get to know her. Over the last several years, I have come to know Clare as a wonderful person and a different kind of expert. She is a brilliant expert who has not lost touch with her humanity. She has earned all the expertise and credibility a professional can have but when talking with her and reading her book, it feels like she is right there with me. Not sitting a bit away from me, as if me, my pain, my suffering, might be too much for her. She's sitting right beside me with an open heart. She is *with* me in a way that few experts allow themselves to be – as real humans.

This book, *Repairing Attachment Injuries in Close Relationships: An Emotionally Focused Guide to Moving Beyond Betrayal*, is her quintessential book. She has always been an excellent writer and an author grounded in science, theory, and knowledge. This book blends science and humanness and, as a seasoned author, Clare's writing offers us – her readers – honest reflections of what is needed to repair a love relationship, a lovely invitation to heal, and many clear glimpses into the science behind what makes healing from a rupture in trust possible.

A couple of years ago, when Clare and I co-wrote a workbook on healing from relationship loss, I shared an analogy I learned from a doctor early in life that she has threaded throughout this book. As you may know, when you break a bone in your body, calcium grows on the outside of the break to provide protection while the healing of the bone happens from the inside out. Your bone knits itself together starting from the centre. The calcium mineral deposit called a callus provides protection, stability, and prevents further damage to the broken place. Interestingly, when the bone is fully healed, that protective calcium callus becomes part of your bone, which strengthens it. As a result, there is a literal reality to being stronger in the broken place after healing!

Part I of this book covers the underlying science of love and loving, including why it hurts so much when a rupture happens in relationships. Chapters 1–3 provide the overview needed to assess how this injury happened to you and to understand the process of healing ahead. Just like with a physical injury, Part I of this beautiful book will help you evaluate your emotional injury. With Clare's support and assistance, you will see where your pain lives on the inside of you, what makes it hurt more, and what you need for it to hurt less. You will gain clarity about yourself and your partner and the emotional communication pattern you have relied on within your relationship, which always plays a role in any relationship injury. You will learn about your emotions and unmet attachment needs, two primary fuels to all relationships' negative patterns.

Stabilisation for your relationship is the focus of Part II. Just like with other types of injuries, after evaluation comes stabilisation which allows for healing to start. In Chapters 4–6, Clare describes the elements needed for stabilisation and will help you learn the three key tasks that each of you need to accomplish to give healing in your relationship the best possible chance. As you may know from previous injuries over your life, stabilisation is the foundation upon which all healing happens. If we continue our old ways – in life and old patterns with our loved ones – we may never get the stabilisation needed to let the healing begin.

As soon as stabilisation starts, healing is possible. Upon stabilisation, your relationship has a chance to heal from the inside out, just like our broken bones and other injuries have done. Part III walks you through this evidence-based healing process called Attachment Injury Repair. In Chapters 7–9, Clare teaches exactly how to build a calcium envelope, so you are stronger in the broken places. Her methods are backed by rigorous science, which is clear and definitive. Thankfully, Clare is the expert on this science and has led thousands of people through this process as a relationship therapist!

The final part of this book, Chapters 10–12, sets you up for your future of continued growth (together or individually). If you have been able to repair together, Part IV of this book will help you maintain your newly earned connection with each other. All love relationships require emotional investment to remain alive, healthy, and strong. After doing the repair process, and with Clare's lovely voice encouraging you along, you will have the muscle memory to continue making the emotional investments needed. Much like a physical injury needs physiotherapy to gain strength and restore range of motion, your emotional injury and repair will need some continued attention to maintain your gains from the repair process. This might seem daunting to imagine now but, trust me, Clare's excellent direction will be with you, step by step. Clare has brilliantly broken important concepts into steps that are manageable, relevant, and efficient.

If you have realised that you are not going to repair your relationship with your partner, these final chapters will help you grieve and heal individually. While very painful, being brave enough to grieve will help to heal your heart, which is such an important step for any future love relationship you may have. Healing happens, individually and together. The most important outcome of this book and the process she has articulated is that you get the healing you need! We all suffer, but due to Clare's book, nobody needs to suffer alone.

Give yourself the gift of this book. You will feel seen, heard, and understood as you make your way through these pages. You will gain clarity and depth about yourself and your relationship that will serve you for decades to come.

Kathryn Rheem, Ed.D., LMFT
ICEEFT Certified Trainer, Supervisor & Therapist
Co-author: *An Emotionally Focused Workbook for Relationship Loss: Healing Heartbreak Session By Session* (2023) and *Becoming an Emotionally Focused Therapist: The Workbook* (2nd) (2022).

Introduction

If you have read any of my other books, you will know that I admit to being a hopeless romantic. As a relationship therapist, I am wholeheartedly in the business of maintaining healthy and happy relationships and I am eternally optimistic about the resilience of humans. I have witnessed first-hand the power of secure connections with those who matter most. It feeds my soul to see people create and maintain loving bonds. I literally fist-pump when I see people form deep, loving bonds in front of my eyes. It is an awe-inspiring sight – one that I feel privileged to witness. Yet, I have focused much of my professional life on what happens when relationships go wrong. I suppose I am pragmatic in the sense that creating secure love is no easy task. As humans who love, we also hurt. To fully open your heart to another involves a risk so great, that it is no wonder that stories and songs have been written about love and pain since time immemorial. Love and pain are indeed, two sides of the same coin.

Personally, and professionally, I have borne witness to the immense pain that comes with the loss of loving bonds. I have seen and experienced the utter devastation of betrayal in close bonds. *And* I have witnessed the wondrous human capacity for healing and growth that can be born from the wreckage of those broken bonds. I have seen people lean into pain and share it in ways that facilitate growth as individuals and together, to heal their bond from damaged trust. So, considering this, I remain eternally optimistic about the resilience of the human spirit and the power of loving bonds to heal and strengthen – even when the hurt is raw and unbearably alive; even when it all feels hopeless. I believe that hurts can be healed and those involved can emerge stronger, wiser, and more connected for all they have survived. As I said, I am indeed a hopeless romantic.

The first thing I want you to know is that *it is possible to heal your bond*. You might think I'm mad, but I need to stress that some people emerge from the wreckage *stronger* for this injury. Although healing may feel hopelessly risky, torturously complicated, and utterly impossible right now, it *is* possible to restore security in your relationship. It takes work and

DOI: 10.4324/9781003466499-1

it takes commitment from all involved, but it *is* possible. You might have received messages about the futility of even trying – that once your trust has been broken – nothing will ever be the same again. This well-meaning advice, while sometimes the case, is certainly not the rule. For those who have been terribly hurt, the protective part of you and those around you might urge you to steer clear of this relationship and to guard your heart from further pain. For those who have been hurtful to someone you care deeply about, you might feel that there is nothing you can do to make things right. You might be feeling utterly hopeless about your ability to stay in this relationship. This is totally understandable, and you might indeed come to the conclusion that this relationship cannot be healed. Just know that if you arrive at such a decision conscious that you took your time to carefully process this pain, then it is a more trustworthy decision. However, there is another part of you that has picked up this book. A part that is not ready to give up on this relationship, that is hopeful for change. That part is not ready to walk away from this relationship. I hope to feed and nurture that hope with practical tools, backed up by research and sound theory to guide you through the recovery process, should you want this, and should your partner be willing to join you in healing. As you work through this book (and require that same level of investment from your partner), you will follow a path to healing that many have followed before you. I will be there with you, as I have with so many of the special humans I have been privileged to work with. I will help you to find some answers, to have a map to follow, and practical tools to restore the security in your loving bond. *I can't guarantee that it will save your relationship, and I can't say it will be easy, but I can promise that you will grow from the process.*

My mission in writing this book is to help you to navigate this body blow to your relationship and to emerge stronger for it. I will give you the knowledge and tools to work through this life-altering event and to hopefully restore security in your bond. I will arm you with up-to-date information about human relationships and attachment theory, particularly about the nature of attachment injuries and their impact on the security of loving bonds. I will provide practical strategies as well as self-reflection exercises for you and your partner to work through as you process pain and work towards repairing the trust in your close relationship. This book provides a path to healing and recovery, informed by attachment science and Emotionally Focused Therapy. It aims to empower you to restore broken trust, to guide you as you do the work required to rebuild your attachment bond, and to strengthen it moving forward. For those who are unable to rebuild your bond and decide to separate or to reconfigure your relationship, this book will support you in processing this loss and in moving forward in ways that honour the history of the relationship and the individuals within it.

Types of hurts

Many books about betrayal in close relationships focus on affairs in monogamous relationships. While this is very important and extremely common, it mattered to me to look more broadly at a range of hurts that people can experience in their close relationships. Affairs in monogamous couples are devastating, but so too are abandonments in times of need, violated boundaries in non-monogamous relationships, and betrayals in friendships. Broken trust can be acquired in a myriad of different ways. I wanted to explore many different types of attachment injuries, including those that can happen in families and in close friendships, as well as those that can arise in monogamous relationships and non-monogamous relationships. For that reason, I will focus on four types of attachment injuries that can occur in close relationships. My hope is that this will encapsulate a wider range of hurts and be relevant for more people. This comes from the wisdom of attachment theory that tells us that relational bonds are bonds of the heart, that we need many attachment figures in our lives, and that a rupture of trust experienced in a close bond is as real and painful as physical pain. It forever changes us, and it can be an opportunity for growth.

This book is written for those who are struggling with broken trust and the fallout of betrayal in a relationship that matters to them. It is for:

- Partners who are reeling from the discovery of a betrayal
- People who are hurt and are looking to reach a place of forgiveness
- Those who have been hurtful to someone they love and want to make amends
- People who are hoping to strengthen their relationship into the future after a rupture to trust
- Partners who are leaving or redefining their relationship after a hurt
- Partners where there have been multiple hurts in both directions that need healing
- Partners who are struggling with secrets, lies, and trust issues
- Family members wanting to break intergenerational patterns of hurt and poor communication
- Friends wanting to strengthen their connection after a falling-out
- Therapists who want to support their clients in the attachment injury repair process

Language of betrayal

I have thought about how to best describe hurts in close relationships and how to refer to the parties involved in ways that encapsulate each person's experience without judging or labelling it negatively. This is tricky, and the best I have come up with is to describe one person as the "hurt" party and the other as the "hurtful" party. For some, this will be clear and straightforward and for others, this might feel overly simplistic. I acknowledge that hurt and betrayal in bonded human relationships is rarely as simple as one "hurt" person and another "hurtful" person; however, I feel I need to use these terms for the concepts to translate clearly. Please be assured that we will spend time looking at the intricacy of hurt and betrayal in relationships and how these hurts are often bidirectional and multi-factorial. It is my hope that this will honour both peoples' experiences and the layered and complex nature of attachment injuries.

I will use the term "partner" to convey the mostly dyadic nature of hurts (i.e., involving two people) and in acknowledgement that the vast majority of hurts and breaches of trust occur in our closest relationships, often romantic partnerships. This runs the risk of overlooking hurts that occur in non-romantic relationships (such as platonic friendships and families), and narrowing the impact of an attachment injury to only two people, when in multi-partnered relationships, there may be more than two people involved. When I talk about partners or interpersonal interactions in a way that indicates only two members, that will fit for couples, but my hope is that it also fits for the many pairs inside a multi-partnered system, each pair being its own microsystem with its own special structure within the larger group. I hope that the term "partner" can be seen as a way of describing two parties who have impacted each other regardless of the nature of their loving bond. I hope that this can include family and platonic friendships as well as romantic relationships. We know that the greater the investment in a relationship, the more that is at stake when trust is broken. So, in this way, the term "partner" denotes the shared commitment between people and the shared responsibility for holding each other's hearts.

You might notice throughout this book that I am sparing with the term "couple," opting to use the term "relationship" or "partnership" most of the time. While I acknowledge that many people are romantically pair-bonded and choose to enter into monogamous agreements, others do not. I want to deliberately and transparently embrace all types of relationships, whether they have two members or multiple members, whether there are expectations of exclusivity or agreements of openness, whether they are romantic or platonic. I have no expectation or assumption that the only way to prevent hurt is via monogamy. The concepts I talk about relate to any close relationship, be it romantic, platonic, or a family connection. In fact, relationship structure and definition fade into the background when it comes to matters of the heart. I am talking about something far deeper; I am talking about emotional bonds. And when a bond breaks, it hurts. I am talking about how people bond, how to survive the damage to that bond, and how to heal and strengthen that bond moving forward. The examples of relationships I refer to are a collection of the many people's stories I have encountered in my practice and all individual details have been changed to protect privacy.

This book is about broken bonds in relationships; all kinds of relationships and the hurt that is caused by attachment injuries. After all, love is love and attachment bonds are bonds of the heart and it hurts like crazy when they are broken, regardless of the context.

A note to mental health clinicians and therapists

While this book is written directly to those suffering from an attachment injury, it is my hope that it will assist you in working with your clients who have experienced attachment injuries. As a couples' and relationship therapist, I know how difficult it can be to help clients to heal from relational traumas. I understand the contagion of fear, pain, and hopelessness that can accompany such damage to an attachment bond and how, as a therapist wanting the best for your clients, it can be so challenging to stand steady and to hold the hope for them. Our work involves an overwhelming responsibility. Attachment injuries bring out the most intense emotions in the beautiful humans we work with, and it can be very taxing on our nervous systems as therapists. For us to maintain our balance and to use ourselves as therapeutic tools, we need support. We need resources and we need a map. I know I do. *I sincerely hope that this book can support you as you offer a safe holding space for your clients to access and process their pain and to hopefully repair their precious attachment bonds. Your role is essential in this process, and I know how heavily this can weigh on us as therapists.* I hope that you find comfort and direction in these pages, along with many practical tools to help your clients to salvage their connection. After all, there is nothing like a road map to help you to feel less lost! I hope this book will offer you that map to guide your clients along the journey to healing.

Structure of this book

As you will see throughout this book, I want you to know what we are doing, and why, every step of the way. I want to show you the process as you work through it so that we do this work together. Each chapter will take you further into the process of healing and builds upon the one before it. In Part 1, I will give you an overview of the path to healing and restoring security in your attachment bond. We look at the attachment view on love and betrayal and why broken trust is so devastating to us all as humans. We unpack what an attachment injury is and explore its devastating impact.

We start this journey in Chapter 1 where we explore why, as humans, we need loving connection and why it hurts so much when it all goes wrong, and trust is broken. We begin to explore attachment theory and how we form our loving bonds and acquire our attachment strategies. We also look at why betrayal in our closest bonds is so devastating to us as humans. This chapter will define an attachment injury through the lens of attachment theory and will look at how hurts of this nature impact the security of the attachment bond. I will help you to reflect on your attachment needs and your attachment strategies as we explore the impact betrayal has on close bonds.

In Chapter 2, we will name and validate the traumatic impact of attachment injuries for each person involved. We will explore and highlight the differences in the impact of these injuries for the hurt and the hurtful partner, as well as on others who may be involved, as we build awareness of the ripple-effect this type of relational hurt can have. Chapter 2 will also provide some ideas on how good people come to be hurtful and the possible reasoning or motivation behind hurtful acts. I will define four key types of attachment injuries including sexual and emotional betrayal, violated boundaries, abandonments, and threats to relational safety. This chapter will explore examples of each type of injury, including a range of injuries that can occur in different relationships.

All relationships have communication patterns or cycles that can cause crossed-wires and scrambled signals. This is never more the case than when there has been a breach of trust. Chapter 3 will focus on how partners can become stuck in cycles of distress that can block them from healing and add to their distress. This negative interactional pattern can flare when there has been an attachment injury, either stemming from a cycle that pre-dated the hurtful event or it can evolve because of the hurt. Either way, it is common for partners to find themselves caught in a pattern that blocks their capacity for healing and further erodes their connection. In this chapter, we will look at how these cycles can impact the recovery from an attachment injury, and we will map out the healing process using the Attachment Injury Resolution Model. I will provide a clear overview of the repair process so that the reader is informed about the roadmap to recovery.

In Part 2, we take all that we have learned about the attachment significance of relational hurts into the current attachment injury and look at how to do the work required to build a safe context for healing. In Chapter 4, I will identify three key tasks each for the hurt partner and the hurtful partner that will create the context for healing. These tasks will allow us to begin the work of restoring the safety in the bond. We can begin to identify the cycle that is blocking the healing and look at each partner's role in contributing to that cycle. You will be guided to reflect on your level of defensiveness and reactivity and how these coping strategies contribute to the negative interactional cycle. These coping strategies are framed as needed or "earned" protections that serve a role of keeping a person safe but can also prevent the process of repair. These important tasks will help you and your special other to step out of the negative pattern that blocks you from restoring closeness and security in your bond.

In Chapter 5, we focus on building awareness about self and connection by exploring the unique attachment context of the betrayal you are facing. You will be guided to reflect on how your most meaningful relationships throughout your life have impacted your expectations and beliefs about closeness with others and about your worthiness of love and support. We look at how past relational injuries can leave scars that might flare in subsequent relationships, and how these powerful experiences can shape how a person shows up in connection, their expectations from connection with others, and how they respond to breaches of trust. This chapter will be important for those who have experienced past hurts and betrayals because these old wounds are bound to be activated by a current attachment injury. Protective coping strategies will come alive in the current context and can add to a sense of isolation and distress. We will explore the impact of historical relational trauma on present coping strategies and how to identify "old" pain from "new" pain. We will look at how to care for the parts of self that need healing and how to lower protective shields when it is safe enough to do so.

Sometimes, hurts in relationships are bidirectional and complex. There is not always a clear "hurt" and "hurtful" partner. In Chapter 6, we look at some of the ways that partners can become entangled in complex patterns of hurt that are not as simple as a "hurt" and "hurtful" partner. This can make the process of attachment injury repair uncertain. I will identify examples of complex hurts such as dual injuries (where partners are equally hurt), eclipsing injuries (when one partner's hurt overshadows the other's hurt), retaliation injuries (when one partner's hurtful act follows a hurt issued by the other), and erosion injuries (smaller hurts that don't completely break trust but erode it over time in a cumulative manner). When the trust is broken in multiple and complex ways, we need to accommodate these complexities into our approach to healing. We will look at how to work with intricate layers of hurt in the attachment resolution process and gain a clear path forward for repair.

Now that we have established safety and understood the meaning of the attachment injury, the impact for each partner, and can see and exit the negative cycle that has been blocking recovery, we can begin the true healing process. In Part 3, we use the Attachment Injury Resolution Model to restore security in the relational bond. To do this, in Chapter 7, we help the hurt partner to explore and express the impact of the attachment injury in a new, more vulnerable way. We will arm the hurt partner with tools for processing their emotions so that they can work through their pain and send clear signals to their partner – signals that pull for understanding and care rather than defensiveness. This represents a powerful new step for the hurt partner to reach into the depths of their pain, and to share it with the other openly and without their protective shield. This is a monumental task for the hurt partner given that the other now appears dangerous – it is a leap of faith.

In Chapter 8, we help the hurtful partner to witness the pain from the hurt partner whilst maintaining their emotional balance. It is so very difficult to confront the impact of your own actions, knowing that you caused pain to someone you care about. The hurtful partner will be supported in this place, to see and gently lower their protective shield and to respond to the hurt partner from a place of compassion and care. When the hurtful partner can remain present and attuned to their partner's pain and let them know how they are impacted by the other's pain, they are no longer alone in it and, together, they can share the load of this hurt. Chapter 8 is about standing steady in the face of big emotions. It is about meeting the hurt partner's pain with accessibility, responsiveness, and engagement – the building blocks to secure attachment. Hurtful partners are encouraged to offer an attuned response to the other where they share their remorse, take an appropriate amount of responsibility for the hurtful events, and offer an apology if required.

When the hurtful partner can keep their balance in the face of their own shame and attend to the other's raw vulnerability, this represents an enormous shift in the relational pattern. Building on Chapters 7 and 8, Chapter 9 focuses on the final and important task of the Attachment Injury Resolution Model – antidote bonding. Each partner will have the opportunity to identify what it is that they need from the other and will be empowered to ask for this. Hurt partners will be guided to ask for what they need to feel safe, and hurtful partners will be empowered to hear and meet these needs. Hurtful partners will be encouraged to reflect on what they have learned about themselves from this attachment injury and to offer this to the hurt partner. This allows them to ask for forgiveness or acceptance and to experience the sense of agency that comes with being an active participant in the repair process. Now, partners are healing together. This is the antidote to the pain of betrayal for the hurt partner and to the helplessness in the hurtful partner. When pain can be healed, it restores trust for the hurt partner and ameliorates the shame for the hurtful partner.

In Part 4, we look to the future. For those who can repair the attachment injury, we look at how to maintain the security in your bond and how to manage the inevitable flares that come from the echo of an attachment injury. For those who, sadly, cannot repair their connection and end or reconfigure their relationship, we will look at grieving this relationship and how to move forward in new ways.

In Chapter 10, we look at how to establish and maintain a new, positive interactional cycle where clear signals make it easier for partners to meet each other's needs. Now, the fear and pain in the hurt partner can be shared when it appears, and the hurtful partner can see a road to reconnection and their role in it. There will inevitably be times when reminders of this attachment injury will flare, and old wounds are bumped. This chapter looks at how to manage these moments in ways that continue to build the security of the bond, rather than weaken it. This is about celebrating the good work that went into repairing this attachment injury and how to maintain it. We look at how to process other relationship concerns unrelated to the attachment injury, how to build security moving forwards, and how to avoid common traps that people can fall into when recovering from an attachment injury. This chapter also looks at the impact of betrayal on romantic partners' sexual connection and how to reconnect sexually when the attachment injury has impacted this important area of the relationship.

For some, the outcome of this process may not be so positive, and the relationship cannot be restored. Chapter 11 focuses on loss, grief, and redefining the relationship. We name and make room for the huge pain of the loss of an important relationship and look at how the reader can process and recover. To love another is to leave yourself open to hurt and when we are injured in a relationship *and* lose a loving connection, the pain and grief is visceral. We will find a pathway into and through the grief and look at practical strategies for riding the waves of emotion until the storm starts to pass. This chapter will allow you to process these painful emotions and to use this suffering as an opportunity for growth.

In Chapter 12, we can conclude this work by briefly exploring the growth that comes from hardship. You will be guided to reflect on what you have learned about yourself, your partner, and your relationship because of this attachment injury. In this way, we can use the suffering for expansion. For those who can restore the security of their bond, Chapter 12 provides a brief opportunity for reflection on each partner's strengths and resilience in working through this painful relational event. Hardships can be incorporated into the story of the relationship – how you struggled and overcame obstacles and fought so hard to restore trust. This injury becomes part of the relationship survival narrative. Now the relationship is stronger in the broken place for having weathered this event.

By the end of this book, my hope is that you will have felt supported and guided as you work through this breach of trust in your precious relationship, that you will have grown in knowledge and experience about attachment and healthy relationships, and that you will have been able to befriend your emotional world and to share it with your special other. I hope the exercises and guides in this book help you to repair your bond and to grow stronger from suffering. That is my wish for you and for all of us; all imperfect humans finding our way in life and love. It is so much easier with a hand to hold in the dark.

Part I

Broken bonds

Learning about attachment and the impact of betrayal

Chapter 1

What is an attachment injury?

You are hurting. Being betrayed by someone you trust or being hurtful to someone you care about is devastating. The damage is immense and the fallout all-encompassing. It can feel like there is no way out and that something so precious to you could be lost forever. As I have said earlier, I want you to know that you *can* rebuild your bond, you *can* work through this injury. It is possible to recover from a blow such as this to your bond – so long as all parties are willing to put the work in. To do that we must begin by understanding the nature of love and connection – of attachment bonds. Let's start our work by exploring why, as humans, we need loving connection and why it hurts so much when it all goes wrong, and trust is broken. We will do this by looking at attachment theory and how we form our loving bonds and our attachment strategies. That will explain why betrayal in our closest bonds is so devastating to us as humans. We will then define an attachment injury through the lens of attachment theory and look at how hurts of this nature impact the security of the attachment bond.

Love and attachment theory

When we open our heart to another, we make them important to our well-being. This means that by virtue of their importance to us, they have the power to lift us to the greatest of heights, or to plunge us to the darkest of depths. It is risky to love another. No doubt you are feeling some of the downsides of that risk right now and the benefits might seem so distant as to render them insignificant. Put simply, it hurts because it matters. When we form a bond with someone, we are letting them matter deeply to us. In attachment terms, they become an "attachment figure." Not just anyone can become an attachment figure for us. We select special people who mean a lot to us, and we bestow on them the gift of our heart. In return, we hold theirs. We do not undertake this lightly and our hope is that the risk is mutual between us and our special others. These special people become a safe place to turn to when we feel uncertain and are a source

DOI: 10.4324/9781003466499-3

of encouragement when we need a boost. By showing our vulnerability when we feel small and wobbly, we are placing our attachment figures in a position of enormous trust. When they hold that vulnerability with love and gentleness, and show us that we matter, and that they believe in us, we are soothed and can go back out into the world with our metaphorical cup refilled. We need emotional connections like this to thrive. This is not because we are needy and weak, but because as humans, our brains are wired for connection. We are a bonding species who flourish in connection and who do not do well in isolation.[1]

Attachment theory has had a lot to teach us about our human need for close and loving relationships. For much of the 20th century, we believed that children should grow up to be independent and that self-reliance was a goal of mature adulthood. Many people still firmly believe this, but thanks to the revelations of John Bowlby's attachment theory[2] and an army of subsequent researchers examining child and adult attachment, we now know that forming loving bonds with responsive others is vital to our well-being as humans. It is clear that we all have an innate yearning for trust and security with one or a few irreplaceable others. Bowlby believed that we need others in this way "from the cradle to the grave."[3] We don't grow out of our attachment needs. Far from being dysfunctional, relying on special others allows a person to flourish and to take what life has to offer.

For some people, acknowledging our need for others as we navigate life might feel obvious and natural. However, for other people, the idea that we are built to connect with others and to rely on them in times of need might feel extremely foreign or even threatening. This reaction is usually grounded in the experiences you have had in close relationships with important people throughout your life. These early attachment relationships teach us important lessons about what it means to be close to another, whether others can be a resource, and whether we are worthy of love and support in times of need. Our earliest attachment figures' sensitivity and responsiveness to our needs are crucial in developing our sense of security in the world and confidence that others will also be responsive to our needs. This security and trust in others, then transfers into feeling more confident in yourself to navigate obstacles. These formative relationships set our expectations for our subsequent relationships, like a blueprint in a way, and impact our belief in our own ability to face life's challenges. They lead to the development of beliefs called "model of other" and "model of self," both of which we are going to talk more about in Chapters 2 and 5.

Attachment theory has crystallised our understanding of our need for a "safe haven" and a "secure base" as humans. Our attachment figures perform these two important functions, and they might look different in different cultures and different family structures. Essentially, attachment figures provide *comfort,* and they provide *reassurance.* We all need somewhere safe to turn when we feel uncertain, and we need encouragement to take on challenges. These are two sides of the attachment coin that help us to develop into fully functional humans, ready to live life to the full. If we can turn to a "stronger, wiser other" when threatened, frightened, vulnerable, sick, or uncertain, then they are a haven for comfort and protection – their loving care helps us to soothe and regulate our emotions. Their support and reassurance that we are loved and safe then become a strong and stable platform underneath our feet to venture out from. This is why it hurts so much when trust is shattered, and you no longer feel that you can rely on your attachment figure. It alters your view of yourself, the other, and your ability to navigate in the world.

Healthy adult attachment bonds

Bowlby was adamant that it is not immature or pathological to need others, believing that this was in fact a biological imperative with adaptive value.[4] Building on Bowlby's ideas, attachment scientists have shown us that the bond that adults form with romantic partners mirrors the bond a child forms with their attachment figures.[5] Our attachment figures as adults serve the very same functions as our primary caregivers did in childhood. In this way, we can conceptualise romantic love as an attachment bond. Partners can offer the same safe haven of support to turn to and a secure base for venturing out from, as a parent offers a child. Actually, it is so natural to want to turn to your special other (or others) when you need comfort, that we never outgrow this need. We gain strength from the knowledge that we have someone watching our back and can, therefore, more bravely engage with the world around us. With this knowledge, we can be curious, can take calculated risks, and can put our best foot forward.

It turns out that there is some truth to the idea of "sharing the load" when it comes to sharing emotionally with safe others (especially our attachment figures). Recent research has backed this up by showing that turning to another for co-regulation of emotion is actually the most efficient use of our brain's resources when under threat.[6] If our special person is there when we need them, responding to our vulnerability by showing interest and care, we feel better. These are the most important elements of an attachment figure; they are accessible, responsive, and engaged.[7] When we are responded to in this way, we learn to regulate our emotional storms, that connection is a good idea, and that we are worthy of love and comfort. This does something very powerful to our inner world; it directly impacts how we see ourselves, others, and the world. We internalise this ability to self-soothe from being soothed by responsive attachment figures. We begin to feel competent in managing our emotional highs and lows and we develop a sense of confidence that others are dependable and reliable. Paradoxically, when we know that we have people to turn to, we don't need them as much. This is what we call "secure attachment."

When attachment is working well, there is a lovely balance between seeking closeness and tolerating distance, there is a flexibility in the bond between intimates. When we know that our few very special and irreplaceable others are there to turn to in life's shaky moments, then we can be brave. The security that these connections offer us is invaluable. This does not mean that we are dependent on our partners. This is what Bowlby called "functional dependence," or what we can think of as effective dependency.[8] In relationship, we grow. The more securely we can feel our important other's responsiveness, the more autonomous and confident we can be. When someone can reach out to a safe other for comfort and reassurance and can travel bravely out into the world, we describe them as having "secure attachment strategies". Someone with secure attachment strategies is likely to be both autonomous and able to seek and accept care from another. They can clearly signal their needs as required and can confidently go out into the world. They are comfortable with closeness and with distance and can flexibly move between the two. This is what we are wired for and if we have it, we thrive, but if we don't have it, life can feel like a steeper hill to climb.

The risks inherent in attachment

What we can take from attachment theory is that it is normal to need others to turn to in times of uncertainty and to use their support as a base to venture out from. I want you to *know* that you are not "needy" or pathological for craving this. Attachment bonds are real, and we all need them. No wonder it hurts so much when someone you love is not a safe haven or if your trust in them is shattered.

If we let someone mean a lot to us and we place them in the privileged position of being an attachment figure, then the threat of the loss of that connection is destabilising and incredibly painful. When these special connections are broken, through betrayal, abandonment, unavailability, or loss, then we will feel this intensely. In fact, research shows that the pain of social exclusion activates the same parts of the brain that are active when we are physically injured. Social pain is equivalent to physical pain as far as the brain is concerned, which makes sense of terms like "hurt feelings," and maybe starts to explain why we turn to others for comfort for both types of pain.[9] In the face of the loss or unavailability of an attachment figure, we will fall into predictable patterns of protest and despair. This protest has been well-researched and shows clearly that we all cascade into protesting the separation and then into the despair of isolation. We might show this in slightly different ways, but researchers have tracked a pattern of emotional responses to the separation or loss of contact with an attachment figure, from babies to adults.[10] Through this research, we have come to learn that we all hurt in similar ways and the loss or withholding of connection is painful. When our attachment figure has been hurtful or broken our trust, we will feel this keenly as a loss – a loss of the safety, dependability, and reliability of our person. We may deal with our emotional pain in slightly different ways, but, as humans, we are united in our attachment needs and the pain we feel when it is unavailable or lost to us.

When we don't have our attachment figure as our secure base and safe haven, we are left alone with our emotional storms. We know that regulating our emotion alone is very taxing and that we rapidly deplete our coping abilities.[11] Without the option of turning to another, we are forced to find alternative ways to emotionally regulate our inner world and to navigate the world around us. Generally, people with unavailable or inconsistent attachment figures manage the distress of this in one of two ways; either by shutting their feelings down or by energetically attempting to gain contact with another. This means that some people will become adept at self-containment, pushing their feelings aside to manage the intensity and preferring to remain task-focused and practical. Others will become practiced in fighting for emotional contact by escalating their emotional signals to ensure a response from another, prioritising the need for soothing through connection above all else. Bowlby believed that these strategies were "back up" strategies, that they were not as efficient as co-regulation with a safe other, and so were only utilised when this was not an available option. We call these "insecure" attachment strategies, and while this term can sound judgmental, it is important to note that we can *all* use insecure strategies when our attachment system is on high alert.

After a breach of trust in a close relationship, you are bound to find yourself gripped by attachment-related pain. When someone you trusted with your heart breaks that bond, I imagine that you know the pain of feeling so alone in the face of overwhelming emotion. When one you trusted starts looking like the enemy, this is an extremely destabilising place.

What is an attachment injury?

An attachment injury is an event that profoundly impacts the way the hurt partner views the other, themselves, and the relationship. More than just a small tear to the fabric of the attachment bond, an attachment injury represents a slash in the bond between partners. An attachment injury has been defined as *a perceived abandonment, betrayal, or breach of trust in a critical moment of need.*[12] I would hasten to add to this definition that, a betrayal or breach of trust *at any time* in a bonded relationship is likely to be devastating to the security of the bond, not just in a critical moment of need. In my experience, perceived breaches of trust are always jolting to the bond and abandonments are particularly sensitive to need. The extent of the injury is likely to be determined by the level of vulnerability experienced by the hurt party at the time.

An attachment injury is defined by its attachment significance to the people involved. Given what we know about attachment bonds, we can see the power of a single event to rupture a relationship and redefine its security.[13] As such, I am not as focused on the actual event or whether others would find that same event troublesome. It is unique to you and your relationship. It carries special meaning and therefore brings with it an especially acute wound. The answers to the critical questions of *Are you there for me?*, *Do I matter to you?*, *Can I count on you?*, and *Am I safe with you?* are now left hanging unanswered or are answered with a resounding "no" for the hurt partner. Events such as abandoning one partner as they face a traumatic health crisis, breaking a promise of sexual fidelity, or keeping a secret from the other that threatens their life together will all have different attachment meanings for different people. Regardless, the incident that caused an attachment injury has a negative impact on the attachment bond between partners, rendering it insecure. This event cannot simply be forgotten; it is used to define the safety of the relationship and acts as a barrier to intimacy and connection.[14] Each time it is raised and not resolved, it only deepens the divide. For both partners, an event like this does not only shake the foundation of your bond together – it also shakes the foundation of your self-concept.

For the hurt partner, the injury is traumatic and they are left with a sense of helplessness, isolation, and intense fear about the other's availability.[15] The discovery of an attachment injury tilts your world on its axis and calls into question everything you thought you knew. All the things you counted on – as safely predictable and clearly negotiated – have been obliterated. Discovering that your partner has become someone you don't recognise takes your secure reality and spins it on its head. No longer does your partner seem safe, dependable, and reliable. After this devastating event, they now appear unknown, unreliable, and even dangerous. Suddenly, the very worst is true, all options are now possible, even things you thought could never happen in your world. Your relationship is no longer a dependable safe haven of comfort and predictability.

People have described the experience of an attachment injury to me in life-or-death terms such as "suffocating," "drowning," "being stabbed in the back," and "being shot through the heart." They define their life in terms of *before* this event and *after* this event. They recall no longer trusting their ability to see, to think, to reason. They question every moment of the relationship history as they look at it through a newly acquired lens. They wonder how they trusted so blindly, how the other could hurt them in this way, they mobilise into rage, they collapse into self-recrimination, they rally to repair or end the relationship before they are ready, and they sink into hopelessness and despair. Each time the hurtful event is raised, the emotion is alive, raw, and overwhelming. From the moment of the injury, it is used as the standard by which the hurt partner measures the dependability of the other[16] – "how could you?" It has been argued that wounds to attachment bonds such as these are a form of trauma with a small "t."[17] This is truly a relational trauma.

For partners who have been hurtful, causing an attachment injury is acutely painful. While not blindsided in the way hurt partners are, knowing that you have caused pain to someone you deeply care about is excruciating. Most people do not set out to be hurtful. They might have been thoughtless or impulsive or blinkered, but they usually are not deliberately hurtful. They may have been avoiding the truth of their actions or telling themselves a story that enabled them to be hurtful without fully facing the reality of their actions. They may have buried their head in the sand, remaining focused only on what is right in front of them. However, to see the pain clearly on another's face is often unbearable. It can be hard to stay present to witness this hurt without becoming triggered yourself. The helplessness that comes with knowing that you have broken the other's trust in you and being unable to wind back time can be overwhelming and consuming. The awareness that you have damaged the fabric of your relationship bond brings with it an enormous weight of responsibility and shame, and that can be tremendously difficult to bear. This is even more the case when you have born hurts in this relationship too – hurts or unspoken needs that have gone unuttered and now might be eclipsed by this event.

In relationships rocked by an attachment injury, this violation or breach of trust by an attachment figure indicates to the hurt partner that the other can no longer be counted on for care and support when needed.[18] Many describe this as the worst part of their experience of an attachment injury – that the very person you would turn to for comfort when your world is turned upside-down is the one causing the pain. Never will you have felt so hurt and so alone. It is inherently disorganising when the person closest to you is also the source of your pain – when you long to reach to them for comfort but you must pull away to protect yourself from further hurt. It is this disorganisation that impacts the bond so profoundly. Hurt partners are in a "no-win" situation where they can vacillate between seeking and withdrawing from their partner, which is difficult for the other to respond to.[19] Attempts to offer comfort or reassurance from the hurtful partner are often impossible for the hurt partner to accept or to trust.[20]

For hurtful partners, this only exacerbates their sense of helplessness and inability to repair the ruptured trust. In this way, each partner tries their best to manage the pain of being hurtful or causing hurt and only amplifies the distance between them. The more one copes in the way that feels right to them, the more they trigger the fears of the other, causing them to rally their protections in response. This cycle of protective coping strategies erodes closeness and gets in the way of repair. We are going to look at this cycle of interaction in Chapter 3.

Broken bone analogy: how do we heal an attachment injury?

It has been so helpful for me to think about attachment injuries using an analogy brought to me by my mentor and friend, Dr Kathryn Rheem, so I wanted to share it with you as we start to look more deeply at these concepts. If we think about the injury to your bond as a physical injury like a wound with a broken bone:

1 Firstly, we all need to assess the damage. We need to know why it hurts, the extent of the injury, how deep it goes, and we need to clean out the wound. This means understanding the attachment injury. What happened? What was the nature and extent of the betrayal? Is anything being held back? This disclosure and assessment period will allow both partners to decide whether they are willing to commit to the work of healing this relationship. This is the work we will be doing in Part I of this book. We will explore the attachment significance and meaning of this hurtful event in the context of your attachment bond. We will assess the injury and outline the path to healing required, should you choose that.

2 Next, we need to stabilise your relationship, in the same way that we would stabilise a broken bone. We splint a broken limb to stop it from being "walked around on" and receiving more damage. In Part II of this book, we will stabilise the injury to your bond. To do this, we need to get to know and step out of negative patterns of communication that so often accompany a hurt of this magnitude. These negative patterns or cycles keep the hurt alive and can block the healing process, leaving your bond raw and unstable. We can then begin to explore and share the meaning for all parties underneath the pain of this injury. Stepping out of stuck patterns of communication about this injury and sharing differently with each other is like a splint that stops the broken bone from being further damaged. Once this work is done, the inflammation can reduce, and the broken limb is safe from additional trauma. In this way, the relational system is stabilised. We call this "de-escalation," and it is a vital precursor to the healing of your bond.

3 Now that we have stabilised the wound and have gained more understanding about its impact, we can do the repair work. For a broken bone to heal well, the pieces need to lie straight, to be in proximity to each other, and to remain steady. This then allows the osteoblasts (bone cells) to find their way to the most tender places, to form new connections, to grow new bone, and to knit together again. As the bone cells do this important work, they are encapsulated in a "calcium envelope" that supports this new growth. This envelope then hardens into a callous that literally makes the bone "stronger in the broken place." What a beautiful metaphor for the healing process for your relationship! We help your relationship to heal in a similar way. We create connection through the vulnerable sharing of pain and attending to it together. We align the broken pieces through new understanding, empathy, and care, all which act as a protective "calcium envelope" around the break as it heals. We aim for healing through shared pain, shared goodwill and, where needed, amends to be made and trust to be regrown. The amazing part of this work is that, in the same way that actual bones end up stronger in the broken place, so to can emotional bonds. You can heal individually, *and* your relationship security can be restored. It may even end up stronger in the broken place. Stronger for having survived this trauma, stronger for having created new patterns and reaching for each other in new ways. This is the work of Part III of this book.

4 As with physical injuries, you might need to tend to the aftermath of the injury with some physiotherapy to make sure that the muscles around the broken bone grow strong and support the healed limb into the future. Part IV of this book looks at how to keep your relationship strong and healthy. We will look at how to manage reminders of the breach in trust, how to continue to grow security in your bond together, and how to move forward in new ways. For those who are unable to heal their relationship, we will look at how to navigate this loss or reconfiguration so that you can still grow from this hardship and move forward positively into your future relationships.

What are attachment strategies?

To change tack ever so slightly, I want to arm you with some more wisdom from attachment theory, particularly as it relates to how we cope when under threat, and how this can impact how we show up in relationships. There is nothing like an attachment injury to flare our most protective defences. And while these defences there for good reason, they can play a role in preventing healing from hurt. They are so good at keeping you safe, that they can block closeness. Just as with bones, closeness is actually required to repair.

An attachment strategy is the term used to describe a person's way of navigating their attachment relationships when they are under threat. Stemming from our experiences with, and expectations of others, an attachment strategy is our way of *signalling our needs* and our way of *managing our own emotional world.*[21] An attachment strategy describes what a person does (internally and externally) when their attachment system fires into action. When we perceive that our needs for contact and comfort from our special other are in jeopardy, we become emotionally thrown off balance. This is so destabilising that we need to turn to our protective, coping strategies to manage this threat. These are the things that we do when turning to another for co-regulation is not an option. The state you find yourself in and what you do when triggered like this is actually your best attempt to regain emotional equilibrium in the absence of being able to use the most efficient channel of regulation, which is turning to a safe other. When your trust has been broken by an attachment figure, they become a source of pain, not closeness or emotional safety. For that reason, attachment strategies are *adaptive*. We see attachment strategies as coping or protective strategies. Coping strategies perform two important functions:

1 they help us to manage our emotions in the moment and,
2 they aim to protect us from more attachment-related hurt.

In this way, our attachment strategies are *adaptive coping strategies* that have been learned in relationships. They are established in your earliest relationships and become a tool to reach for when your attachment alarms go off in your subsequent relationships. While they protect you from hurt or help you to manage in the moment, they don't always help you to clearly signal what you need from your person, and this is where problems can arise.

It is normal to have a range of attachment strategies, some that might be considered "secure" and some that might be termed "insecure." Different relationships can call for different attachment strategies. It is important to remember that the attachment strategies you use do not define you. They are simply your range of coping options that help you to navigate relationships. Some will be more helpful to you than others. You will most probably find (if you're anything like me or the people I work with in my practice), that the attachment strategies you use don't fall neatly into a specific category of "secure" or "insecure," but that you have a unique combination of strategies that you have learned over time. I like to think of this as an "attachment strategy tool kit" that is made up of many different attachment tools for coping in different situations. Some may now be obsolete, and others might still be needed. Some, while not helpful in your closest relationships, might keep you safe in the wider world. For instance, remaining logical in emotionally charged situations or keeping a protective shield up in certain circles is helpful and adaptive to that context. Our aim in life is to keep expanding our attachment strategy tool kit by adding more secure strategies and developing our ability to select the most helpful strategy in any given moment. Let's look more at some different attachment strategies and how they can impact our expectations in close relationships and the signals we send about our needs.

Secure attachment strategies

A person who tends to use secure attachment strategies is likely to have a positive view of relationships and connection. They generally have a sense that attachment figures will be helpful when needed, that they are worthy of love and support, and that the world is a safe place, ready to be explored. They are neither anxious about other people's potential unavailability nor about relying on another for emotional support. Research shows us that people with secure attachment strategies are likely to have experienced their earliest caregivers as responsive to their bids for comfort and reassurance – reliably there when they need them. They become comfortable in signalling their emotional needs and accepting assistance from their attachment figures as required. This instils in them a sense of confidence that others can be relied on as a resource and that they are worthy of this care. The co-regulation offered by a safe other builds a securely attached person's ability to withstand and manage their own emotions, which has a compounding effect on their belief in their ability to navigate life. We know that secure attachment strategies are related to effective emotional regulation skills and higher psychological well-being.[22] Examples of secure attachment strategies are letting another know when you need help or comfort, offering help or comfort to another without becoming overwhelmed, clearly signalling your needs in ways that do not trigger the other, setting healthy boundaries, seeking repair when hurt, being willing to forgive another's transgressions (when appropriate), riding out inner emotional storms without becoming overly dysregulated, trusting in one's own ability to manage challenges, calling a special other to mind to sustain you in a wobbly moment, and knowing that others are there if you need them.

When people tend to use "insecure" attachment strategies, it means that they may not have experienced their prior or current attachment figures as accessible, responsive, and engaged. If our attachment figures are absent or frightening to us as children, we can't develop our ability to clearly signal to others our need for assistance or comfort, which then impacts our ability to manage our inner emotional world, and of course, we can then struggle to develop our ability to freely explore and learn about the world.

Experiences like this in relationships can teach a person that co-regulation with a safe other is not easily available or rewarding, so they must find other ways of managing their emotions and navigating their closest relationships. Most humans respond to the lack of attachment security by either turning the heat on their emotional signals up or down, and some do both. What this means is that we either *hyperactivate* our emotional signals (turn up the heat) or *deactivate* our emotional signals (turn down the heat) towards our attachment figures. We did this as tiny babies through crying and clinging, and we still do this as adults. These ways of managing when our attachment system is under threat are called "insecure" attachment strategies and they are divided into three groups: anxious, avoidant, and fearful-avoidant.

Anxious attachment strategies

People who tend to use anxious attachment strategies have learned that their attachment figures are likely to be unreliably available and they manage this by energetically pursuing the connection. They learned (for good reason) that they need to turn up the heat on their emotional signals, in order to get on their attachment figure's radar. Bowlby called this "attachment protest" which is a perfect way of describing the intent behind anxious, pursuing behaviours. People who use anxious attachment strategies live with a high amount of *fear* that their special person will not be there for them and will ultimately reject them. As a result, they are often on the lookout for perceived threats to their bond. This burden of worry can prevent them from fully engaging in other things, they can become consumed with worry about the status of their relationship. No one can just "get on with life" and put their best foot forward when their most important relationship seems to be under threat, or their safe other is not there for them or has been hurtful. Understandably, those with anxious attachment strategies will be vocal when they sense distance from their special other and will seek contact in any way they can, often in escalating intensity.

Anxious attachment strategies include signalling the need for safe contact with the other by protesting perceived distance, increasing the intensity of the plea for connection through raising your voice or using more evocative language, clinging, escalating demands, or becoming critical. Anxious attachment strategies can also include scanning for possible threats to the relationship (born of worry about possible abandonment), seeking reassurance that you are loved, and throwing lots of energy at the problem of the disconnection. Because anxious attachment strategies involve turning up the emotional heat, you can be perceived by others as overwhelming, confrontational, irrational, or intimidating. These attachment strategies are driven by fear of the loss of connection. As a result, the other's *lack* of response is unbearable. People who use anxious attachment strategies see *connection* as the solution to their emotional uncertainty and aim to desperately seek it to soothe their jangling attachment alarms.

Avoidant attachment strategies

Avoidant attachment strategies help a person to turn down the heat on their emotional signals. People who tend to use avoidant attachment strategies have learned that their attachment figures are unavailable and dismissing of their needs for comfort and reassurance. As a result, they have come to the sad conclusion, often very early in life, that it is not a good idea to take their attachment needs to another – that it doesn't make things any better. Instead, they learn to manage the storms of their emotions by pushing them down and not taking them to another for soothing. Without the help of co-regulation with a safe other, they are left to cope alone. Biologically, this is no easy task, and this is where avoidant attachment strategies help a person to cope when safe co-regulation with another is not an option. Coping alone is taxing and those with avoidant attachment strategies must suppress their natural need for others, squash their emotional pain, and stay very practical and logical to manage all by themselves. In fact, to help them to achieve this, a person may utilise drugs, alcohol, or other things to avoid their emotions. Bowlby called this "compulsive self-reliance," and sadly, this is an image that is still held up in some societies (particularly Western) as a healthy and mature way of coping. As a result, people who use avoidant attachment strategies reconcile coping alone as their preferred option and often state with pride that they "don't do emotions" and can handle things on their own.

Avoidant attachment strategies can include, moving away from your own or your special other's emotions (sometimes appearing dismissive or unfeeling), retreating to regulate alone, preferring to stay very logical and problem-focused, going into self-defence, or trying to avoid conflict. Because avoidant attachment strategies mean that you self-regulate, you may come across to others as cold or distant – as not needing anyone. Your attempts to prevent conflict in relationships by "putting out fires" can look like you are not engaged.

Fearful-avoidant attachment strategies

Some people use a combination of both anxious and avoidant attachment strategies. We describe these strategies as "fearful-avoidant" attachment strategies, but sometimes they are called "hybrid" or "disorganised" attachment strategies. These are the result of fear about the reliability of the other's responsiveness and avoidance of closeness to protect against hurt and rejection.[23] This means that a person may anxiously pursue their loved one for contact, but then feel frightened by the risk of hurt in becoming so emotionally close, that they then pull back to avoid emotional intimacy. Fearful-avoidant attachment strategies are associated with having had frightening, erratic, or abusive early caregivers who were inconsistent, unpredictable, and unsafe. To have to rely on caregivers like this puts a child in an untenable position where their very natural attachment needs drive them to seek connection with caregivers who do not offer them a secure base or safe haven. This dilemma has been described as a "violation of human connection."[24] Such a violation of trust is completely destabilising for a child and severely impacts their ability to trust others later in life. It is then an act of supreme bravery and endurance for people with this early experience of relationships to consider opening their heart to another. Despite emotional connection being so painful, people with fearful-avoidant attachment strategies show amazing courage when they still seek love and closeness but can become terrified of allowing another in. They can become extremely fearful of hurt, betrayal, or loss and can become emotionally dysregulated in the face of such an enormous risk. As a result, fearful-avoidant attachment strategies can involve the sending of confusing signals to attachment figures such as, energetically pursuing for connection, rapidly followed by panic with this closeness, and then retreating and shutting down to avoid vulnerability and potential hurt. A sort of rapidly cycling "I want you...I don't want you." This can confuse or even push away well-intentioned partners who long to provide the healing experience of a safe, loving connection. Alternatively, the inconsistent signals can be triggering for the other, reminding them of their own attachment trauma (Figure 1.1).

Attachment strategies and betrayal

Naturally, our attachment strategies impact how we respond to betrayal in our closest relationships and the forgiveness process. We know that people with anxious or avoidant attachment strategies tend to process the behaviours of attachment figures in a negatively biased way, usually without conscious awareness that early life attachment experiences may be influencing their attributions.[25] Attachment strategies have a survival function, they protect the self from hurt in close relationships. However, they also can make it difficult to tune into the emotional needs or the experience of the other. This can impact the healing and forgiveness process by limiting the opportunity for attunement and understanding – factors that can be very important in processing breaches of trust, repairing hurt, and forgiving transgressions. Following a breach of trust, for those who are anxiously attached, the fear of rejection and abandonment takes a high

Attachment Strategies

Attachment Strategies are adaptive coping strategies that are learned in close relationships. They help us to navigate relationships, manage attachment distress, maintain our attachment bonds & to regulate our inner state. We develop attachment strategies early in life & we continue to add more attachment strategies to our "attachment strategy tool kit" throughout our life. Some will continue to be helpful & others might block us from the relationships we want. We can always learn more secure attachment strategies.

Secure Attachment Strategies

People with a secure attachment strategies are likely to have good emotional regulation skills & can clearly signal their needs to their special others. They feel worthy of love & care & can take this in from others.

People with secure attachment strategies have learned that others are there for them, that they can manage their own emotions & can bravely take on challenges in life, safe in the knowledge that others are there when needed.

They trust their own ability to cope & have effective emotional regulation skills. They tend to be hopeful about relationships & are open communicators.

Anxious Attachment Strategies

People with anxious attachment strategies are likely to feel concerned about their special others' availability & have learned to strenuously signal their needs to make sure that they are heard & responded to.

They are likely to have experienced their attachment figures as inconsistently reliable, to doubt their own ability to cope alone & to doubt their worthiness of love & connection.

As a result, those with anxious attachment strategies can become preoccupied with their attachment figures' responsiveness & to look out for cues of impending abandonment. This leaves them feeling uncertain & anxious in relationships.

Avoidant Attachment Strategies

People with avoidant attachment strategies have learned that it is better to cope alone than to share their emotional needs with others. They tend to stay away from their emotions & to use practical ways of coping.

These coping strategies are often learned in environments where emotions were not shared & were dismissed or even shamed. People with avoidant attachment strategies learn that turning to others is not helpful & they resort to self-reliance.

This means that they have to rely on strategies that distance them from the intensity of their emotions such as suppression, distraction, or problem-solving.

Fearful-avoidant Attachment Strategies

People with fearful-avoidant attachment strategies (also known as a hybrid or disorganised attachment strategies) might display a mixture of anxious pursuit of connection & avoidance of connection. This stems from fear of being hurt in close relationships.

People with fearful-avoidant attachment strategies have often experienced their early attachment figures as frightening or intrusive & may have experienced trauma in close relationships.

Understandably, they naturally crave safe connection but struggle to trust that others will not hurt them. This can lead to mixed signals to the special people in their world.

Clare Rosoman 2024

Figure 1.1 Summary of attachment strategies.

level of internal management, leaving less room for processing hurt and finding empathy or understanding for their partner. The pain overwhelms and makes it very difficult to attune to the other. Conversely, those with avoidant attachment strategies are more likely to turn inwards and to emotionally distance themselves from the pain of betrayal or from the plight of the other. This can stultify the healing process by preventing opportunities for self-reflection and for attuning to the other.

It is clear that the *hurt* partner needs a lot of empathy and care in order to heal. However, we also know that the ability of the hurt partner to attend to the experiences of the *hurtful* partner is integral to forgiveness in romantic relationships. Empathising with a partner who has been hurtful, while extremely difficult, significantly reduces the desire for retribution and facilitates repair.[26] Sometimes, our attachment strategies make this process challenging by drawing our attention away from the relationship and into a self-protective space. *When we are protecting ourselves, the other person looks like the enemy, and when they have been hurtful, this can feel justified.* The problem with this is that when people perceive hurtful acts as intentional, the process of letting go of the negative feelings that go along with that event is more arduous. These beliefs can colour our view of the other and block healing. When in the grips of anxious or avoidant attachment strategies, a hurt person is more likely to decide negative things about their partner, to retreat emotionally, to react defensively, and to be unable to attune to the intricacies of the hurtful partner's world. In turn, the hurtful partner is likely to do the same – to retreat to a defensive and protective position, where they can shield themselves from witnessing the pain of the other. This leads to an awfully stuck place that contributes to feelings of helplessness and hopelessness. Tackling this negative pattern is where we will begin our healing work. More on that soon!

Notes

1 Berscheid, E. (2003). The human's greatest strength: Other humans. In U.M. Staudinger (Ed.). *A psychology of human strengths: Fundamental questions and future directions for a positive psychology* (pp. 37–47). Washington, DC: American Psychological Association.
2 Bowlby, J. (1969/1982). *Attachment and loss: Volume 1 attachment.* New York, NY: Basic Books.
3 Bowlby, J. (1979). *The making and breaking of affectional bonds.* London: Tavistock.
4 Bowlby, J. (1988). *A secure base.* New York, NY: Basic Books.
5 Shaver, P.R., & Hazan, C. (1988). A biased overview of the study of love. *Journal of Social and Personal Relationships, 5*(4), 473–501.
6 Coan, J.A., & Sbarra, D.A. (2015). Social baseline theory: The social regulation of risk and effort. *Current Opinion in Psychology, 1,* 87–89.
7 Johnson, S.M. (2008). *Hold me tight: Seven conversations for a lifetime of love.* New York, NY: Little, Brown.
8 Shaver, P.R., & Mikulincer, M. (2016). *Attachment in adulthood: Structure, dynamics and change* (2nd ed.). New York: The Guilford Press.

9 Eisenberger, N.I., Lieberman, M.D., & Williams, K.D. (2003). Does rejection hurt? An fMRI study of social exclusion. *Science*, 302, 290–292.
10 Tronick, E., Als, H., Adamson, L., Wise, S., & Brazelton, T.B. (1978). Infants response to entrapment between contradictory messages in face-to-face interaction. *Journal of the American Academy of Child and Adolescent Psychiatry*, 17, 1–13.
11 Coan, J.A., & Sbarra, D.A. (2015). Social baseline theory: The social regulation of risk and effort. *Current Opinion in Psychology*, 1, 87–89.
12 Johnson, S.M., Makinen, J.A., & Millikin, J.W. (2001). Attachment injuries in couple relationships: A new perspective on impasses in couples therapy. *Journal of Marital and Family Therapy*, 27, 145–155.
13 Brubacher, L. (2018). Attachment injury resolution model in emotionally focused therapy. In J. Lebow, A. Chambers & D. Breunlin (Eds.). *Encyclopedia of couple and family therapy* (pp. 165–169). Cham: Springer Science and Business Media.
14 Johnson, S.M. (2004). *The practice of emotionally focused couple therapy: Creating connections* (2nd ed.). New York: Brunner/Mazel.
15 Zuccarini, D., Johnson, S.M., Dalgleish, T.L., & Makinen, J.A. (2013). Forgiveness and reconciliation in emotionally focused therapy for couples: The client change process and therapist interventions. *Journal of Marital and Family Therapy*, 39(2), 148–162.
16 Zuccarini, D., Johnson, S.M., Dalgleish, T.L., & Makinen, J.A. (2013). Forgiveness and reconciliation in emotionally focused therapy for couples: The client change process and therapist interventions. *Journal of Marital and Family Therapy*, 39(2), 148–162.
17 Johnson, S.M. (2002). *Emotionally focused couple therapy with trauma survivors: Strengthening attachment bonds*. New York: Guilford Press.
18 Johnson, S.M., Makinen, J.A., & Millikin, J.W. (2001). Attachment injuries in couple relationships: A new perspective on impasses in couples therapy. *Journal of Marital and Family Therapy*, 27, 145–155.
19 Main, M., & Hesse, E. (1990). Parent's unresolved traumatic experiences are related to infant disorganized attachment status. In M. Greenberg & D. Cicchetti (Eds.). *Attachment in the pre-school years* (pp. 152–176). Chicago: University of Chicago Press.
20 Schore, A.N. (1994). *Affect regulation and the organization of self*. Hillsdale, NJ: Erlbaum.
21 Ainsworth, M.D.S., Blehar, M.C, Waters, E., & Wall, S. (1978). *Patterns of attachment: Assessed in the strange situation and at home*. Hillsdale, NJ: Erlbaum.
22 Shaver, P.R., & Mikulincer, M. (2016). *Attachment in adulthood: Structure, dynamics and change* (2nd ed.). New York: The Guilford Press.
23 Bartholomew, K., & Horowitz, L.M. (1991). Attachment styles among young adults: A test of a four-category model. *Journal of Personality and Social Psychology*, 61, 226–244.
24 Herman, J.L. (1992). *Trauma and recovery*. New York: Basic Books.
25 Dykas, M.J., & Cassidy, J. (2011). Attachment and the processing of social information across the life span: Theory and evidence. *Psychological Bulletin*, 137(1), 19–46.
26 Kimmes, J.G., & Durtschi, J.A. (2016). Forgiveness in romantic relationships: The roles of attachment, empathy, and attributions. *Journal of Marital and Family Therapy*, 42(2), 645–658.

Chapter 2

The impact of an attachment injury

Now that we have looked at the basics of attachment theory to help you to understand love as an attachment bond, and why attachment injuries are so damaging to the security of those bonds, it is time to dive deeply into the impact of attachment injuries. In this chapter, we will explore and validate the traumatic effect of attachment injuries on your relationship, and individually for each person involved. We will look at the differences in the impact of an attachment injury for the hurt partner and the hurtful partner, as well as on others who may be involved, as we build awareness of the ripple-effect this type of relational hurt has. In this chapter, I will provide some ideas on how good people come to be hurtful and the possible reasoning or motivation behind hurtful acts. We will define four key types of attachment injures, including sexual or emotional betrayals, violated boundaries, abandonments, and threats to relational safety.

Attachment injury as a relational trauma

As we know, to open your heart to another involves significant risk of hurt. And hurt you are. The pain that comes from shattered trust is excruciating for all involved – the one who was hurt, the one who caused this rupture, and for those near to you both. The pain you feel provides evidence for the meaning of this relationship. Put simply, if you didn't care about your partner, you wouldn't be suffering in this way. If they didn't matter to you, the breach of trust could be brushed off and you could "chalk this event up to experience" and move on. However, when your trust is broken by someone who matters deeply to you, who you have let close to you – maybe even the closest of all the people in your world – then the hurt is a measure of the love. I know that is cold comfort right now. I particularly want those who have been hurtful to remember that the pain you feel from causing pain is proof of your care. I urge you to cultivate this and to demonstrate this care, because it is your most valuable tool in repairing this injury. Similarly, I encourage hurt partners to access their

DOI: 10.4324/9781003466499-4

pain and vulnerability, rather than their protective rage, because this will be your most valuable tool for repair. But more on that later, let's not get ahead of ourselves.

Hurt of some form is inevitable in close relationships. I don't think that it is possible for us to never err or rupture trust when we form a loving bond with another. In fact, rupture and repair is a healthy part of secure attachment. If you think of your loving bond as being made up of many threads woven into a strong and thick rope, each time you mis-attune or cause hurt, some threads break. Each time you repair through making amends and clarifying shared understanding, threads are woven back into the rope, making it stronger and more resilient. The bigger the rupture, the more threads that are severed. An attachment injury can sever *all* or *almost all* the threads in the rope of connection.

An attachment injury has special meaning on an attachment level, it speaks to the other's responsiveness, reliability, and trustworthiness. It is an abandonment or a violation of trust that creates a shift in the relational bond. I want to be clear that we are not talking about general trust issues or an accumulation of small hurts, but rather a specific event or events that break trust or where one partner is perceived to be inaccessible or unresponsive to the other when they really need them. An event such as this shatters the assumptions we hold, changes the way we see ourselves and others, and induces a sense of existential vulnerability.[1] For some people, this particular hurtful event marks the most outstanding example of a long history of such betrayals (the last straw) and for others, it is an isolated event that is not at all the norm (a bolt from the blue). However you arrive at an attachment injury, the impact is profound, and the work required to repair the bond takes concerted effort from all parties.

As we saw in Chapter 1, each person's attachment history and their learned attachment strategies colour the meaning they place on this hurtful event or chain of events, and on how they respond to relational threats. Obviously, the impact of an attachment injury in a close relationship will be different for the hurt partner as opposed to the hurtful partner.

For Susan, after 17 years of marriage to Paul, she was devastated to discover his affair with a work colleague. As a monogamous couple, she had put her work aspirations on hold to support Paul's career, and to raise their children. As his work hours increased, she was aware of his stress and redoubled her efforts to run their house and to organise their children. Susan was sure that her support of him and of their family would pay off once Paul made his next promotion and could relax a little. She put her needs on hold, choosing to support him and took comfort from the knowledge that soon they would have some time together. When Susan saw a text message on Paul's phone and discovered his affair, she was in utter disbelief. They had been so good. They had regular sex, they agreed on most things, they laughed together, and they were made for each other. How could this have happened? Yes, he had been stressed about work and a little distracted, but she never thought he would turn to another. Not in her wildest dreams would she have ever thought this could happen to them. They were the couple others admired. How could she tell anyone this? How could she go on as normal?

For Callum, he and his partner of five years, Casey, had opened their relationship with clear ground rules around the development of relationships with other partners. They had long discussions where they carefully outlined what felt manageable for them both and where their personal limits were. They agreed on their ground rules for having other relationships and started to reach out to potential partners. They were clear that they were to let the other know if they were interested in someone, they would keep the other in the loop about how the new relationship was progressing, and they agreed to never have unprotected sex with another partner. When Callum discovered that Casey had lied about continuing to see another partner after telling Callum that the relationship had ended, he was hurt. However, when she admitted to having had unprotected sex with this partner and then with him, he was devastated. How could she endanger his safety in this way? What happened to their careful plans and agreements? How could she so recklessly break her promises to him?

Impact on the hurt partner

As you can see from these two examples, attachment injuries are seen as potentially devastating threats to attachment security. They bring a hurt partner's worst fears to life and create a crisis in the relationship. It's been shown that following a betrayal in a close relationship, hurt partners are likely to show symptoms of psychological distress similar to a trauma response, including elevated anxiety (such as racing heart and physical trembling), intrusive images and thoughts, and rumination over the betrayal. Physical impacts such as sleep disturbance, loss of appetite, weight loss, difficulty with concentration, and loss of libido have also been documented after experiencing a romantic betrayal.[2] These symptoms often mirror the symptoms of posttraumatic stress disorder including sensitivity to reminders of the event that caused the breach of trust, fluctuating emotions – from numbness to reactivity, vivid flashbacks, and preoccupation over the details competing with a desire to avoid reminders of it.[3]

When hurt partners speak of their injury, they use attachment language, such as:

"I felt like I didn't matter"
"I was discarded like I was nothing to you"

"I was all on my own"

"You didn't give me a second thought"

"My pain didn't matter to you"

"Where was I when you made that choice?" "You took all we had built, and you ruined it"

"How can I ever trust you again?"

"I've lost faith in you as my person and in us"

"How can you say you love me and then do this?"

"I need your reassurance, but I can't trust your words or let you close"

These painful, heartrending words echo the plea for lost security in the bond. Your sense of attachment security comes from a sense that you are important to the other, that you are cherished and protected by them, that they would never intentionally be hurtful. It is built on a sense that the other is dependable, reliable, and trustworthy – that they would never abandon or reject you. When these fundamental assumptions are violated, we feel this as a traumatic loss.[4] The other, once a source of solace, now is a source of distress. This hurtful event delivers evidence of the others' lack of trustworthiness, dependability, and reliability. It presents an attachment dilemma – connect and risk being hurt again or stay away and risk losing the bond entirely.

Relational hurt seems to involve a unique set of characteristics including the unexpected nature of the event (I never thought that could happen to us), its seemingly incomprehensible nature (this doesn't make sense, how could this have happened?), the strong emotions that come with it (intense shock, disbelief, sadness, fear, and anger), and the tendency of both hurt and hurtful parties to want to retreat from the pain.[5] You might find yourself feeling angry and vengeful towards your partner, while at the same time, feeling sad about the lost connection and even feeling empathy towards your partner. You might oscillate between wariness of the other and longing to restore the openness and trust – the struggle between hope and hopelessness. A significant dilemma for hurt partners is that they simultaneously want to protect themselves by retreating from the hurtful party and they want to restore the relationship by re-engaging.

Hurt that is acquired in close relationships has been explored by researchers and defined as a mixture of sadness felt about a loss coupled with a fear of being vulnerable to further harm.[6] While the emotional experience for hurt partners will almost certainly reference sadness, fear, and anger, the process and experience of emotions may shift over time, in somewhat unpredictable ways. For instance, some people might experience intense anger followed by sadness and then fear of being hurt again, while others might feel sadness initially, only to become angry or fearful further down the path to recovery.[7] Many people describe feeling numb towards or "walled off" from their partner following a hurt of this nature. You might identify with some of these experiences or find that other reactions come up for you during the course of discovering and processing this relational trauma.

Naturally, the meaning of the hurtful event will impact the level of hurt experienced. Some people have theorised that relational hurts stem from a belief that the hurtful act devalues the relationship and its sacredness, or that the hurtful act represents a relational transgression, where one person is seen as the rule-breaker or transgressor and one person is cast as the aggrieved party. Others have suggested that relational hurts are so impactful because they involve a sense of personal injury to the hurt partner's self-worth, value, and basic trust in others.

This dovetails with our discussion about attachment theory in Chapter 1, where we looked at how our beliefs about the value of turning to others in times of need and our worthiness of love and support are shaped in key interactions with our attachment figures. We call these belief-systems *working models of self and other*. They are formed and altered in our close relationships with those who are important to us and whom we let close. Experiences of being responded to and cared for build our sense that others are worthy of trust – that they are resources we can turn to when we need them. Conversely, when our trust is betrayed by an attachment figure, it makes perfect sense that this would alter our trust in others to be reliable and dependable (model of other) and our sense that we are worthy of love and care (model of self). Some attachment researchers have said that a key feature of hurtful events in relationships is that they have the potential to destroy an individual's sense of safety and security, which is *deep, visceral, and generally unconscious.*[8]

Many hurt partners speak of the pain that comes from the loss of their loved one following a breach of trust. Even if they are wanting to repair their bond, the loss of the relationship and the partner they had, is incredibly destabilising. Along with this experience, hurt partners are often taken by surprise by the loss of self, of the diminishment of their self-worth and personal value. The hurtful act by someone so special is devastating to the connection, but also to the individual. It rocks you to your core. This hurtful event represents the demolition of the dream of your relationship and the notion that you are unique and prized.[9] It is not uncommon for people to feel fractured, different, and forever changed, and to struggle to remember their good qualities and strengths. The loss of specialness from being overlooked, rejected, or betrayed can be truly shocking. We can easily lose sight of how important and nourishing it is to know that you are loved and cherished by another, assured of your specialness to them. When this is obliterated by an attachment injury, we grieve its loss acutely. Such a blow to your internal world and the security of your relationship can even alter your view of the world as safe and your ability to navigate it (model of world). Your secure world is literally shattered.

Feeling so thrown-off balance and so uncertain about your partner and your self-worth can provide fertile ground for harmful coping strategies. It might be helpful to know that hurt partners can fall prey to punishing the other and to justifying their actions on account of the other "deserving" it. This is never more tempting than when you feel so hurt and so raw. Adopting an accusing position can allow someone to preserve their view of themselves as right and the other as wrong. While it's possible that this might be true, it can be a dangerous path for all involved. From this vantage point, hurt partners are more likely to judge the transgressions of the other in a very negative light. They might channel their anger towards acts of retribution, or revenge, try to shame the other through public exposure, or to resort to verbal or physical abuse. It is important to remember that, like a cornered wild animal, this is the hurt person's best attempt to protect themselves and to make sure that they fight to right this wrong. While totally understandable, this accusing stance can change you into someone you don't recognise by taking you away from your personal values, and it can block the healing process, causing even more harm in the long run.

As we mentioned in Chapter 1, betrayal of this magnitude can cause you to question everything you thought you knew – about your relationship, your partner, and yourself. It shakes your very foundations. Cherished memories can become tarnished and blackened, and future dreams sour and degrade. Depressive symptoms, such as low mood, feelings of hopelessness, worthlessness, lack of joy, tearfulness, and despair, are commonly experienced after betrayals. Understandably, a hurt of this magnitude damages the hurt partner's ability to trust and flares their protective and defensive strategies. Hurt partners can go into self-protection mode so profoundly, that if the attachment wound is left unaddressed, then healing is not possible and the relationship's ability to survive and thrive is under threat.

Impact on the hurtful partner

Knowing you have been hurtful towards someone you care about is truly awful. For some who have been hurtful, especially those who have acted out of character and gone against their values, it can be almost impossible to comprehend how you became this person. It may seem surprising, but hurtful partners can be just as impacted as hurt partners when it comes to the very real threat of losing the relationship. Hurtful partners will often say things like:

"I don't know how else to fix this"
"I've said I'm sorry"

"Why won't you believe me?"
"Haven't I done enough to show you how much I care?"
"I can't make you trust me again"
"Tell me what else I could do to make this right, I'm all out of ideas"
"I'm doing all I can to make things right, when will you forgive me?"
"How much longer do I have to be punished for this?"
"I can't talk about my issues now that we are focusing on this concern"
"You'll have to learn to trust again, I can't do any more than I have"

Witnessing the harm you have caused and feeling helpless to make amends creates a special kind of "pit of shame" for hurtful partners. This shame is actually your best tool for repair, but for most people, touching shame is unbearable and they will do anything to avoid it or to move away from it. Hence, hurtful partners will tend to respond in two counterproductive ways. The first is that they tend to adopt a defensive stance, where they attempt to defend their actions and to minimise the damage through explaining or justifying. This serves a purpose of trying to stem the bleeding and minimise the damage to the relationship and to the partner, but it just alienates them. The second is to seek comfort for what they are going through. It is important to know that any endeavour to preserve your self-concept as good or right or justified, while understandable, will send a signal to the other that you care more about managing your discomfort and "saving face," than about attending to their pain and distress. It indicates to the other that your priority is to exhaust your precious resources on protecting, defending, and spotlighting yourself, leaving very little for tending to their distress. Ultimately, this will exacerbate the mistrust and block the healing.

Many partners who have caused ruptures in trust describe feeling utterly helpless to repair their relationship and to prove their trustworthiness to the other. They have usually tried everything they can think of to explain and to reassure, in a seemingly futile attempt to restore the bond. Helplessness is profoundly difficult for us as humans to bear, especially when the stakes are so high. You might become frustrated at your lack of agency in repairing this rupture. When it matters so much and you feel, at worst totally responsible and at best partially responsible for the damage, of course you want to jump into action to resolve the issue. Sadly, these attempts can make repair more difficult, increasing the sense of helplessness for all.

It is common for partners who have caused hurt in their relationship to feel that they are being punished, that there is no way out, no way to make things right again. They most often have tried to make amends and to apologise, to no avail. You might find yourself in this position, where you are frustrated by the lack of options, where it feels unfair that you are continually held responsible for so much pain with no way to repair it. You might even feel angry towards your partner. This is a very difficult place to be. You might feel exasperated that each time you talk about the hurtful event, it just ends up worse, and you and your partner feel even further apart. You might feel that your own concerns are now eclipsed by this attachment injury and cannot be discussed. That there is no room for your needs. It is a challenge to remain steady in the face of your partner's anger, bitterness, and pain without becoming triggered into your own self-protective strategies. Unfortunately, your frustration can leak out in your interactions with your partner. If you expect your partner's rage and wariness to be reduced or resolved by now, you will find that your aggravation acts as a danger signal to the other, only enhancing their uncertainty. I urge you to reflect on your frustration and to reframe it as energy – energy that you are wanting to put into repairing the relationship. I will help you to channel that energy into healing, but for now, notice how it impacts the signals you send.

Sometimes, we prefer to feel anger if the alternative is to feel guilt. Partners who have damaged the relationship's trust often tell me that they feel awfully guilty for causing pain, and terribly ashamed of the choices that led to this attachment injury. Guilt is a healthy emotional reaction that appears in response to hurting someone who matters to you. The discomfort of this experience will force you to pay attention to this injury and to make amends. Guilt acts as a personal homing beacon that alerts us when we have upset an important person in our world. That swirling uneasiness in your gut that keeps you peeking at the hurt party to see how impacted they are comes from guilt. Guilt propels us to attend to the tender spot in the other and to make a repair. Guilt is other-focused, and you are likely to be feeling a lot of it.

Shame on the other hand is self-focused. Shame is an emotional reaction that tells us about our self-worth. Shame lets us know when we are not proud of ourselves. It acts as the tap on the shoulder that says, "Am I okay about who I am right now?" Shame is adaptive for a social species like humans because it acts as a social brake.[10] In evolutionary terms, it stops us from doing things that could get us rejected from the herd, and if you do find yourself excluded, the expression of shame helps with being allowed back in. Shame is a tricky emotion because it makes us want to curl into ourselves and to hide from others. We don't want anyone to see our shameful places, we don't even want to look at those places ourselves. Shame can pull you away from others or it can push you to make amends with others. It can send you spiralling into more dark places within yourself and make it impossible for healing work to happen, or it can be immensely helpful in repairing the security of your bond. We will look more at working with guilt and shame and getting this balance right later in this book because it is so crucial to being able to repair your bond and grow as an individual.

Knowing that you have been hurtful is difficult, in and of itself, but knowing that you could lose the person who matters so much as a result is unbearably painful. Given that you find yourself in the position of having caused harm, how you manage the fallout of this attachment injury can determine whether you can mine this event for meaning by learning about yourself and your relationship, and whether you can repair your bond. Using this difficult time as an opportunity for personal reflection and growth can lead to substantial changes in your world – internally and externally. That is the important work that I hope you can undertake as you work through this book. It is brave and courageous to stay with this process. I am full of admiration for partners who can stay the course to confront pain they have caused and be active in the healing process. You are working on your relationship's behalf. That is no easy feat.

Ripple-effect of attachment injuries

The meaning of the hurtful event and its impact on the bedrock of trust in the relationship is impacted by many factors and in turn, it can impact many other people in your world. Your level of commitment to this relationship, whether you have children together, whether this is an isolated incident or part of a pattern of breaches of trust will all impact how deeply this is felt by those immediately involved. Additionally, each partner's past experience in relationships and their earliest attachment relationships will have taught them important lessons about closeness, lessons that could be confirmed by this injury. This can create a larger ripple-effect of hurt between you. How you each respond to the other when there are reminders of this hurt or as you discuss the details of the critical events will also impact a sense of shared pain and helplessness and can cause further waves of hurt.

If this attachment injury impacts more than the two of you, then the ripples will travel further. For instance, if you are in an open or polyamorous relationship, then there will be other partners that are impacted by this breach of trust and by the trouble in this dyad. If there are children who are aware of the hurtful events or extended family or friends that are involved or impacted, this will extend the impact of the injury and possibly bring tension and hurt to more relationships within the larger system. Sometimes, external influences can exacerbate the rupture between the primary partners. Tensions can flare if other parties in extended family systems weigh-in on the troubles or attempt to influence the outcome. If there has been secrecy and hiding, then those who were lied to are likely to feel extremely hurt, even if they are not the primary partner or directly impacted. This can cause significant damage to relationships. There can be multiple ruptures across several relationships, all which may need tending to.

If the hurtful act involves risky behaviour (e.g., exposing yourself and your primary partner to sexually transmitted diseases), financial loss, legal troubles, or loss of employment, then the extent of the damage can turn a ripple into a tsunami.

How good people can be hurtful

As you grapple with the impact of this breach of trust in your relationship, I imagine that you have spent much time attempting to understand how and why it happened. This is important work that will ultimately assist you in repairing your bond, but it can take some time to organise. When a relationship is rocked by an attachment injury, the first questions people ask is "I thought we were happy, how could this happen?" and "I thought I could trust you, how could you do this to me?" The first question stems from an assumption that for trust to be broken, there must be something wrong with the foundations of the relationship, it must be cracked some-where and unless we can find the crack, it will forever be weak. The second question relates to concern about the possible motivations of the hurtful partner. Is the crack within my partner and what does it mean? Some-times, hurt partners also blame themselves by asking how they might have contributed to the other being so hurtful. They look for the crack within themselves.

Most of the time, the factors that contribute to an attachment injury are multiple and layered. In some cases, they are clearly apparent for all to see, and in other cases, they are more elusive. For instance, one part-ner's affair might be clearly driven by their need for connection in the context of a very troubled relationship with their partner. In this instance, there are many possible "cracks" that can be uncovered and explored and potentially repaired. For another relationship, one partner's hiding of their alcohol addiction might be difficult to understand in the context of a loving and honest relationship. It might be stemming from personal issues within one partner that are yet to be discovered and understood.

In seeking to understand how good people can become hurtful to those who matter most to them, I want to be clear that I am not condoning hurtful acts. The partner who has been hurtful bears the responsibility for the impact of their choices. Understanding the motivations behind hurt-ful actions is part of coming to grips with this attachment injury. This is important for both the hurt partner and the hurtful partner. We will do this not to excuse or justify behaviours that have been damaging to trust, but to understand the vulnerability that might have been there before this event and the factors that could be preventing the healing of the rupture afterwards. We are beginning this process now, but it is one that takes considerable time and that we will return to throughout this book.

If we endeavour to understand how hurtful acts can happen by looking at the research on heterosexual monogamous couples, we learn that sexual relationships outside the primary relationship can have a range of motivations. For some people, they can have extramarital sex without being dissatisfied emotionally or sexually in their primary relationship[11] and for others, affairs can be motivated by deeper concerns. It is helpful to divide these into three categories; *relationship* factors such as, unresolved conflict and unmet needs for love, affection, and sex, *situational* factors such as, being clouded by stress or being intoxicated, and *personal* factors, such as self-esteem enhancement or drive for autonomy.[12] What this shows us is that behind a hurtful act, there could be a range of motivations, both personal and interpersonal, and it could be serving a range of needs.

There are also significant gender differences in reasons for extramarital affairs. Men said that they were sexually motivated to engage in their affair because they were curious, and they wanted to try new things, and while they were emotionally motivated to feel loved and appreciated, this was second to sexual motivation. On the other hand, women were found to be more emotionally motivated to engage in an affair, citing a desire for closeness and love as being more important than sexual motivation.[13] This is in line with research showing that women may seek closeness and intimacy elsewhere if dissatisfied emotionally in their primary relationship and that men are more sexually motivated to engage in affairs, especially if dissatisfied sexually in their primary relationship.[14]

In reflecting on the attachment injury that has devastated the trust in your relationship, the hurtful event may indicate an issue that one partner needs to explore more deeply. I have found that behind hurtful acts there is often an *unexpressed or unacknowledged need*. When acted on impulsively or taken in covert and harmful ways, this is extremely damaging to the relationship. Obviously, it is important to uncover these deeper needs to make meaningful changes moving forward. For some people, throughout their life, they may have become so disconnected from their own emotions and needs that they have very little awareness of what they might be. They can find themselves acting on unacknowledged needs with very little awareness of why. In reflecting on these patterns, it is clear to me that when an individual has had experiences throughout their life of their needs not being heard or acknowledged, they learn powerful lessons about expressing them. They can become disconnected from them. If a person has repeated experiences in their most meaningful relationships (particularly growing up) of their needs being unimportant, dismissed, or ridiculed, then it makes total sense why they would stop sharing them. When another's need is always more important and you learn that you must *squash* your needs, it can build a level of resentment and teaches you that the only way to meet your needs is to take care of them yourself, often in covert ways. This pattern can be outside of or on the fringes of conscious awareness and can show up despite having more positive relationships later in life where your needs could potentially be embraced. Patterns like this are important to flush out and to elucidate as part of coming to terms with this attachment injury. Examples of taking needs in covert ways are secret spending, having a sexual relationship that violates the agreements of the primary relationship, not respecting the other's consent sexually, or breaking promises.

In a similar vein, partners who have been hurtful can also express that the hurtful act was something they were engaging in purely to manage their inner world (e.g., to manage stress or to lift their spirits) with no intent to hurt the other. These hurtful acts often happen without awareness of the impact on the other or by not considering the impact it could have on the other. When motivated in this way, hurtful partners are seeking to manage their emotions in a way that makes sense to them. Altering these patterns of emotion regulation or of meeting their needs in this way might prove difficult, even if they become aware that it causes their partner hurt. People might find themselves reverting to old habits and either disengaging from thoughts about the impact or by minimising the perception of harm. They might tell themselves a story about why they need to do this thing, why it's not that big a deal, or how their partner shouldn't be so impacted by it. They might agree to no longer engage in the behaviour or make promises to themselves and their partner that they go on to break. Examples might be gambling, illicit drug-use, or using online porn or chat sites (things that go against relationship agreements). Put simply, they may not have been deliberately hurtful, but their impact is damaging, nevertheless.

Hurtful partners can often cite the lack of clear boundaries around expectations or unclear agreements as the source of the hurt. Those in monogamous relationships are often clear about sexual exclusivity but may not be so clear about emotional boundaries with someone other than their partner. When an emotional connection is formed with someone other than the primary partner, hurtful partners might defend their actions by expressing confusion around the "rules" of their relationship, and a belief that so long as the relationship wasn't sexual, they did not consider it to be violating their agreement of monogamy. Those in non-monogamous relationships tend to put more work into negotiating the relationship agreements and to clarifying the nature and extent of other partnerships. Despite this careful planning, hurts can happen if those agreements are broken. Examples might include having unprotected sex with another partner or sharing something with one partner that you had promised another to keep confidential.

When the attachment injury occurs, hurtful partners might maintain that they were torn between two competing priorities, and that no matter which one they attended to, they would suffer negative consequences. An example of this could be being pulled between a pressing work commitment and attending their partner's important medical appointment. In these cases, as with many of the examples above, there is a clear difference between intent and impact.

Occasionally, hurtful acts happen with a direct awareness of the negative consequences and impact on the other. These breaches of trust represent a rebellion against, or rejection of, the shared agreements of the relationship and can even be directly punitive, controlling, or intimidating towards the other partner. In these cases, the hurtful act is a more violent attack on the foundation of the relationship and on the partner's wellbeing. It obliterates trust and creates a power-imbalance in the relationship. Research shows that some partners in monogamous relationships cite anger at their partner as motivation for extramarital affairs. Unless the hurtful partner can take responsibility for their damaging impact on the other and on their bond, and they can uncover the underlying needs that might have been driving their behaviour, then it will be impossible for trust to be restored.

In a healthy relationship, partners share responsibility for protecting the relationship from threats and from causing damage to the bond by violating each other's trust. I strongly believe that partners are each *solely* responsible for their own behaviour and their own choices within their relationships; so long as there is shared power. For instance, if one partner violates a relationship agreement or violates the other's rights to physical and emotional safety, then the responsibility for that action lies squarely with them. These actions cannot be blamed on the other party or external forces. The relational dynamic might have set the scene for damaging influences to creep closer, but the partner who chose to engage in a damaging behaviour is responsible for their choices.

Four subtypes of attachment injuries

As you can see, while similar in their impact on the security of the bond, attachment injuries can take many forms. The most basic measure of whether a hurtful act could become an attachment injury is to ask yourself, if your partner was witnessing this behaviour or had knowledge of it, would they be okay with it? If not, then it is probably a violation of the relationship's expectations and agreements (spoken or unspoken) and it has the potential to shred the delicate fabric of your trusting bond.

All attachment injuries involve a sense of betrayal or being abandoned in a time of intense need. All leave the hurt partner questioning their value to the other and cause them to redefine the hurtful partner as untrustworthy. All attachment injuries create insecurity in the relationship bond. Separate from the specific details, hurtful acts will most likely have a key theme of the hurtful partner centring their own needs over the other.

To allow us to explore different attachment injuries, I have created four subtypes to understand the intricacies of particular breaches of trust. This will hopefully help you to identify the core injury you are managing and to allow us to be more targeted in our healing work. If we return to the analogy of an attachment injury being like a broken bone that needs stabilising before it can heal, there are many ways that a bone can be broken. These four groups of attachment injuries follow the same theme:

1 Sexual and emotional betrayal – Compound fracture
2 Violated boundaries – Occult fracture
3 Abandonment at a time of need – Fragmented facture
4 Threatening the safety or livelihood – Spiral fracture

Betrayal: sexual and emotional

Compound fracture – A break where a portion of the bone protrudes through the flesh.

If a monogamous or non-monogamous relationship has agreed-upon expectations about sexual and or emotional exclusivity, then any secret emotional or sexual behaviour with another party that contravenes these expectations will compromise those commitments and break trust. The hurt is often caused by the secrecy and concealment of the actions that defy the relationship ground rules. These agreements might have been clearly spelled out or implicitly established, and the violation of these relationship tenants is ruinous to the bond. As we have established, it is the meaning of the hurtful actions in the context of the relationship, and the promises made to each other that shapes the significance of the event for those involved.

This breach of trust is like a broken bone, but the break is "compound" in that the broken part of the bone protrudes through the flesh. This type of break is painful and horrifying, and plain for all to see. This mirrors the devastating nature of sexual and emotional attachment injuries because they are universally experienced as extremely distressing, cause trauma that extends beyond the break in trust, and are often seen by others outside of the relationship. They also involve another party who may or may not also be injured and whose needs can become a part of the dynamic.

Infidelity in monogamous relationships has been defined as *a secret romantic, sexual, or emotional behaviour that constitutes a breach of trust in that it violates the expectations and agreements of the primary relationship.*[15] In research spanning 160 cultures, it has been revealed that infidelity in monogamous relationships is the most common reason for a relationship to break up.[16] Infidelity is often particularly damaging because monogamy between heterosexual couples is commonly viewed as the only socially acceptable form of romantic pairing. In same-sex relationships, however, social norms have not been applied as rigidly, possibly due to gay, lesbian, and bisexual people having to struggle to keep their sexual identities a secret for fear of social judgement. Consequently, fewer rules regarding relationship structure and definition may have been imposed on them, and they have embraced diverse relationship structures. As a result, lesbian, gay, and bisexual people have the freedom and creativity to derive their own rules that may vary greatly from one relationship to another.[17] Along with some heterosexual people, gay, lesbian, and bisexual people are choosing to have non-monogamous relationships where multiple relationships can flourish with established ground rules between members. For non-monogamous relationships, these ground rules and agreements form the backbone of trust between partners, and violation of those commitments is experienced as an attachment injury.

In many monogamous relationships, there are clear expectations preventing sexual behaviour outside of the primary relationship, but it may be a little less clear what would constitute an emotional attachment injury. There might be an expectation that the partner will be the one you are closest to emotionally as well as sexually. However, even if a person is sexually monogamous with their partner, they may have multiple attachment figures, and this can make defining what would represent an emotional betrayal difficult. Generally, emotional infidelity is considered to be emotional involvement with a third party that steps outside of the primary relationship's ground rules, such as sharing more with another than your partner, withholding details of the relationship from your primary partner, or being more committed to another. Interestingly, research looking at heterosexual and lesbian females and heterosexual and gay men in monogamous relationships showed that all four groups reported emotional affairs to be more distressing than sexual affairs.[18] Examples of emotional affairs in monogamous relationships include secretly sharing your deepest fears with someone other than your partner, turning to them at the expense of your primary relationship, or prioritising spending time with another person when your partner really needs you. In non-monogamous relationships emotional violations might include sharing emotionally with one partner in a way that violates an agreement with another partner.

Interestingly, research on heterosexual couples shows us that men are more likely to be distressed by their partner having a sexual affair, while women are more likely to be distressed by their partner having an emotional affair.[19] Sexual affairs seem to elicit anger and blame from the hurt partner, while emotional affairs seem to evoke greater feelings of hurt.[20] The level of distress about an emotional affair seems to be higher in those who were very committed to their relationship, and the level of distress about a sexual affair seems to be higher in those who felt their relationship lacked sexual connection.

Violation: trampled boundaries

Occult fracture – fracture causes pain but is difficult to locate.

Emotional and sexual betrayal involves violation of established relationship boundaries. However, I wanted to create another subtype of attachment injuries to identify breaches of trust that are not limited to sexual and emotional betrayal. This subtype of attachment injuries relates to violations of the relationship agreements concerning honesty, trust, openness, and transparency. This type of injury centres around secrecy and its consequences. An "occult" fracture of a bone can be difficult to detect, causing pain and weakness long before the break is identified. Violations of boundaries can act in the same way. Trust is broken, and the source of the break can take time to uncover.

Sometimes the violation takes the form of lying by omission or of keeping part of your life secret from the other. This could include hiding a special interest (such as a secret fetish or hobby), not sharing a health concern (such as receiving treatment and not telling the other), pretending to go to work when actually no longer employed, engaging in clandestine habits (such as online gaming, spending, or use of pornography), or withholding information that the other would want to know (such as about the state of the shared finances). These types of betrayals can involve deceptive decision-making where one partner makes a unilateral decision that impacts the other, such as becoming pregnant or interfering with contraception without the other's knowledge, or taking on financial risk without the other's consent. The consequences of this can be severe because, once discovered, trust is broken, and history must be re-written as new information comes to light. The foundation of the relationship is called into question. The lack of openness and honesty undermines the creation of true security in the bond and then the subsequent discovery of the secret violation is devastating. In a way, withholding information from the other is a covert means of meeting your own needs and of taking the other's power and choice away. This is shattering to trust between partners.

Abandonment: absence at a time of need

Fragmented fracture – bone broken in many pieces.

We never need our attachment figures more than when we are vulnerable and scared. This is fundamental to how we cope with difficult times as humans and is how we define our special others. If we know that they are there for us in times of need, then we can trust in them as a resource to lean on when times are tough. So, if your attachment figure is not responsive to you when you really need them, this has a monumental impact on the security of your attachment bond. We know that the presence of a loving other during times of stress reduces threat-related brain activity, perception of pain, and emotional regulation.[21] Humans do not do well in isolation, it is taxing to our nervous systems.

If we think of attachment injuries that arise from abandonments as a broken bone, this is a "fragmented" break because there is the original break of trust and the additional pain that comes from having to cope alone. We are most vulnerable to an attachment injury in times of stress and change, but particularly when sick, pregnant, or scared. When the other is not there as support, it sends a signal that you are all alone, that you can't count on your partner. As humans, we seem to be most vulnerable and most in need of our attachment figures' presence and responsiveness when we are facing major life-transitions or when our identity or mortality is threatened. The greater to vulnerability, the greater the need for the other's responsiveness and presence.

Abandonments can take the form of one partner not responding to the other's call for help in a time of urgent need, not being close at hand as the other faces a major health crisis, or not being there to face a hardship together or celebrate an important milestone together. Not protecting the other from abuse by a third party can certainly feel like an abandonment as can being distracted by something else at a time when the other is in need. Attachment injuries that come from being abandoned at a time of vulnerability are profoundly painful. They hurt because they redefine your special other as unavailable and untrustworthy and they shake your faith in yourself as deserving care. This violation of trust indicates to the hurt partner that the other can no longer be counted on for caring and support when needed. On top of this abandonment, you are left on your own to face adversity. Subsequently, the injury will only be compounded if the hurt partner approaches the offending partner about the events and is met with defensive responses such as dismissal or denial. Over time, if the fractured bond is not repaired then feelings of despair and alienation develop.[22]

Danger: threats to relational safety

Spiral fracture – Bone is broken with a twisting force.

The fourth subtype of attachment injuries is those injuries that threaten the safety of the relationship. By threatening the safety, I mean that they compromise the emotional or physical safety between partners, or they jeopardise the security of the shared life together. This type of injury could include one partner gambling away the shared savings, making a unilateral decision to take on more debt, engaging in risky behaviour that could bring about legal troubles or threaten the livelihood of either partner, physical violence (or the threat of violence), or endangering the other to sexually transmitted diseases. It can involve one partner being deliberately hurtful with their words, such as, through the weaponising of the other's vulnerability. This could mean metaphorically hitting someone "below the belt," or using disclosures they have made about their worst fears or toughest times against them later. When this happens, the injuring partner looks like the enemy – like they want to inflict the most damage possible to the other. It is extremely difficult to come back from this type of injury. It is devastating to the shared trust, the life together, and to the security of the relationship. The breach of trust is brutal and frightening and its consequences likely to be far reaching. This type of injury breaks trust like a broken bone, but the added threat to safety of the relationship is like a "spiral" fracture where the break has been caused by a twisting force.

The hurt from this type of injury is profound. Not only does it break the trust between partners, it also legitimately redefines the hurtful partner as unsafe in the other's eyes. When the attachment figure is both the source of and solution to pain, this is inherently disorganising for the hurt partner and it places them in an untenable position.[23] Restoring safety in this type of injury will take time and willingness to confront the deeper issues underlying this injury and commitment to making the relationship emotionally and physically safe (Figure 2.1).

Now that we have explored the impact of attachment injuries and looked at the differences between the many and varied ways that people who love each other can cause them, it is time to give you a map for healing so that you can have a bird's eye view of the repair process and what it entails. In the next chapter, we will look at how Emotionally Focused Therapy can help partners to rebuild their bond, how distress shows up in relationships, and how we can target the attachment injury using the Attachment Injury Resolution Model to restore security in your bond once more.

Attachment Injuries

An attachment Injury is defined as a betrayal, breach of trust, or abandonment in a critical moment of need that is devastating to the security of the relational bond. It is an event that profoundly impacts the way the hurt partner views the other, themselves & the relationship. More than just a small rupture to the fabric of the attachment bond, an attachment injury represents a break in the bond between partners that redefines the relationship bond as insecure.

Impact of Attachment Injuries

An attachment injury is experienced as a relational trauma. It shatters the trust between partners. It is an event(s) that has special meaning on an attachment level that redefines the hurtful partner in the hurt partner's mind as unresponsive, unreliable & untrustworthy.

Hurt partners typically describe the attachment injury as traumatic, shocking & unbelievable. The fact that the one they trusted the most could hurt them so deeply is completely destabilising. This hurtful event delivers evidence of the others' lack of trustworthiness, dependability & reliability. It presents an attachment dilemma - connect & risk being hurt again or stay away & risk losing the bond entirely.

Hurtful partners are often deeply troubled knowing that they have caused pain to their loved one & experience a mixture of guilt, shame, & helplessness. Hurtful partners can be just as impacted as hurt partners when it comes to the very real threat of losing the relationship. They might want to defend, justify, reassure & explain & can feel utterly helpless in making amends.

Types of Attachment Injuries

Betrayal
Sexual & Emotional

Hurt caused by the secrecy & concealment of actions that break the relationship ground rules. If a monogamous or non-monogamous relationship has agreed-upon expectations about sexual & emotional exclusivity, then any secret emotional or sexual behaviour with another party that breaks those agreements will also break trust.

Violation
Trampled Boundaries

Breaches of trust that are not limited to sexual & emotional betrayal. This subtype of attachment injuries relates to violations of the relationship agreements concerning honesty, trust, openness & transparency. This hurt centers around secrecy & its consequences. E.g. lying by omission, keeping secrets, or deceptive decision-making.

Abandonment
Absence at a Time of Need

Hurt stemming from being abandoned at a time of intense need. When your attachment figure is not responsive or available to you when you really need them, this impacts the security of your attachment bond. We are most vulnerable to an attachment injury in times of stress & change, but particularly when sick, pregnant, or scared.

Danger
Threats to Relational Safety

Those injuries that threaten the safety of the relationship by compromising the emotional or physical safety between partners, or they jeopardise the security of the shared life together. E.g. gambling away the shared savings, engaging in risky behaviours that could bring about legal troubles, being violent or threatening.

Clare Rosoman 2024

Figure 2.1 Attachment injuries.

Notes

1 Johnson, S.M., Makinen, J.A., & Millikin, J.W. (2001). Attachment injuries in couple relationships: A new perspective on impasses in couples therapy. *Journal of Marital and Family Therapy*, 27, 145–155.
2 Lonergan, M., Brunet, A., Rivest-Beauregard, M., & Groleau, D. (2021). Is romantic partner betrayal a form of traumatic experience? A qualitative study. *Stress Health*, 37, 19–31.
3 Furrow, J.L., Johnson, S.M., Bradley, B., Brubacher, L.L., Campbell, T.L., Kallos-Lilly, V., Palmer, G., Rheem, K.D., & Woolley, S.R. (2022). *Becoming and emotionally focused therapist: The workbook* (2nd ed.). New York: Routledge.
4 Johnson, S.M. (2005). Broken bonds. *Journal of Couple & Relationship Therapy: Innovations in Clinical and Educational Interventions*, 4(2–3), 17–29.
5 Fitness, J., & Warburton, W. (2009). Thinking the unthinkable: Cognitive appraisals and hurt feelings. In A.L. Vangelisti (Ed.). *Feeling hurt in close relationships* (pp. 34–49). New York: Cambridge University Press.
6 Vangelisti, A.L. (2001). Making sense of hurtful interactions in close relationships. In V. Manusov & J.H. Harvey (Eds.). *Attribution, communication behavior, and close relationships* (pp. 38–58). Cambridge: Cambridge University Press.
7 Feeney, J.A., & Fitzgerald, J. (2012). Relationship education. In P. Noller & G.C. Karantzas (Eds.). *The Wiley-Blackwell handbook of couples and family relationships* (pp. 289–305). New Jersey: Wiley-Blackwell.
8 Shaver, P.R., Mikulincer, M., Lavy, S., & Cassidy, J. (2009). Understanding and altering hurt feelings: An attachment-theoretical perspective on the generation and regulation of emotions. In A.I. Vangelisti (Ed.). *Feeling hurt in close relationships* (pp. 92–119). New York: Cambridge University Press.
9 Abrahms-Springs, J. (2020). *After the affair: Healing the pain and rebuilding trust when a partner has been unfaithful* (3rd ed.). New York: Harper.
10 Schore, A.N. (2003). *Affect regulation and the repair of the self*. New York: W.W. Norton.
11 Atkins, D.C., Dimidjian, S., & Jacobson, N.S. (2001). Why do people have affairs? Recent research and future directions about extramarital affairs. In V. Manusov & J.H. Havey (Eds.). *Attribution, communication behaviour & close relationships* (pp. 305–319). Cambridge: Cambridge University Press.
12 Selterman, D., Garcia, J.R., & Tsapelas, I. (2021). What do people do, say, and feel when they have affairs? Associations between extradyadic infidelity motives with behavioral, emotional, and sexual outcomes. *Journal of Sex Marital Therapy*, 47, 238–252.
13 Glass, S.P., & Wright, T.L. (1992). Justifications for extramarital relationships: The association between attitudes, behaviour and gender. *Journal of Sex Research*, 29, 361–387.
14 Mark, K.P., Janssen, E., & Milhausen, R.R. (2011). Infidelity in heterosexual couples: Demographic, interpersonal, and personality-related predictors of extradyadic sex. *Archives of Sexual Behaviour*, 40, 971–982.
15 Blow, A.J., & Hartnett, K. (2005). Infidelity in committed relationships II: A substantive review. *Journal of Marital and Family Therapy*, 31, 217–233.
16 Grøntvedt, T.V., Kennair, L.E.O., & Bendixèn, M. (2020). Breakup likelihood following hypothetical sexual or emotional infidelity: Perceived threat, blame, and forgiveness. *Journal of Relationship Resources,* 11, 1–9, e7.
17 Martell, C.R., & Prince, S.E. (2005). Treating infidelity in same-sex couples. *Journal of Clinical Psychology*, 61(11), 1429–1438.

18 Leeker, O., & Carlozzi, A. (2014). Effects of sex, sexual orientation, infidelity expectations, and Love on distress related to emotional and sexual infidelity. *Journal Marital and Family Therapy,* 40, 68–91.
19 Buss, D.M., Larsen, R.J., Westen, D., & Semmelroth, J. (1992). Sex differences in jealousy: Evolution, physiology, and psychology. *Psychological Science,* 3(4), 251–255.
20 Green, M.C., & Sabini, J. (2006). Gender, socioeconomic status, age, and jealousy: Emotional responses to infidelity in a national sample. *Emotion,* 6(2), 330–334.
21 Johnson, S.M., Moser, M.B., Beckes, L., Smith, A., Dalgleish, T., et al. (2013). Soothing the threatened brain: leveraging contact comfort with emotionally focused therapy. *PLoS One,* 8(11), e79314. https://doi.org/10.1371/journal.pone.0079314.
22 Johnson, S.M. (2004). *The practice of emotionally focused couple therapy: Creating connections* (2nd ed.). New York: Brunner/Mazel.
23 Main, M., & Hesse, E. (1990). Parent's unresolved traumatic experiences are related to infant disorganized attachment status. In M. Greenberg & D. Cicchetti (Eds.). *Attachment in the pre-school years* (pp. 152–176). Chicago: University of Chicago Press.

Chapter 3

Healing an attachment injury

We have looked at attachment injuries and why they are so devastating to trust in close relationships. Now, it is time to look at the repair process. In this chapter, I will introduce you to an evidence-based model for building security in close relationships called Emotionally Focused Therapy (EFT). Luckily, this model of therapy is backed by science and has a specific approach for helping troubled partners to repair attachment injuries. Next, we will focus on how partners can become stuck in cycles of distress that can block them from healing and add to their distress. All relationships have communication patterns or cycles that can cause crossed-wires and scrambled signals. This is never more the case than when there has been a breach of trust. This negative interactional pattern can flare when there has been an attachment injury, either stemming from a cycle that pre-dated the hurtful event or it can evolve because of the hurt. Either way, it is common for partners to find themselves caught in a pattern that blocks their capacity for healing and further erodes their connection.

Before we start looking at how to repair this attachment injury, we need to do some groundwork in understanding where relationships go wrong and what we know about strengthening attachment security between partners. Hang in there with me as I introduce you to EFT and to some of the common ways that partners can become disconnected, especially when there has been an attachment injury. I want to assure you that we are going to be exploring the impact of this injury on the communication in your relationship later in this chapter, as well as outlining the repair process so that you have a sense of direction in our work. But first, let's talk about EFT – the most effective model of couples' therapy out there.[1]

Introduction to Emotionally Focused Therapy

When working with the good people I see in my practice, I am an ardent proponent of EFT. As an international EFT trainer, I passionately share this model with therapists all around the world. I am sold on EFT as

DOI: 10.4324/9781003466499-5

an effective model of therapy for building attachment security within individuals and between people who matter to each other. EFT was developed by Professor Sue Johnson and Professor Leslie Greenberg in the late 1980s.[2] Sue Johnson has gone on to develop her model more over time by integrating knowledge about adult attachment and bonding.[3] Therapists and clients alike all over the world have experienced the power of EFT.

As a model for working with couples, families, and relationships, EFT has garnered a wealth of scientific evidence for its effectiveness. EFT is also proving itself to be a powerful model for assisting individuals (Emotionally Focused Individual Therapy, EFIT). Over the last 30 years, considerable research has gone into the development of this model of therapy and into investigating its efficacy in helping couples move from distress to recovery. So far, the research has mainly looked at monogamous dyads, and 86%–90% of couples taking a course of EFT reported significant improvement with and 70%–75% recovering from their distress.[4] The positive effects of EFT on couple satisfaction and connection have been shown in even the most distressed relationships[5] to both continue to improve after therapy ends, and to remain stable over time.[6] We now have evidence that a course of EFT not only changes the security of the bond between partners, it also changes individual partners' attachment strategy.[7]

This is wonderful because EFT is going to be your most helpful tool in repairing the ruptured trust in your relationship. Put succinctly, EFT is all about creating secure attachment bonds between people who matter to each other. It does this by helping partners to improve their connection by firstly understanding their own emotional world more clearly and then sharing their needs and fears in ways that can be heard and felt by their partner. EFT is based on the idea that sharing emotional vulnerability in a clear way reduces missed signals, misunderstandings, and incorrect assumptions, and it creates a strong and secure bond between partners, built through mutual risk and trust. Like two pieces of Velcro facing each other – vulnerability is what draws and sticks partners together. In EFT, we help partners to build security in their bond by assisting them to be accessible and responsive to each other and engaged with each other (the accessible, responsive, engaged (ARE) of secure attachment we discussed in Chapter 1). This form of therapy is so effective because it goes right to the heart of the matter (where the pain, fear, and longing lives) and works on building attachment security between partners. It is all about human bonding.

When there has been a breach of trust in a close relationship, the non-blaming attachment-based focus of EFT is effective in helping partners to identify stuck patterns of communication, in reducing defensiveness, and in creating healing moments that can restore the attachment security. The focus on emotion in EFT means that this model can assist hurt partners to lower their protective defences and to process the pain of betrayal in adaptive and healthy ways. Likewise, EFT can help hurtful partners to manage their defensiveness and to process their sense of helplessness and shame in ways that can restore the trusting bond.

EFT has three distinct stages that track the relationship change process as it moves from distress to recovery. In Stage 1 of EFT, we help partners to identify and untangle themselves from negative interactional patterns (cycles of distress) that happen when partners are hurt and disconnected. This stage is called "stabilisation," which works nicely with our broken bone analogy, where we are stabilising the broken limb to prevent further damage and to set the scene for the repair work. In Stage 2 of EFT, we "restructure" the attachment bond by diving deeply into vulnerable places within each person and encouraging the sharing of tender emotions. When people can take their sore spots to each other and risk being fully seen, and are met with acceptance, this powerfully transforms the relationship's bond. Along with our broken bone analogy, Stage 2 is where the bones are supported as they knit together, leaving them stronger in the broken place. EFT has a special model called the Attachment Injury Resolution Model, especially for this healing work in Stage 2, which I will tell you more about later in this chapter. In Stage 3 of EFT, we consolidate these changes and look at ways to protect and nurture the bond moving forward. This acts as the physiotherapy that keeps a healed injury strong and prevents re-injury.

Stage 1 EFT: cycles of distress in relationships

The first task in Stage 1 of EFT is to identify the cycle of distress (the negative and stuck interactional pattern) that could be causing disconnection in your relationship. One of the most important gems that EFT has to offer is its take on relationship distress. Instead of attributing blame to either party or trying to "fix" communication problems by teaching communication skills, EFT looks at the patterns of communication between partners and tracks how they impact each other. This means that we look at problems in terms of the "team" rather than at the individual level.

When there has been broken trust in a relationship, patterns of communication usually become extremely loaded. The stakes could not be higher, and every tense moment partners have serves to further the disconnection and to cement in the cycle of distress. This leaves the original hurt unresolved and the resultant mistrust festering. When hurts are alive and tensions are running high, each partner is likely to be absorbed in overwhelming emotion and to act on it defensively. We are rarely our "best selves" in these high-stakes moments. With attachment alarm bells clanging, we tend to surprise even ourselves with the enormity of our feelings, the rigidity of our thoughts, and the desperation behind our behaviour.

Despite the chaotic nature of this experience, as humans we all basically do our version of one or two things when our attachments are under threat; we either reflexively dive into battle to fight for our needs or we retreat and duck for cover (and sometimes we try them both).

In tense moments, each partner usually feels that they are being crystal clear about their needs and can't imagine why the other doesn't understand them. They then come up with theories about why the other isn't hearing their messages, like "She just wants to fight" (no one wants to fight – people only choose this as a desperate measure to gain contact or to defend themselves), "He just doesn't care/I don't matter to him" (usually the opposite – it is distressing because you matter so much to him but he is not showing care in ways that make you feel cared for), "She's impossible to please" (it can certainly look this way when needs are not clearly stated), or "They just have to be right" (yes, it can look like this when someone is defending themselves). Partners might have strong ideas about exactly what the other needs to do to "fix" the problem and become critical about the other's responses ("If he would just…if she could change… if they stopped doing…"). These theories or assumptions about the other's behaviour and motives become self-perpetuating as each partner becomes more defensive and reactive and less clear about their deeper, more vulnerable needs and fears. The bond between them suffers, becoming brittle and insecure. The attachment injury remains unresolved, and the "broken limb" keeps being walked around on, causing immeasurable pain and worsening the damage.

This becomes a repetitive pattern that EFT therapists call a relational cycle. This cycle usually is self-perpetuating where the *way* each partner signals their needs is experienced by the other as negative and triggering. For instance, it might make sense for one partner to get louder when they perceive the other's distance, or one might become quieter and pull away when they sense tension with the other. This way of signalling a threat to the connection can become a trigger of alarm for the other – it is a signal of danger that rings attachment "sirens and alarms." For instance, one partner getting verbally louder might be experienced as threatening for the other, or one partner's silent retreat might be experienced by the other as abandoning. Harsh words or stony silence leave an indelible mark on the attachment security when tensions are running high.

A negative relational cycle is formed by partners reaching for their attachment strategy when feeling that their relationship is under threat. If you recall our discussion of attachment strategies in Chapter 1, we spoke of how they are coping strategies that help someone to maintain their emotional balance in their relationships. They are learned in our earliest relationships and shaped in our subsequent relationships throughout our lives. I think of a coping strategy as a "protective stance," something we do to cope when we feel off balance emotionally and adrift from our special person. Unfortunately, this protective stance will inevitably be triggering for the other. For instance, the more someone turns up the volume to get on the other's radar, the more the other is off-balance and turns away to regulate their stress. The more they turn away to cope, the more the other feels abandoned and turns up the heat to make contact. They get stuck doing what they feel they must, which is alarming for the other. In fact, the way one partner signals need and how they cope with being off-balance is usually an *exact trigger* for the other's coping strategy, which blocks them from being able to respond in caring ways. Both partners end up triggering the defences of the other – both look dangerous to the other – no wonder they end up disconnected and hurts can't be resolved! Of course, in these moments partners are *not* each other's safe place – they are more and more scary to each other, and the signals become more and more scrambled. The problem with this type of cycle is that *the consequence of experiencing your partner as triggering and emotionally unsafe worsens the impact of the attachment injury making repair impossible.*

Sometimes a pattern like this predates an attachment injury. It might have evolved as a result of smaller hurts, disappointments, or misunderstandings and left its mark on the security of the connection, leaving it vulnerable to further damage from bigger hurts. In these cases, the attachment injury worsens or amplifies a pre-existing negative cycle. Other times, there has not been a marked negative interactional pattern before an attachment injury occurs, but the injury itself is so triggering to all parties, that their protective attachment strategies come to the fore, creating a strong, negative cycle of distress. Almost always, an attachment injury will have a profound impact on a relationship's cycle of interaction, blocking the healing conversations that need to happen to repair this rupture to the bond.[8]

Common cycles of distress following an attachment injury

When our attachment figure has been hurtful, or we have caused hurt, and we are in "self-protection mode," we are self-focused and threat sensitive. This makes perfect sense and is a sensible way to try to regulate emotion and to guard against further harm. The problem with this protective or defensive way of coping is that it obstructs empathy and compassion for the other, fuels negative thoughts about the other, and makes sharing vulnerably impossible. We know that to heal and to restore trust in a loving bond, this requires empathy, understanding, and vulnerability. It is through shared vulnerability and gentle responsiveness that bonds are restored. Before we can be responsive, we must tackle the obstacle that prevents this healing work – the negative relational cycle. Relationship experts have identified three different patterns or cycles that are often seen in distressed relationships, so let's have a look at each.[9]

Pursue-withdraw cycle

The most common cycle we see is angry demand paired with defence or dismissal. In EFT, we call this a *pursue-withdraw cycle*. In this cycle, we have one partner who uses anxious attachment strategies and one partner who uses avoidant attachment strategies. The anxious partner reaches for coping strategies aimed at seeking connection – they want reassurance of the other's care, but they seek it in a way that pushes the other away. This might look like angry "protest" where they demand more of the other's time or are critical of the other's lack of response or lack of care. The more avoidant partner reaches for coping strategies aimed at preventing conflict – they want to reduce the emotional intensity and to create distance between them, but this signals to the other that they want to be away from them. This might look like shutting down, dismissing concerns, busying themselves with other things, staying very logical, or defending their position. Both people's coping strategies are triggering to the other. In a pursue-withdraw cycle, the anxious pursuit of one partner is just as triggering as the withdrawal of the other.

Pursue-withdraw cycles are a delicate dance where the more one partner steps forward, the other steps back, and the more one steps back, the more the other steps forward. This does not mean that we are blaming either partner or their attachment strategies for "starting" this cycle or for being more at fault. This interaction is co-created and both partners have an equal impact on the other – even if it doesn't appear that way. One partner's coping behaviour primes the attachment alarms of the other. The natural tendency of the partner using avoidant attachment strategies is to cope individually, but this is seen as a threat to closeness by the partner who uses anxious attachment strategies. The partner using anxious attachment strategies has a natural tendency to energetically seek contact (connects to regulate), but this is triggering for the partner who uses avoidant attachment strategies (retreats to regulate). When one partner stonewalls or shuts down, they block the other out, triggering the intense pain of abandonment. When one partner feels abandoned, this triggers a cascade of protest, clinging, and pain which is often experienced by the other as difficult to come close to. The more one partner protests the distance, the harder it is for the other to move closer, and the more one partner backs away to regulate themselves, the harder it is for the other to remain calm in the face of impending loss. It is easy to see here how emotional disconnection can happen and the relationship can start to feel emotionally unsafe. Both partners rely on their best coping strategy to manage the distress between them, but their way of coping is like a foreign language to the other. They just end up tripping the other's alarm system, making it difficult or even impossible for them to meet their attachment needs in that moment.

Paul and Susan, a heterosexual monogamous couple we met in Chapter 2, had a pursue-withdraw cycle before the discovery of Paul's affair. Susan would normally be the one to raise issues, and Paul, to avoid conflict where possible. This cycle only occasionally flared for them when Susan felt that Paul was very distant, but it would be fairly quickly resolved. She would complain about this lack of presence and Paul would try to brush off her concerns initially before promising to be more connected to her and the family. Paul kept his need for Susan's support and reassurance to himself. After the affair was revealed, Susan was extremely hurt and seethed with anger about the sacrifices she made for their relationship. She could not look at Paul without feeling fear and rage – *who was this person, how could he do this, how would they ever repair this, what would it mean for their life and their family together?* As a result, Susan's expression of anger and pursuit for answers to these questions meant that she relentlessly demanded that Paul explain and atone. This was her best attempt to cope with this huge threat to their relationship. She was trying to find a way to protect herself and to make sense of this injury. Despite this, Susan's anger was unbearable for Paul who didn't have a good explanation for his choices. He certainly didn't feel safe to explore what might have been driving his hurtful actions with her when she was so angry. He desperately wanted to repair the broken trust but felt unable to say anything that would reassure Susan. Paul felt utterly helpless to remain steady in the face of Susan's angry protest and to say anything that he hoped could soothe her. Susan desperately tried to keep her balance by alternating between seeking reassurance from Paul and protecting herself from hurt by pulling away from him. Paul tried to maintain his emotional balance by remaining logical and keeping his vulnerable emotions at bay, but his answers were never helpful to Susan, and he withdrew further. Susan felt so alone in her distress and completely baffled as to how Paul could remain so calm – it was like he didn't care! Susan was desperate for an explanation that would offer her some shred of understanding of how her person could become so hurtful. The more she sought answers, the more Paul withdrew emotionally, and the more they both felt alone.

Withdraw-withdraw cycle

Another typical cycle we see in relationships is a *withdraw-withdraw cycle* where there are two partners who use avoidant attachment strategies. Both are harmony-loving and used to coping individually. As a result, they are likely to try to resolve concerns on their own and to avoid turning to each other for emotional connection, preferring to connect through doing things together rather than sharing deep, vulnerable feelings. Both see coping alone as the best way of dealing with their emotional worlds and have good reasons for having learned this attachment strategy. Both understand that they need time alone, especially when processing something internally. Problems and disagreements may be mutually sidestepped for the sake of keeping the peace. In my experience, partners like this can have very low conflict because both are keen to avoid it, but they will also rarely share their deeper feelings. This means that partners in a cycle like this don't get to "practice" the skill of sharing vulnerably, of expressing clear needs, or of having to repair a rupture to their bond when things go wrong between them. This can lead to a brittle, fragile attachment bond that does not hold up well if the relationship is challenged in any meaningful way. In other words, all seems okay on the outside, but the reality is, their situation is extremely precarious.

When there is an attachment injury, partners in a withdraw-withdraw cycle are ill-equipped to process it in profound ways that restore the connection. Sonia and Emma were in a relationship like this. As a monogamous, lesbian couple, they had lived amicably together for five years and naturally seemed to want the same things out of life, rarely disagreeing about big decisions. There were some grumbling issues over how they spent their shared finances, with Emma wanting more travel and adventures and Sonia being more concerned about having savings in the bank and needing to support her ageing mother. These differences were never fully resolved between them. Sonia carried stress from her job as well as feeling extremely responsible for her mother's health care. She kept these worries inside, rarely letting Emma know about the depths of her despair. After a back injury, Sonia commenced prescription pain medication and noticed coincidentally that it improved her mood, along with managing her pain. She continued to take this medication long after the injury was resolved without telling Emma. Emma noticed that Sonia was more withdrawn and didn't seem herself, raising her concerns with Sonia in a quite timid manner. Emma was keen to not have any conflict over her concerns, so was indirect in her delivery. When Sonia always had a reason for her withdrawal, often citing tiredness, Emma was at least partially reassured. Neither spoke about what was really bothering them. Despite the lack of conflict, Emma could feel more distance than usual between them, and she began to wonder if their connection was as solid as she thought. She managed her worries on her own and reminded herself of Sonia's stressful job and the weight of being the sole carer for her mother. Sonia grappled with her reliance on this medication but kept seeking it whilst denying to Emma that there were any issues. When Sonia had three separate, but minor, traffic accidents, Emma became even more concerned. When the final accident involved interaction with the police, Sonia tearfully admitted to Emma that she had been regularly taking the prescription medication. She confessed to taking it long after it was needed for her back injury and disclosed that she thought she was dependent on it. Emma wondered if this ever would have come out if Sonia hadn't been in this last car accident. The secrecy of Sonia's medication use and her dismissal of Emma's observations broke the trust between them. Sonia felt deeply ashamed that she had put others in danger. Both partners retreated into themselves and were unable to openly share their pain and hurt, leaving the wound to their attachment bond gaping.

Pursue-pursue cycle

Sometimes we have two partners who use anxious attachment strategies and become caught in a *pursue-pursue cycle* that involves lots of heat and escalation. In this cycle, both partners are concerned with the other's availability and seek emotional contact but do this in confrontational and heightened ways that can be difficult for the other to respond reassuringly to. Despite both partners agreeing that connection is the answer to their distress, they can battle for their attachment needs to be met, becoming combative or even competitive in their quest to be "right" and to be soothed by the other. While both are battling to be heard, they are equally unavailable to the other, and equally alarming to the other's attachment system. The more they each pursue the other for their attachment needs in this way, which is likely to be intense and may have elements of demand and criticism, the more it is impossible for the other to come close. When met with this kind of approach, even a person with the same attachment strategy is going to be thrown off balance. It is so unbearable for either partner to be disconnected from their special person that they can rapidly escalate and become blind to how their attempts to get their needs met actually block the other from being able to come towards them. In cycles like this, small things become big things very quickly and partners become gridlocked with neither willing to give ground.

This cycle is particularly seen when there has been an attachment injury. It might not have been the pre-existing cycle, but after the breach in trust, it can be a reactive cycle that flares when the stakes are so high. This was the case for Callum and Casey who we met in Chapter 2. They had an open relationship with clear ground rules around other partners and sexual safety. Callum and Casey were both anxiously attached and became caught in a cycle where they would escalate their demands of the other when either partner perceived that the other was emotionally unavailable. This cycle was particularly sparked if either did not completely adhere to the agreements, they had made around other partners.

When this happened, they would have heated arguments about the nature and specificity of their agreements, and each would defend their position and accuse the other of not caring about their primary relationship. New relationship energy (the feelings of positivity that come from forming a new relationship with another partner outside the primary dyad) was particularly threatening to them. They were both committed to their non-monogamous relationship but struggled to know that they mattered to the other when they were engaged with other partners. Both had attachment histories that taught them that attachment figures are unreliable, so their fear was understandable. When Casey told Callum that a relationship with another partner had ended, this was not the total truth. In fact, she continued to see her other partner and broke their agreement about sexual precautions. It was only after Callum saw some communication between Casey and her other partner that he realised that the relationship was still alive, that they had had unprotected sex, and that Casey had shared far more about their primary relationship with this other partner than they had agreed. This break in trust threw fuel on the fire of their pre-existing cycle. Now, in addition to each feeling uncertain about their importance to the other, every misattunement became evidence of further betrayal and impending abandonment.

The impact of attachment injuries on relationship cycles

As you can see in the above examples, when a cycle pre-dates an attachment injury, then it can become amplified by the break in trust. Partners can use their existing coping strategies in more exaggerated or escalated ways. It makes sense that a shock of this proportion will intensify coping strategies. They are after all, learned ways of navigating relationships, managing attachment threats, and regulating emotions. However, sometimes the positions each partner holds in the cycle can actually *reverse*. For instance, if the partner who normally pursues is hurt, they might increase their protest or they might shut down with the sting of rejection that comes from the attachment injury. If you normally pursue for connection, you might find yourself completely withdrawing from it after you have been hurt. You might avoid tough topics for fear of what you might discover, and you might find yourself using distraction and avoidance like you never have before. If the partner who normally pursues is the one who has caused harm, this can also contribute to a total withdrawal out of helplessness and shame. This is an understandable reaction to an attachment injury. It turns your world upside down and can make you abandon old ways of coping. Likewise, if you normally tend to withdraw, after being hurt, you could find yourself going into what EFT therapists call "reactive pursuit" where you pursue for answers and insist on repair in demanding ways that can push the other away. You could also do this if you are the one who normally withdraws but because you have been hurtful to the other, you might go into reactive pursuit to put things right. There is never a better time or reason to step out of old patterns for the sake of your relationship.

Complex cycles

What we know about attachment injuries is that they are *disorganising* to the individual *and* the to the relational system – the interaction between partners. An attachment injury is a relational trauma that topples each partner's sense of reality and upends the relationship dynamic. Getting to know the cycle that is at play in your relationship is a vital first step in the healing process and one we are going to do in the next section of this book. As you start to observe the cycle that you and your partner were in before the attachment injury and subsequently since the injury, you might notice one or both of you use fearful-avoidant attachment strategies. This means a combination of anxious pursuit for connection coupled with avoidance of connection. When this happens, as is so often the case for those who have endured trauma in their earliest relationships and for those who have experienced an attachment injury, the cycle is likely to be more complex and less predictable. You might see in yourself or in your partner, a mixture of longing for emotional contact in addition to an intense fear of it. It makes all the sense in the world that you long to restore your bond, but you are also so afraid of the further hurt from the other's criticism, blame, or carelessness with your heart.

Matt and Dina were a heterosexual partnership who identified as polyamorous, but they did not have additional partners currently. They saw their relationship as extremely passionate and felt that they had a special and rare connection. Their relationship was tremendously volatile with wonderful times of deep connection interspersed with destructive conflict that left them both emotionally bruised and wary. For this reason, they felt that they needed to be more secure in their connection together before developing relationships with other partners. When they were in a good place, their relationship was loving and harmonious, but when either partner felt that the other had misunderstood them or had intentionally been thoughtless or hurtful, the relationship would awaken old wounds and mixed coping strategies. Matt would pursue contact with Dina only to retreat when it felt too much or that he was getting it wrong with her. Her criticism reminded him of his childhood trauma, stemming from an abusive and frightening father who would eviscerate him as a child. Harsh words or a negative tone from Dina sent Matt reeling into protective shutdown coupled with bursts of rage in an attempt to "never again" feel so disempowered. One moment he would angrily pursue and completely shut down the next. Dina experienced trauma in her earliest relationships with a mother who was emotionally unstable, erratic, and frightening. She managed as an adolescent by controlling her food intake in an attempt to feel in control of something in her world and developed a severe eating disorder. As an adult, Dina managed her struggle with food and body-image effectively, but it was a constant worry for her and for Matt. Matt's explosions awoke echoes for Dina of being at the whim of her mother's unpredictable outbursts which caused her substantial anxiety. Dina would seek closeness with Matt only to shy away from him really seeing her for fear of his rejection or the sting of his frustration. Her signals were just as confusing to Matt as Matt's were to Dina. Their bond suffered from the constant ruptures and repairs so that when Matt, in a burst of anger during a particularly bad fight said, "I never wanted to be with someone with an eating disorder" this was devastating to Dina. She experienced this as an attachment injury and her view of Matt as her safe place was shattered. No matter what Matt said or did to attempt to reassure her and to repair, his words spoke to Dina's worst fear – that she truly was unlovable. Matt's lack of ability to make things right with Dina went straight to the helpless place within him that never could get it right with his father – that he was a failure. This injury pressed right on the raw spots within each partner and amplified their pre-existing cycle – their bond was in tatters.

Stage 2 EFT: Attachment Injury Resolution Model

EFT as a model of relationship therapy has an evidence-based and effective method for resolving attachment injuries,[10] with positive results that last over time.[11] This is called the Attachment Injury Resolution Model, and we are going to follow this model throughout this book. It is important to me that you are fully aware of the process you will need to follow to repair the trust in your relationship. Personally, I wouldn't like to embark on a journey without a clear map and without knowing what would be required of me, and I don't imagine you would either.

The Attachment Injury Resolution Model gives us a clear path from disconnection to repair. With the help of this process, partners can transform the hurtful impact of an attachment injury and restore the security in their bond. Hurt partners are helped to experience the emotional depth of the pain and to disclose it in increasingly vulnerable ways (rather than from a self-protective stance), and hurtful partners are supported to respond with emotionally engaged empathy and remorse (rather than defensiveness). In this vulnerable process of reaching and responding, of risking and being safely caught, the hurt is processed, forgiveness is facilitated, and trust is restored.

AIRM Phase 1: stabilisation

We start the repair work by exploring the impact of this injury on both partners. We explore the pain behind the protest or the shutdown of the hurt partner and look at how their attachment strategies impact the other. Then, we look at how the hurtful partner copes with knowing that they have caused pain – how they defend themselves or attempt to keep their balance in the face of the other's raw pain. This allows us to get to *know your relational cycle*, how you impact each other when this painful topic comes alive. So far, we have started to look at some of the types of cycles that partners can become caught in when they are distressed and how an attachment injury can impact those cycles. My hope is that you are starting to recognise your cycle and how the injury has impacted it.

We pinpoint the *attachment meaning* of this event for all parties involved, particularly the hurt partner. As you learn more about attachment theory, it might be clearer now why this event has had such a monumental impact on your bond. We explore the meaning of this event for each person involved and how it has impacted their view of self, other, and the world. We also look at how it has changed each person's feeling of security in the relationship. This process is important for reflection on the layers of meaning surrounding this attachment injury and for altering the assumptions that partners might be holding about the other. To return to our analogy of the broken bone, this part of the work allows us to assess the damage and to treat the wound carefully.

Next, we look at how the negative interactional cycle is blocking the much-needed healing, and we help you to be able to *step out of it*. To do this, we start to glimpse the softer emotions that are beneath the protective shields you each wear, and to risk revealing a little more of the softer places underneath. Revealing these vulnerable places represents a shift out of defensive positions and into territory conducive to healing. *When partners can catch their cycle and take deliberate steps to lean towards their partner in more accessible ways, we have the required safety to begin the healing work!* This is a key marker of change that we rely on as an indicator of there being enough safety between you to go deeper. When we achieve this, we have stabilised the broken limb, it is in a cast, and no longer being bumped and walked around on. Now we have created a *context for healing*.

AIRM Phase 2: healing

In Phase 2, we have the required safety to do the repair work. This work calls for *vulnerable sharing of pain* from both parties. That is the most efficient way to repair ruptures and to build security in your attachment bond that I know of. To do this, we firstly support the hurt partner in expressing the emotional impact of the attachment injury in a profoundly vulnerable way. This means connecting with the impact of the injury, the essence of the hurt, and integrating the elements of the experience to share with the other.[12] This is so difficult to do when you are cautious about trusting your partner! It asks for you to lower your carefully placed and hard-earned protections and to let your partner really see your pain. This is an act of immense bravery on the part of the hurt partner and represents their hard work on their relationship's behalf.

In turn, we help the hurtful partner to take in the hurt from the other and to register deeply, the hurt partner's experience. This is so difficult to do when your own pain and shame come alive! We ask the hurtful partner to let themselves be moved by the other's pain and to access the natural ache of regret and remorse that arises when you let yourself fully engage with the impact of the injury for the other person. Next, we help the hurtful partner to express their regret and remorse in a meaningful and emotionally alive manner and to take responsibility for causing the other pain. This is where amends can be made, and apologies can be shared where needed. The hurtful partner can also share their regret about the damage to the bond and how they have also been impacted by this injury. This is a signal directly from one heart to another – it speaks straight to your attachment bond saying, "it hurts me to know that I hurt you – your pain matters to me – you matter to me."

For both partners to reach to each other with vulnerability is so powerful in restoring the trust in the relationship. It breaks the isolation for both parties – once more, they are in this together. Now, pain can be shared, partners are once again accessible, responsive, and engaged, and security can tentatively grow. Just as each partner reaches out with vulnerability to the other, so too do the osteoblasts (bone cells) from the ends of broken bone to grow new bone in the space left by the break. The bones can now knit back together.

AIRM Phase 3: growth

In the final phase of the Attachment Injury Resolution Model (AIRM), we support the hurt partner to witness and accept the other's reparative reach. This means being able to hear and trust in the hurtful partner's remorse for the hurt they caused and to accept their apology if one was called for. This allows the hurt partner to let go of some of their fear and mistrust, safe in the knowledge that the hurtful partner has reflected on this event, has learned from it, and can offer assurance that they will not be hurtful in this way again. This learning is important for both partners so that they can create a shared narrative around the attachment injury – how and why it happened, how they worked through it, and how, together, they can prevent an injury like this from occurring again in the future.

In the last piece of work to restore the security in the attachment bond, we help the hurt partner to take the bravest reach of all, that is, asking for what they need from the other. When you have been hurt so terribly by one so close, and you have guarded your heart for so long, it is terrifying to lay yourself bear and ask for reassurance and love from the person who hurt you so deeply. But, reach you must if you want to restore this bond. When the hurt partner can bravely ask for what it is that they *truly need from the other* to heal from this pain, and the other can respond with love, and acceptance, and reassurance, then this is the "antidote bonding event" that redefines the relationship as secure once more. Now, the hurtful partner can demonstrate their love and care and provide evidence that they are more invested in soothing the other than in attending to their own comfort. Usually, the hurtful act involved prioritising your own needs over your partner's and this bonding event repairs the damage of the original injury. It is the hurtful partner's accessibility and responsiveness that is the antidote to the pain of the attachment injury.

Partners sharing in mutually vulnerable and emotionally accessible ways pave the way for attachment repair. Reconciliation, the restoration of trust, and a softer emotional connection evolve as a direct result of this process.[13] This is far more powerful than a simple apology followed by acceptance or non-acceptance. This process involves the *intention to repair* and the *willingness to risk* from *both* partners – they are working on their relationship's behalf to forgive and to rebuild their connection. Not only is the break in the bone repaired, because of the calcium envelope that formed around it, it is now stronger in the broken place (Figure 3.1)!

In Part I of this book, you have already completed the groundwork for Phase 1 of the Attachment Injury Resolution Model by learning about attachment theory, attachment strategies, attachment injuries and their impact, and the cycles of distress that show up in relationships, particularly when there have been breaches in trust. In Part II, we will dive into the work of Phase 1 as it specifically applies to you and your relationship. This will create a context for healing by outlining what you each need to bring to the process, identifying the blocks to healing that might emerge for either partner, managing your reactivity, exploring the meaning of this event, looking at the elements of forgiveness, and how to manage complex attachment injuries where the hurts might have been cumulative and bidirectional.

The Attachment Injury Resolution Model

From Makinen & Johnson, 2006 & Zuccarini et.al., 2013

Phase 1 AIRM Goals

Explore the impact of the injury on the **hurt** partner	Explore the **hurtful** partner's response & impact on them
Unpack emotional experience & attachment significance of the event for each partner	Identify the negative cycle that blocks healing & access glimpses of softer emotion

Phase 2 AIRM Goals

Accessing & processing the **hurt** partner's primary emotions relating to this injury + Helping them to vulnerably share this with the other	Accessing & processing the **hurtful** partner's primary emotional responses + Helping them to express responsibility, remorse & apology

Phase 3 AIRM Goals

Hurt partner takes in the apology & can now ask for attachment needs – for reassurance	The **hurtful** partner is responsive to these needs ANTIDOTE BONDING EVENT

Clare Rosoman 2024

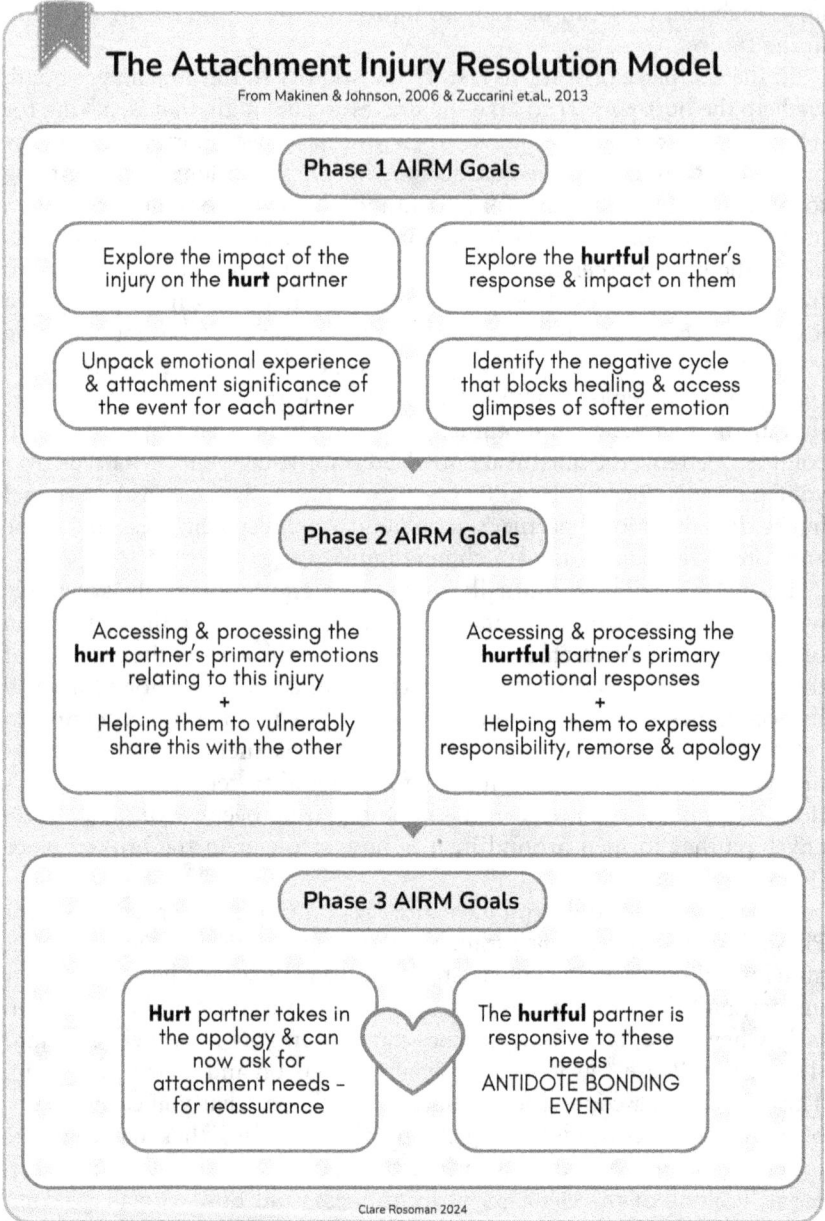

Figure 3.1 The Attachment Injury Resolution Model.

Notes

1 Beasley, C.C., & Ager, R. (2019). Emotionally focused couples therapy: A systematic review of its effectiveness over the past 19 years. *Journal of Evidence-Based Social Work*, 16(2), 144–159.
2 Greenberg, L.S., & Johnson, S.M. (1988). *Emotionally focused therapy for couples*. New York, NY: Guildford Press.
3 Johnson, S.M. (2020). *The practice of emotionally focused couples therapy: Creating connection* (3rd ed.). New York: Routledge (First ed. 1996).
4 Johnson, S.M., Hunsley, J., Greenberg, L.S., & Schindler, D. (1999). The effects of emotionally focused marital therapy: A meta-analysis. *Journal of Clinical and Counselling Psychology*, 6, 67–79.
5 Dagleish, T., Johnson, S.M., Burgess Moser, M., Wiebe, S.A., & Tasca, G. (2015). Predicting key change events in emotionally focused couple therapy. *Journal of Marital and Family Therapy*, 41(3), 260–275.
6 Johnson, S.M., & Talitman, E. (1997). Predictors of success in emotionally focused marital therapy. *Journal of Marital & Family Therapy*, 23, 135–152.
7 Wiebe, S.A., Johnson, S.M., Lafontaine, M., Burgess Moser, M., Dalgleish, T.L., & Tasca, G.A. (2016). Two-year follow-up outcomes in emotionally focused couple therapy: An investigation of relationship satisfaction and attachment trajectories. *Journal of Marital and Family Therapy*, 43(2), 227–244.
8 Brubacher, L.L. (2018). *Stepping into emotionally focused couple therapy: Key ingredients of change*. New York: Routledge.
9 Gottman, J.M., & Levenson, R.W. (2002). A two-factor model for predicting when a couple will divorce: Exploratory analyses using 14-year longitudinal data. *Family Process*, 41, 83–96.
10 Makinen, J.A., & Johnson, S. (2006). Resolving attachment injuries in couples using emotionally focused therapy: Steps toward forgiveness and reconciliation. *Journal of Consulting and Clinical Psychology*, 74, 1055–1064.
11 Halchuk, R.E., Makinen, J.A., & Johnson, S.M. (2010). Resolving attachment injuries in couples using emotionally focused therapy: A three-year follow-up. *Journal of Couple & Relationship Therapy: Innovations in Clinical and Educational Interventions*, 9, 31–47.
12 Zuccarini, D., Johnson, S.M., Dalgleish, T.L., & Makinen, J.A. (2013). Forgiveness and reconciliation in emotionally focused therapy for couples: The client change process and therapist interventions. *Journal of Marital and Family Therapy*, 39(2), 148–162.
13 Zuccarini, D., Johnson, S.M., Dalgleish, T.L., & Makinen, J.A. (2013). Forgiveness and reconciliation in emotionally focused therapy for couples: The client change process and therapist interventions. *Journal of Marital and Family Therapy*, 39(2), 148–162.

Part II

Stabilisation

Creating the context for healing

Chapter 4

Beginning the healing process

In this next section, we will begin the healing process. To do this, we firstly need to create a *context* for repair. For a broken bone to heal, we need to assess the extent of the injury and stabilise the limb to prevent further damage. Once stabilised, there is a safe context for healing. This too is the first step in recovering from an attachment injury. We need to bring all that you have learned about the attachment significance of relational hurts into your current situation to build a safe context for healing from this attachment injury.

To embark on this work, I will identify three key tasks for the hurt partner and three key tasks for the hurtful partner that will create this context for healing. These tasks will allow us to begin the work of restoring the safety in the bond. They are vital to stemming the bleeding and preventing further damage to your precious attachment bond. Next, we will begin to identify the cycle that is blocking the recovery process and look at each partner's role in contributing to that cycle. I will help you to reflect on your level of defensiveness and reactivity, and how your coping strategies might contribute to the negative interactional cycle. We know that these coping strategies might be much needed, "earned protections," but they might also be preventing the process of repair. This self-awareness is crucial to being able to identify and exit the negative pattern that blocks you from restoring closeness and security in your bond.

What each partner needs to bring to the process

To begin the work of repairing your attachment bond, there are some things that are essential to setting off on the right track. These include emotional safety, shared vulnerability, and an open heart (at least partially). Of utmost importance is the creation of emotional safety. I ask both the hurt and the hurtful partners to prioritise making the relationship a safe space in which to discuss painful material. This means being aware

DOI: 10.4324/9781003466499-7

of and taking responsibility for the hurt that you have caused the other, for how you show up in this relationship (especially when heated or when defending yourself), and for the mutual creation of a respectful space in which to begin to heal. Attachment injuries bring with them big emotions and extreme reactions – explosion of emotion, lashing out, recrimination, or polar-level shutdown. These reactions, while completely understandable, set the tone for healing and can, unfortunately, completely block it. At the end of the day, you are *both* responsible for the escalation between you, but you are each *solely* responsible for what you *say and do when you are reactive*. I need to stress that where there is open warfare or cold distance, it is impossible for either person to lower their guard or to show their soft underbelly.

If you are serious about this relationship and about repairing your tattered attachment bond, I need you to know that the only way you can do that is through vulnerably sharing your pain and remorse. Vulnerability is present when we let the tender places within our heart be seen and when we can respond to the other's tender places with softness. This requires an open heart and immense bravery. Shared vulnerability is the "secret sauce" for building attachment bonds and for repairing them when broken or frayed. When vulnerability meets vulnerability, bonds grow. When your heart is open to the other, you can share your deepest hurt and you can be impacted by the other's emotions. This allows you to find each other and to connect. It allows you each to feel empathy for the other's experience and this is vital to healing and to forgiveness.

Three tasks for the hurtful partner

As we have said, knowing that you have caused hurt to someone special to you is truly devastating. When you care deeply about another person, it is natural and inevitable that there will be times when you misattune and cause each other pain. When that pain is so great that trust is broken and your attachment bond is ruptured, then understandably this is incredibly painful for the hurt party. For the one whose actions caused the breach of trust, the anguish of being unable to wind back time and prevent the hurt is often tremendous. Hurtful partners will undoubtably struggle with feelings of guilt, shame, and despair. Sometimes, you might distance yourself from the enormity of the broken trust by numbing, staying logical, or trying to "fix" the problem. When these attempts are not effective, there is often an overwhelming fear for the future of the relationship, bringing with it a deep feeling of helplessness. It is this helplessness that we need to tackle first! This book and the Attachment Injury Resolution Model will guide you to process the emotional sequelae and to hopefully reconcile with your partner and repair your bond. However, there are three things that you firstly need to do, to set the scene for repair work. It turns out that you are not as helpless as you may feel.

Three tasks for the hurtful partner to create the context for healing:

1 Demonstrating your commitment
2 Providing transparency
3 Witnessing the pain

Commitment

Your first key task is to demonstrate your commitment to this relationship. Without this first and seemingly obvious step, there will be no way to begin to restore trust between you and your partner. You might feel that your good intentions should be obvious to your partner. After all, you're here, aren't you? It would be easier in many ways to give up on the relationship. Surely, they can see how important this is to you. In my experience, your commitment to the relationship cannot be overstated. If you think you are already demonstrating commitment, find some additional ways to show this for good measure. If you feel it, you need to show it. *And show it some more.* Hurtful partners often tell me that they are committed to repairing this rupture in trust, that they are sure they can be trusted once more, and that they feel frustrated that their partner cannot see and feel this. It would be so much easier if your partner could just step into your shoes and see for themselves how important they are to you and how trustworthy you are. Unfortunately, because of the attachment injury, your partner has learned to mistrust your words, to second-guess your motives, and to question your actions. Suddenly, your words are not enough to reassure the other, so your *actions* need to clearly signal your good intent and commitment to this relationship without room for doubt or question.

Displaying your commitment to the relationship could look like regularly checking in on how your partner is feeling, being more involved in the organising of activities together, letting them know that you are thinking of them by remembering key events in their day, sending them good luck messages before a stressful task, planning future events, asking what you can do to help them, being proactive in seeing things that need doing and taking them on, researching a place to go together, a TV show to watch, or a finding solution to a problem in your home. You demonstrate your commitment when you share the mental load of organising of your life together, when you prioritise the relationship, and when you centre your partner's needs. Showing that this relationship and your partner *matters* to you is key.

When there has been a breach of trust, demonstrating your commitment to the relationship serves two important roles in preparing for healing.

The first is that it shows that you are *invested* in the relationship, and the second is that it shows that you can *prioritise* your partner's needs over your own. These elements are usually absent when an injury happens. To the hurt partner, the hurtful event signals a disregard for the relationship and for their needs. Hurt partners tell me that they are left feeling that their needs and feelings were not on the hurtful partner's radar at all, and that they are shocked that the other could be so cavalier about the impact of their actions on the relationship. For this reason, showing your commitment to your partner and to your bond goes a long way towards building hope that this injury can be healed. Without clear demonstration of commitment to the bond, there is no way that a hurt partner will engage productively in repairing the injury – they will remain cautious, defended, and closed.

Transparency

If the attachment injury that has rocked your relationship had elements of secrecy and hiding, then the transparency of the hurtful partner is vital in creating a context for healing. If secrecy and hiding damaged your bond, then ongoing secrecy or the appearance of such will simply exacerbate the damage. Ongoing secrecy is like stomping around on the broken limb, splintering the bone more. Sadly, I hear all too often that a hurtful event is uncovered by a hurt partner, leaving them to wonder how long it would have continued if they hadn't discovered it for themselves. Similarly, when hurt partners unearth more details that have been initially withheld, their hurt is compounded. When details are retained, only to come to light later, it is impossible to begin to heal this rupture to trust. With each new piece of information, the hurt is intensified by the additional details, plus the knowledge that it was kept from them. This worsens the damage, making the repair work far more difficult.

For hurtful partners, it is crucial that you do not continue to hide details about the event that caused the attachment injury. Your transparency is the antidote to the damage caused by your secrecy. I know that being open about the details is harrowing and that it will inevitably lead to more hurt and pain, but withholding is worse for your relationship in the long run. The process of revealing the details of the hurtful event is excruciating for you both; however, it is akin to the doctor needing to X-ray the bone and to explore the wound to assess its magnitude before the course of treatment can be determined. *Hurt partners deserve to know the extent of the hurtful event to have agency in choosing whether to attempt to repair the damage.* If a hurt partner is not in possession of all the facts, then their decision to stay and repair the relationship or to leave is only based on partial information. For them, to stay and commit to a healing process without knowing the depth of the wound would be unethical and even deceptive – it would mean that any repair to the foundations of your relationship would be lacking strength, undermined by the lack of transparency.

If you have been hurtful, your task is to be transparent about the event that ruptured trust. The amount of detail that you are required to share is determined mostly by the hurt partner, but your sensitivity is also required because this can be tricky terrain. We will talk more about the limits of disclosure of details about the event later in the section on managing information for hurt partners. When sharing the details of the hurtful event, it is important that the hurt partner knows enough information that they no longer feel anything is being kept from them – that they know the extent and nature of the injury – but not necessarily the fine details that could worsen their pain.

Managing the level of detail is something that the hurt partner needs to monitor carefully, because the hurtful partner cannot be the gatekeeper of information. For them, to do this would replicate the secrecy present in original injury. Transparency can be demonstrated by being willing to talk about the injurious event and to answer questions non-defensively, as much or as little as the hurt partner needs. Because this can be so difficult, you and your partner might need to agree to how frequently and for long you will both engage in these discussions to ensure that they are productive and do not exceed either partner's ability to self-regulate.

As a short-term strategy to stabilise the limb after a break in trust, transparency can extend to your devices and your calendar or schedule. This is especially the case when the use of devices played a role in the hurtful event. Likewise, being open about your plans and your whereabouts can be helpful in creating a context for healing. Being open with your devices and about the unknown corners of your life can be extremely helpful in offering the hurt partner reassurance that nothing is being hidden from them. Your willingness to be transparent in these practical ways sends a clear signal that you are wanting to regrow trust, and it recognises that your word alone is not enough to offer reassurance right now. For this reason, it is far more powerful for the partner who has been hurtful to *freely offer* this transparency, rather than the hurt partner having to request or demand it.

It is important to note that this level of openness can constitute a lack of privacy for many people, which may feel unjust at times. For this reason, this needs to be a short-term stabilising strategy to prevent further damage. This level of transparency is *not* a long-term strategy for creating security in your relationship. The loss of one person's privacy through the reliance on complete transparency cannot be the only way that a hurt partner feels safe in the relationship over the long term. There is a difference between secrecy and privacy in close relationships. Privacy means maintaining a sense of personal integrity and space without damaging trust. Secrecy, however, means holding back information or parts of yourself in a way that damages trust between partners and stifles the other's choices. All humans are entitled to privacy, but secrecy works against connection. If you are wanting to repair your bond, now is probably not the time to stand firm on your personal boundaries around privacy. While your need for privacy is totally understandable, after an attachment injury, it is very difficult to earn back trust when your word alone is not enough. Your actions have a heightened significance at this time, and it is possible that your request for privacy, even if reasonable, will feel threatening to the other. The more you are willing to give up your personal needs for privacy for a period of time in order to repair the closeness, the faster you will earn the hurt partner's trust. In this way, being willing to sacrifice some of your personal privacy demonstrates a commitment to the repair process and to supporting the regrowth of trust. It is a powerful signal of safety for the hurt partner. It allows your actions to be louder than your words until your words can be trusted once more.

Witnessing

The third task for hurtful partners to set the scene for repair is to be able to witness the other's pain. This is extremely difficult, especially when you care about the person in pain and particularly when you are the one who has caused their anguish. Being able to stand firm in the face of the other's pain is crucial to being able to repair this attachment bond. However, this task is easier said than done! To witness the other's pain without defending, explaining, protesting, minimising, or deflecting can feel completely impossible. It is totally understandable that you will want to do any of these things, and you probably have. In your attempts to resolve the injury, you might have rushed to solutions, assurance giving, logical arguments, appeasing, or counterattacking. You might have thrown your hands up and said, "Well it's up to you if you want to trust me again, there's nothing else I can do!" While these responses might help you to blow off steam or to temporarily regain your balance, they have the nasty side effect of throwing the other further off-balance. These ways of coping might make sense to you in the moment, but they can leave the hurt partner feeling alone in their pain, unwitnessed.

While you are busy explaining or minimising or blaming your partner, their pain is going unaddressed, their protest unsoothed. When you try to rush them to healing or place the burden of having to trust again in their hands alone, you accentuate the distance between you, and leave them to manage their pain on their own. Unfortunately, these responses will have only deepened the wound and prevented it from healing. These actions will signal to the other that you are wanting to gloss over the hurtful event, to rush to resolution, or to minimise your accountability for their hurt. When hurtful partners appear to not take accountability or responsibility for causing the other pain, this signals to the hurt partner that it could happen again. It tells them that their pain is not central to you – that your comfort is more important than their pain. It keeps their threat-perception high and prevents them from dropping their guard and regrowing trust. For pain to be processed and to lessen in intensity, it must have a witness. This means an engaged, caring witness who can allow themselves to be moved by the other's pain. When witnessed in this way, a hurt party is left feeling not just heard, but *felt*. When pain is unwitnessed, the hurt party can be left doubting their reality and feeling foolish for being upset or, alternatively, they can double down on their protest and work even harder to *make* you see their pain.

It requires a lot from a human to witness another's pain, knowing that you caused it and that you cannot immediately fix it. A key step in this process is taking responsibility for the actions that caused the other pain. You might have had your reasons for acting the way you did, but it is important that you can hold yourself accountable for your impact on your partner. It is clear to me that most people struggle with witnessing the other's pain, and I can understand why. It brings up our worst feelings of shame, inadequacy, and powerlessness. These are not emotions anyone likes to have, but they are even more difficult to experience when so much is at stake. I want to come alongside you in this process and help you to do this important work, step by step. Throughout this book, we are going to look at how to witness the other's pain in detail. *Knowing that this will be required of you is the first step.* I urge you to reflect on the notion of witnessing your partner's pain, on what blocks you from attuning to the other, and how you can hold firm and be with them the next time their pain flares. In conjunction with this work, we are going to follow a process where the hurt partner is supported to share their pain in vulnerable ways – not in reactive, escalated ways. You cannot be expected to withstand unbridled reactive emotion or abusive behaviours on account of your actions. No matter what the attachment injury was and how justified your partner is in feeling anger and rage, one of their key tasks (as you will see below) is to learn to manage their reactivity if they, too, want to repair this relationship (Figure 4.1).

Three tasks for the hurt partner

As we explored in Chapter 2, suddenly discovering that your partner has broken your trust is truly devastating. When your partner suddenly looks like the enemy and everything you thought you knew about your

Three Tasks for the Hurtful Partner

Creating a Context for Healing After an Attachment Injury

Commitment

When trust is broken & your word is not enough to reassure your partner of their importance to you & how seriously you take this rupture in your relationship, demonstrating your commitment in your actions is crucial to creating a **context for healing**.

Some ways you can show your commitment are:

- Checking in on how your partner is feeling
- Planning things to do together
- Remembering key events in your partner's world
- Sharing the load for organising your life together

What are some ways that you can show your commitment to this relationship?

Transparency

When secrecy was involved in an attachment injury, it is important that you do not continue to hide aspects of the event that caused the attachment injury & that you are as open as you can be about the details (whilst still being sensitive to the other's feelings).

Your transparency is the antidote to the damage caused by your secrecy.

NOTE: This level of transparency is not a long-term strategy for creating security in your relationship. It is a short-term stabilising strategy.

How can you be more transparent about this hurtful event?

How can you increase transparency regarding your devices, plans etc.?

Witnessing

To witness the other's pain without defending, explaining, protesting, minimising, or deflecting is extremely difficult & involves taking responsibility for causing pain. **This is vital for healing**.

How can you stay steady & able to witness & hold your partner's pain?

How can you hold yourself accountable for causing pain & damaging trust?

Clare Rosoman 2024

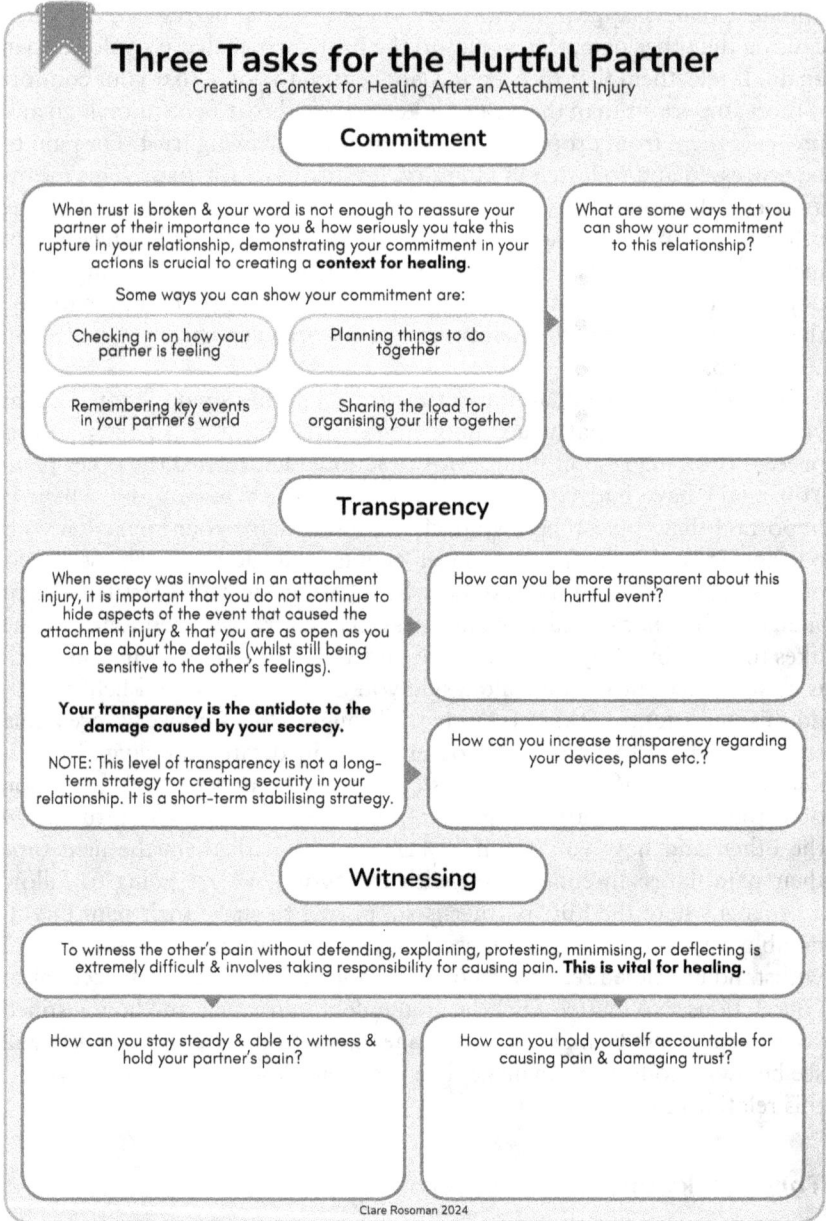

Figure 4.1 Three tasks for the hurtful partner.

relationship is called into question, it is shattering to your safe world. No doubt, there are times when enormous waves of intense emotion knock you over and threaten to drown you, and there are times when you catch a glimpse of the horizon again and feel a little more optimistic. Feeling an intense range of emotions is completely understandable and normal. After all, it wouldn't hurt if it didn't matter. You are facing an absolute crisis where it can feel like there are no good options – stay and risk being hurt again or leave and lose something so important to you. As you are rocked by a kaleidoscope of emotions, you are likely to be questioning whether, in fact, this relationship can be repaired and whether you have it in you to do the work required. Attempting to repair an attachment injury is not for the faint of heart. That you are reading this book says there is a part of you that is hopeful that you can recover from this relational trauma. While you might feel utterly demolished, it may help to know that you can influence the healing process more than you realise. What you bring to the healing process can greatly impact the capacity and extent of repair possible. This book and the Attachment Injury Resolution Model will guide you to process the emotional fallout from this breach of trust, and to hopefully repair your bond and restore your trust in your partner, but there are three things that you firstly need to do, to create a context for repair work.

Three tasks for the hurt partner to create the context for healing:

1 Owning your reactivity
2 Managing information
3 Open heart (even just a little)

Owning your reactivity

Your hurt, anger, and even rage are totally understandable and justified. You have a right to feel all that you do following such a breach of trust. I want to you to hear and feel that – *your hurt matters and your need for repair is the most important priority in attachment injury repair.* Among others, your fury, your fear, and your sadness are reasonable reactions to this injury. You are entitled to them. However, I want to caution you that the *way* you express your indignation and righteous anger can stall or even prevent healing. Hurt partners can find themselves yelling, screaming, calling their partner names, or taking drastic action such as becoming violent, making threats, waking their partner at odd hours of the night and demanding answers for hours on end, or exposing the injury to others to shame and alienate the hurtful partner. While understandable attempts to express pain and to address the significance of the event, these actions can add further damage to the bond, some of which can never be repaired.

If you want to heal this breach of trust and preserve what you can of this relationship (whether you stay together or redefine it), your first key task is to manage your reactivity. This means managing how you express your anger and hurt when the injury flares for you. It means holding yourself accountable for how you show up in this relationship, even when you are hurting, even when your actions feel warranted. Put simply, your level of hurt does not justify you taking abusive actions towards your partner. If you want to restore this relationship, even if you choose not to be together in the same way, then you simply must honour each person's humanity in the process. In short, your delivery matters. I will help you to reach behind your protective shield and to access the vulnerable places and I will help you to feel safe enough to share them with your partner, but I need you to reflect on your reactivity and work on managing that before this will ever be possible.

You might be reading this thinking, "My problem is that I don't rage, I don't share my hurt at all. I don't even know where to begin to express my pain, so I keep it inside." If this is you, then I want you to understand this as another form of reactivity that I consider to be a protective shutdown. Instead of raging and lashing out, some people go quiet and turn inward when hurt. Sometimes, they can even outwardly appease and comply with the other to not make a fuss. They might appear to move on from the hurt, try to return to normal interactions, to reassure the other that they are fine, that they understand why it happened, and that they have forgiven the other. This can be a form of self-protection, aimed at easing tension and pouring oil on troubled emotional waters. While less destructive to the other person involved, this form of coping with a relational hurt of this magnitude is equally detrimental to the healing process because the hurt partner's pain is completely inaccessible. It remains hidden and suppressed, a burden for them to privately suffer. Carrying pain of this scale alone is exhausting and endless. Avoiding touching the pain within and not sharing it with the hurtful partner robs you of the opportunity of being heard, held, and healed. We all need this when we are vulnerable. Pain born in relationship needs to be healed in relationship. To repair this rupture, we need to be able to access the pain to process and heal it. You cannot do this work alone. Healing requires you to share your heart and to let the other help you with your pain.

Managing information

Given that secrecy and hiding may have been prominent features in the hurtful event, it is likely that hurt partners can find themselves compulsively combing over the details of the event and searching for answers. This is an understandable reaction to mistrust. When your trust is shattered, it is natural to attempt to protect yourself from further hurt. Vigilance to possible secrecy is an adaptive way of trying to prevent this – never again will you be blindsided in this way. Mining for details and answers is an attempt to no longer have anything hidden from you – nothing lurking in the depths of your partner's world that could pose a threat to your security. This makes total sense, but it is an illusion. No matter how well we try to know another, they will always remain a mystery in some ways. No matter how much we try to understand a hurtful event, it will always contain unknown, perplexing, and unfathomable elements. Vigilance of this nature will simply exhaust you physically and mentally, and it won't bring back the trust or closeness you are hoping to restore.[1] In fact, it can even drive partners further apart.

So, what is the solution then? It is important for hurt partners to know enough of the detail about the hurtful event (or events) so that they do not feel that anything is being kept from them, but not so much that they are left traumatised by what they are hearing. As I mentioned in the earlier section on transparency for hurtful partners, it is essential that the hurtful partner is not the gatekeeper of information because this runs the risk of replicating the withholding that was present in the injury. I want to place the responsibility for exposure to information about the hurtful event firmly in the hands of the hurt partner. However, this comes with a warning: I urge you to be circumspect about the *amount* of information you seek and the *level of detail* you require. Only you can know how you feel once you are given the information, and if you ask for too much and then are negatively impacted by what you hear, you could just end up feeling worse. Too much information can be traumatising – it can leave a visual image in a person's mind that can put down roots and grow. Hurt partners have told me that certain images or phrases have stuck with them long after the injury is resolved that they wish did not take root in their minds. To avoid this, you need to regularly ask yourself *why* you need to know; "Will this help me to feel that nothing is being kept from me? Will this help me to understand/let go/feel reassured? Will this additional detail leave me feeling worse?" I recommend that hurt partners seek some details and then reflect on how they feel after hearing them before asking for more. You can easily fall into a trap of seeking more and more detail, that, like picking at a scab, just becomes harmful and corrosive to all involved. It is an illusion that knowing all the facts will relieve your suffering. Some details do not need to be known for you to feel that you have knowledge of the hurtful event and that you can move on and heal from its impact.

Open heart

Despite the immense hurt and the risks inherent, if you are willing to enter a repair process, then I want you to know that this requires you to have an open heart – even just a little. What I mean by this is that you need to be willing to let your partner impact you – to reach you. This is extremely difficult when you have been so hurt and your trust in the other's goodness is so rattled. I have seen many hurt partners who are unable to open their heart to the other remain unmoved by their partner's attempts to share their remorse and sadness. This, while reasonable, leaves no room for the hurtful partner to make amends, to wend their way back into your heart. The idea of opening your heart to the other might feel horrifying when all you want to do is protect yourself and never allow them to hurt you again. However, when someone's heart is closed, there is no way to restore the connection. We know that the single best way to build bonds is through shared vulnerability and this is just not possible when your heart is closed, and your vulnerability is safely sectioned off behind a protective wall. What an awful dilemma it is to feel that the only way you can protect yourself is to wall yourself off from the other, especially when you long to preserve this important relationship. I want to offer some reassurance that opening your heart to the other is a gradual process and that your partner must create a context where it is safe for you to do so in small ways. This book will guide you both in this process, but open your heart you must, if you are to repair your bond.

When you can open your heart to the other, even a little way, it means that you can hear about their experience and that you can take in new perspectives and ideas about the hurtful event or events. This is important in facilitating empathy for the other's suffering and for your own. Letting yourself feel the other brings you closer, and it aids in forgiveness.[2] In addition, being open to the other's experience allows you to expand your view of the motivation behind the attachment injury and its impact on the hurtful partner, as well as on you. You can expand your understanding of this hurtful event. Connecting like this represents a risk on your part, but it is an important part of healing and the creation of a new narrative about the hurtful time and its impact on your relational bond (Figure 4.2).

Identifying the cycle that blocks healing

Now that you are clear on the tasks and ingredients that each partner needs to bring to the process of healing, it is time to tackle the biggest obstacle to recovery from an attachment injury – the negative relational cycle. In Chapter 1, we looked at attachment strategies and in Chapter 2, we looked at how attachment injuries strongly evoke these strategies. In Chapter 3, we looked at how partners can become stuck in repetitive patterns of responding to each other in ways that increase their disconnection. Now it is time to put this all together to get to know the negative relational cycle that could be preventing you and your partner from recovering from this attachment injury.

Three Tasks for the Hurt Partner

Creating a Context for Healing After an Attachment Injury

Owning Reactivity

Big emotional reactions are totally understandable & justified after a breach of trust. If you want to repair your bond, you will have to manage how you express your anger & hurt when the injury flares for you. This means holding yourself accountable for the ways you show up in this relationship, even when you are hurting, even when your actions feel warranted.

Being hurt is not an excuse for abusive behaviour

Acting on impulses can create more damage

Reactivity keeps you in a protective position

Reactivity blocks repair by shutting off vulnerability

What are some things you can do to manage your reactivity better?

Managing Information

When secrecy was involved in an attachment injury, it is understandable that you want to seek answers & to ensure that you are never blindsided again.

It is important for you to know enough of the detail about the hurtful event so that you do not feel that anything is being kept from you, but not so much that you are left traumatised by what you are hearing.

Your partner cannot be the gatekeeper on information, but you need to carefully ask yourself if it will help or hurt you.

How much do you need to know to feel that nothing is being kept from you?

How do you feel after asking your partner for more details about the event?

Open Heart

You & your partner cannot restore the security in your bond if your hearts are closed to each other. Healing requires you to allow yourselves to be impacted by each other's vulnerability.

What fears come up when you think about letting your partner close enough to impact you?

What support do you need to share your pain & to be open to your partner's experience?

Clare Rosoman 2024

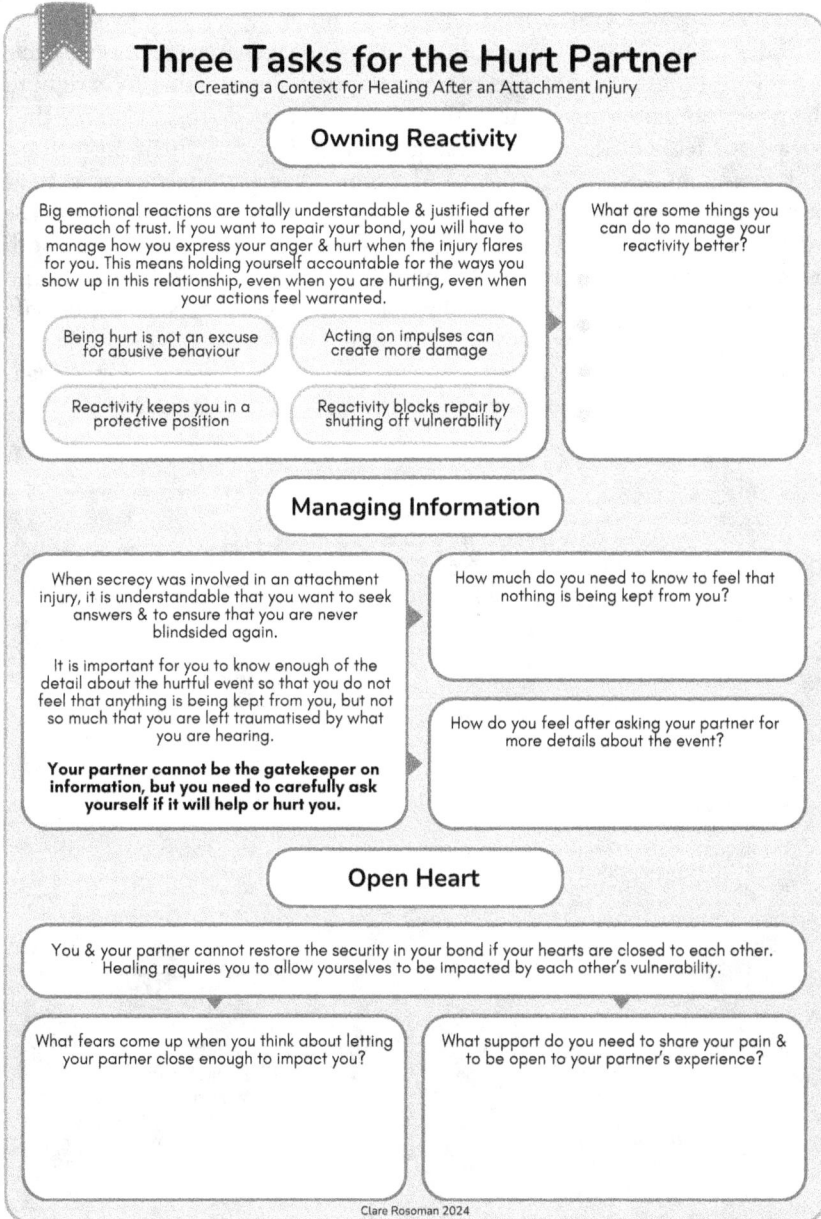

Figure 4.2 Three tasks for the hurt partner.

When under threat, it is normal for people to manage their emotional disequilibrium in the best way they know how. Sadly, the things that people do to cope when thrown off-balance are often experienced by the other as threatening. As you can see in Figure 4.3, a negative relational cycle becomes established when each partner copes in the way that feels right to them but is destabilising for the other. The more they do this, the more they trigger the fears of the other, causing them to rally their own protections and coping strategies in response. The more that each partner tries their best to manage their inner turmoil in ways that make sense to them, the more they amplify the distance between them. Unfortunately, when both partners are using their protective coping strategies, it erodes closeness and precludes repair. Our self-protections are so effective at keeping us safe that they prevent our loved ones from coming close.

When there has been an attachment injury, it is common for a negative relational cycle to become pronounced and active. It usually prevents

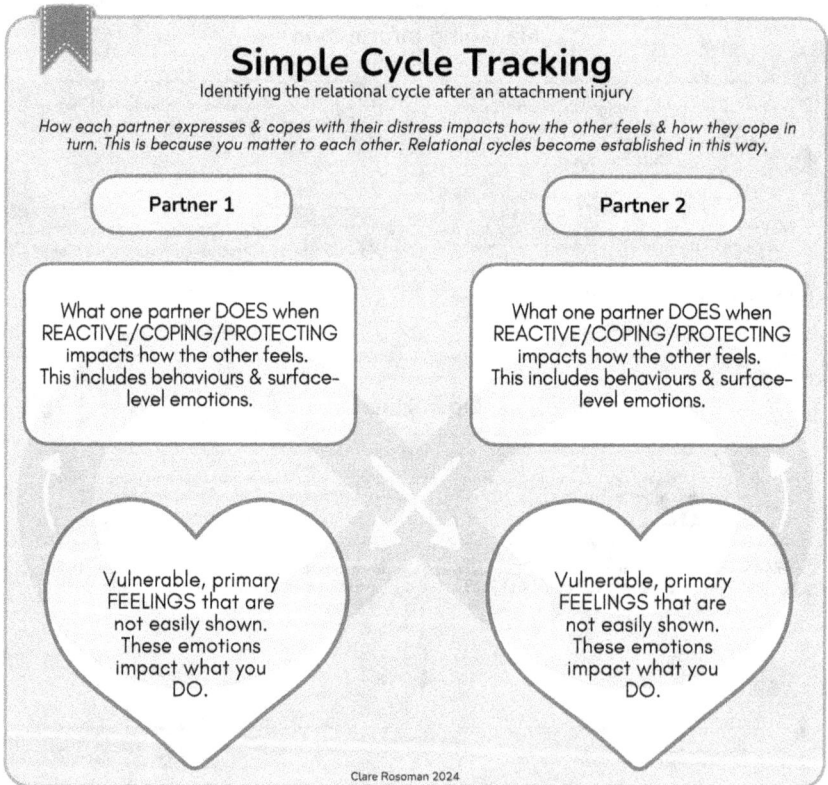

Figure 4.3 Simple cycle tracking.

the repair of the injury to the bond because the relationship feels unsafe and the other looks dangerous, so both partners rally their self-protections with a vengeance. When someone is protecting themselves, they do not show vulnerability, softness, or empathy for the other. Their priority is on defending and protecting themselves from further hurt. As a result, they can appear to the other as scary, contemptuous, and erratic, or as cold, dismissive, and unreachable. It's no wonder that a cycle like this prevents healing after an attachment injury. Both partners are armoured up and ready for battle. When the other looks like the enemy, the possibility of peace talks seems very bleak. I want to emphasise that while your protections might be necessary, you simply must agree to lay down your arms. *If you want to repair this relationship, you don't have to take your armour off until it is safe to do so, but you do need to put down your weapons.*

For this reason, we need to get to know your negative relational cycle and help you to step out of it. When reading about the different relational cycles that partners can become caught in in Chapter 3, which cycle fitted best for you and your partner? – the pursue-withdraw cycle, the withdraw-withdraw cycle, the pursue-pursue cycle, or the complex cycle? To identify the cycle that could be blocking healing in your relationship, let's start by reflecting on your commonly used attachment strategies and what you find triggering in your relationship. This will help you to get to know the signals in your relationship that feel threatening for you and that throw you emotionally off-balance. When you can slow and observe your internal process and how it impacts your actions, you can gain more awareness about how your attachment strategy helps you to cope with being dysregulated in this way. Using Figure 4.4, take some time to reflect on your responses and reactions in your relationship when painful triggers are present. To gain a full picture of your negative relational cycle, this exercise needs to be completed by *both* partners on a separate sheet each.

When you are aware of what triggers your attachment alarm, what you do when triggered, and how you might impact your partner, you can connect your experiences to map the cycle you and your partner create together. We can link how you both cope in ways that confirm each person's fears and continue to send dangerous signals to each other that create more distance. When stuck in this way, it is no wonder that you become disconnected and each feel alone. The wound between you goes unsoothed and trust cannot regrow. The distance and wariness that develop in a negative cycle actively work against recovery from this attachment injury. Getting to know your negative cycle is imperative in tackling it. To piece together the elements of your cycle, use the information you both gathered in Figure 4.4. In Figure 4.5, see if you can construct the moves of your negative cycle. Try to be objective in your reflection of each partner's role in the cycle.

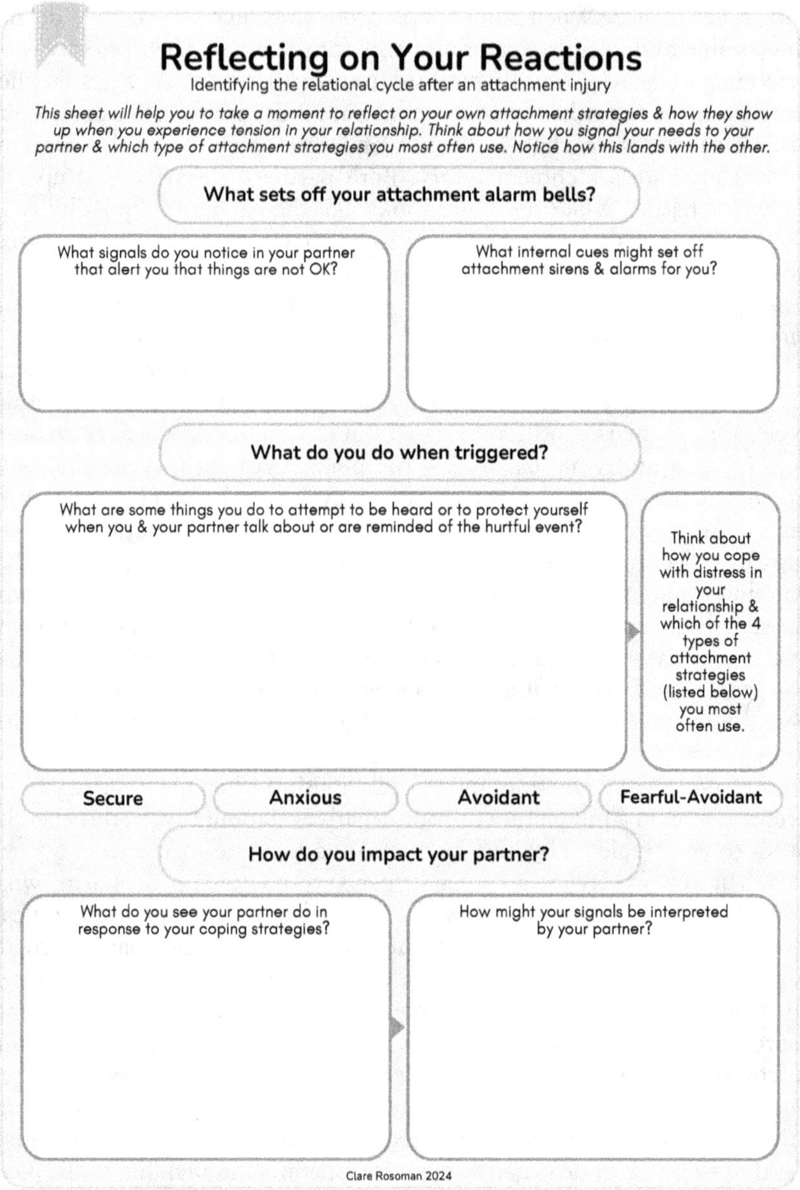

Reflecting on Your Reactions
Identifying the relational cycle after an attachment injury

This sheet will help you to take a moment to reflect on your own attachment strategies & how they show up when you experience tension in your relationship. Think about how you signal your needs to your partner & which type of attachment strategies you most often use. Notice how this lands with the other.

What sets off your attachment alarm bells?

What signals do you notice in your partner that alert you that things are not OK?	What internal cues might set off attachment sirens & alarms for you?

What do you do when triggered?

What are some things you do to attempt to be heard or to protect yourself when you & your partner talk about or are reminded of the hurtful event?

Think about how you cope with distress in your relationship & which of the 4 types of attachment strategies (listed below) you most often use.

Secure	Anxious	Avoidant	Fearful-Avoidant

How do you impact your partner?

What do you see your partner do in response to your coping strategies?	How might your signals be interpreted by your partner?

Clare Rosoman 2024

Figure 4.4 Reflecting on your reactions.

Start by thinking about what happens between you when the topic of the attachment injury comes up:

- Who raises, it and how? How are reminders dealt with?
- What happens between you when you talk about the hurtful event?
- How do you each feel on a surface level compared to deep inside?
- What do you show your partner? How do you signal your distress?
- What do you tell yourself about the incident or the other's reaction in the moment?
- What are you really needing from your partner at an attachment level that would soothe you in some small way?
- Can you see how what you each show the other might be different from what you feel on a vulnerable, primary level?
- Can you see how your way of reacting taps into your partner's deeper vulnerable emotions?

Figure 4.5 will help you to track and name the elements of your negative cycle. The negative cycle using the "infinity" symbol was first used by EFT Trainer Scott Woolley,[3] and it has been invaluable in helping partners to track the pattern of distress that they become stuck in. It guides you to look at what you do when you are triggered, what you tell yourself about this event or about your partner, what emotion you display to your partner compared to how you feel inside, and to identify what you are really crying out for at an attachment level. You will notice the infinity symbol in the background showing how you impact each other in a feedback loop that can feel infinitely stuck and repetitive. There is also a dotted line across the infinity loop, showing the behaviours, thoughts, and emotions that are "above the line" and easily within conscious awareness compared to the emotional experiences that are more vulnerable or "primary" that are "beneath the line" and more difficult to access. Take your time to work through this together as well as separately, to notice your cycle as it comes alive. Remember, the first step in being able to exit a negative cycle is to recognise it. This is how you start to identify and catch your negative interactional cycle. Being able to spot and exit your negative cycle is the first and most important step in creating a context for healing an attachment injury.[4]

Cycle that predated the attachment injury

As you become more aware of the negative relational cycle that could be preventing you and your partner from repairing this rupture to your bond, you might notice that this cycle actually predated the attachment injury. This is very common; in fact, all healthy relationships will have

Getting to Know Your Cycle
Identifying the relational cycle after an attachment injury

This sheet will help you to identify the elements of your negative relational cycle. Think about what happens between you when the topic of the hurtful event or breach in trust comes up.

Partner 1	Partner 2

Partner 1

What do you do? What do you show your partner?

What do you tell yourself? What is the meaning you make?

Surface emotion that you show:

What are your primary, vulnerable emotions that are harder to show?

What are your deepest, attachment needs?

Partner 2

What do you do? What do you show your partner?

What do you tell yourself? What is the meaning you make?

Surface emotion that you show:

What are your primary, vulnerable emotions that are harder to show?

What are your deepest, attachment needs?

Clare Rosoman 2024

Figure 4.5 Getting to know your cycle.

a negative cycle that can rear its ugly head in moments of disconnection and misattunement. I don't think that there is any way to intimately connect with another without having a negative pattern pop up from time to time. It's not that you have a cycle that is the issue, it's how you work with it to gain more understanding of the other (and yourself) and to create more flexibility in responding that allows you to flourish as a unit. Following a breach of trust, it is understandable that your pre-existing cycle will become amplified. Each time you disconnect, this becomes evidence of the hurtful partner's untrustworthiness and the hurt partner's inability to move on. With greater pain comes heightened emotions and the need for stronger defences – how could this not flare an existing negative cycle?

Alternatively, you might notice that you and your partner had a different cycle before this event that has changed since the attachment injury. For instance, a hurt partner, who used to pursue for connection, can shut down after a betrayal of their trust and withdraw from connection. A withdrawing partner who is hurt can go into "reactive pursuit" where they pursue for resolution and reassurance in a way that is out of character for them. Pursuing partners, who are hurtful, can shutdown out of helplessness, and withdrawing partners, who are hurtful, can pursue out of a feeling of urgency to make amends or to defend themselves. A hurt of this magnitude can evoke fearful-avoidant attachment strategies in either partner creating a mixture of anxious pursuit and avoidant withdrawal. This can contribute to an unpredictable cycle when pursuers can suddenly withdraw, and withdrawers can anxiously pursue in any given moment.

If your cycle has changed, it can be helpful to get to know your "old" cycle as well as getting to know your "new" cycle. You could do this by using another copy of Figure 4.5 to track each cycle. Later in this book, when we come to look at repairing an attachment injury and building security moving forward, we will need to look at the historical ("old") cycle as a way of coming to understand where there may have been vulnerabilities in your relationship that allowed hurts to grow. This will help us to know how to strengthen the attachment security in your relationship as it emerges from an attachment injury, and you begin to create security for the future.

Exiting the cycle

As we come to the end of this chapter, I want to leave you with the goal of exiting the negative cycle. You have worked so hard to reflect on how your attachment strategies flare when reminded of this painful event, and what you bring to your negative relational cycle. You have linked your way of coping to your partner's and seen how you impact each other in ways that add to the disconnection and block the healing from this injury.

This is meaningful, important work on your relationship's behalf that is creating a strong and stable platform for us to do the repair work required. I encourage you to embrace the "tasks" you have been allocated and to work on being aware of your moves in your relationship pattern. Each time you choose to intentionally step out of the negative cycle, you are taking a step towards restoring the trust in your loving bond.

In the next chapter, we are going to look at the deep wounds that an attachment injury can cause and how it can awaken past hurts. We are going to look at how to work with the emotional fall-out of an attachment injury by slowing and understanding your reactions and being able to soothe the parts that hurt. We will help you to manage big reactions, so that can show up differently with your partner – clearer about your pain and your needs. We will look at understanding guilt and shame and how to use these emotions to re-establish closeness rather than increasing distance.

Notes

1 Abrahms-Springs, J. (2020). *After the affair: Healing the pain and rebuilding trust when a partner has been unfaithful* (3rd ed.). New York: Harper.
2 Kimmes, J.G., & Durtschi, J.A. (2016). Forgiveness in romantic relationships: The roles of attachment, empathy, and attributions. *Journal of Marital and Family Therapy*, 42(2), 645–658.
3 Woolley, S. (2023). Personal communication.
4 Brubacher, L.L. (2018). *Stepping into emotionally focused couple therapy: Key ingredients of change*. New York: Routledge.

Chapter 5

Echoes of trauma

In Chapter 4, you took the time to reflect on the interactional cycle that takes hold when this injury comes alive between the two of you, and you built your awareness about your own reactivity and its impact on that cycle. Now, I want you each to take some time to reflect individually on the very personal meaning of this injury for *you*. Specifically, the new wounds it has created in you and the old wounds it might be flaring. I'd like to encourage you to spend some time holding yourself in this painful place. This chapter is about your own inner work to prepare you for healing this rupture of trust with your partner. It means meeting your pain with compassion and finding order in what can feel extremely chaotic. When big emotions flare – and attachment injuries certainly are some of the biggest emotional wounds we can bear – it can feel like you are spinning out of control and that your emotions have no rhyme or reason – that they are unpredictable and ever-changing. This chapter is all about finding the meaning in the madness, the order in the chaos, leaning into the pain to find the embedded wisdom, and being able to soothe the parts that hurt with self-compassion. This will set the stage for the repair process in earnest in Part III. *Knowing yourself and being able to hold your pain will help you to seek repair or to provide repair in the most effective way.* This self-work is important in ensuring attachment injury repair.

Blueprints for relationships and coping skills

As we touched on in Chapter 2, our most meaningful relationships throughout life shape our expectations and beliefs about closeness with others. They teach us powerful lessons about others' reliability and trustworthiness, and about our worthiness of love and care. The experiences you have in your closest relationships growing up teach you what to expect from others and whether they can be a resource to lean on in times of trouble, or whether it is safest to cope alone. These expectations are like blueprints, built from deep learning that is done "in relationship," and

DOI: 10.4324/9781003466499-8

form what Bowlby called internal "working models."[1] These models tell us what it means to love and be loved, what we deserve in our closest relationships, and what we can expect from those we love. These working models (expectations born of experience) form as a direct result of the relationships we have with our attachment figures – of how we are loved in our formative years. We develop a *model of other* – which is a concept of what we can expect from others – and a *model of self* – which is a view of our self-worth.

Model of other

Our *model of other* includes our expectations, built from experience in close relationships, of the benefits or consequences of turning to another for comfort and reassurance in times of need. Throughout your life, if you have had positive experiences of attachment figures being accessible, responsive, and engaged with you, then you are likely to have learned that others are a positive resource to help you to ride out life's tough moments. You are likely to have a positive model of other, which means that you are fairly optimistic about turning to others when you need them and their ability to assist you. Alternatively, if your attachment figures throughout your life have been frightening, rejecting, dismissing, neglectful, or shaming, then you are likely to have developed a negative model of other, for very good reason. You will think twice before turning to another in a time of need because you have experienced the sting of being emotionally dropped or traumatised in those vulnerable moments. Repeated experiences of being missed in this way compound these hurtful experiences and deepen your wariness of relying on others. For you to risk letting another see the vulnerable places within you, or to trust them with your heart, is an enormous risk. It represents the fragile hope that another can be safe and soothing.

Model of self

Our view of ourselves as worthy of another's love and support, of our emotions making sense, and our trust in ourselves to cope forms what we call our working *model of self*. Growing up, when caregivers are accessible and responsive to you, you will naturally feel worthy of their love and support. Their loving and safe presence shapes your positive view of who you are. This means that we absorb some of our special person's soothing ability as well as some of their view of us as lovable and worthwhile, which can sustain us when we feel uncertain.[2] Their love and support set the stage for feeling worthy of such gifts from others throughout your life and provide a benchmark for other relationships. Conversely, if you had caregivers who were *not* reliably responsive to you, this will have a profoundly negative impact on your view of yourself. You are likely to blame yourself and to develop an idea that you are not worthy of love and support, at all, from anyone. Sadly, when given less-than-ideal caregiving, it is adaptive for vulnerable humans to blame themselves for their attachment figure's shortcomings, rather than blaming the other. This allows them to preserve the relationship above all else and the sense of self suffers as a result.[3] The scars left from this type of learning can last a lifetime because they impact a person's growing sense of identity and value. While possible to undo, it takes concerted work given the influence that our attachment figures, particularly our earliest ones, have on our development.

Emotional regulation skills

When attachment figures are not accessible, responsive, and engaged, not only are our working models of self and other impacted negatively, so too is our capacity to regulate our emotions. As humans, we need safe co-regulation with others to find the order in our emotional experiences. This is the most efficient use of our resources and the quickest way to restore balance. If we are lucky enough to have trusted others to help us, we develop an expanded range of emotional regulation and coping skills. The safe presence of our caregivers helps us to manage our emotions and changes the way our brains respond to our emotional ups and downs, expanding our tolerance, and building our resilience.[4] When anyone is left alone to manage their emotional storms without co-regulation with a safe other, it is overwhelming and frightening. When we are left on our own, we have fewer tools available to us and must rely on less-effective ways of managing big emotions. In this way, your earliest attachment relationships shape how you cope with your emotions, by determining whether you can turn to others and experience successful co-regulation (that later becomes self-regulation), or whether you are left alone to manage in the best way you can, which will generally feel precarious and energy-taxing. How a person learns to manage their emotions, in turn, impacts the beliefs they hold about their inherent ability to manage what life throws at them. If you always feel thrown off-balance by your own emotions, you naturally will come to mistrust them and even to fear them.

While these working models act as blueprints for relationships, they are more amenable to change than you might think. In fact, they are adapted and refined within every close relationship we have. Since our self-identity forms and grows from the loving reflections we get from our most important relationships, relationships can become fertile grounds for growth and healing.[5] New, positive experiences of being responded to caringly and reassuringly can soothe and redefine long-held expectations that others are unreliable and untrustworthy. In this way, our working models of self and other can be revised and sculpted in positive relationships as we "earn security" with our loved ones.[6] As our expectations of connection become more positive, so too does our view of our worthiness of love and support. In connection, we grow. When you can encounter your emotional world with balance and in co-regulation with a safe other, then you realise that your emotions make sense, that you can find the wisdom in them and learn from them.

While this is hugely positive, it also stands that positive expectations about relationships can be dashed where trust is broken. When there is an attachment injury, it will obviously be painful if it replicates or approximates past, negative experiences you have had in relationships. However, it is also painful when it destroys long-held, positive beliefs about others' trustworthiness. In short, attachment injuries can open up an "old" wound and they can create a "new" wound. Next, let's look at how past experiences in relationship can impact how you might respond to or cause attachment injuries, and how to explore the difference between past and present pain.

How the past impacts the present

When people have been exposed to traumatic experiences or abusive environments as children, especially when it has been over a prolonged period of time, it changes the way they navigate life. Bessel van der Kolk says that when a person is traumatised, they continue to organize their life as though the trauma were still going on, "unchanged and immutable."[7] In this way, new encounters can become contaminated by *remnants of the past*, even if only through watchfulness and fearful expectations. Your partner's hurtful actions or your hurtful actions towards your partner are significant in and of themselves. However, you might find yourself interpreting your partner's actions or this hurtful event through the lens of prior traumatic experiences in close relationships. This can have a profound impact on your relational dynamic, on how you signal your needs and fears to your partner, and how you respond to a breach of trust. Almost as though the past trauma provides a lens through which you view your current relationship. For instance, if you experienced an abandonment by a parent at a crucial time growing up, it stands to reason that you are going to be more alert to signs of impending abandonment by your romantic partner. If, like your parents, your partner abandons you at a time of intense need, your reaction is going to be stronger than it might have been if you had never had this experience in your formative years. There already is an "old" wound that has scarred over, and you have learned that this type of hurt can happen, you have lived it, and you bear the scar to show for it. This makes it more familiar – more sensitised – and makes you more protective of that hurt place within you. Of course, a similar hurt is going to press right into that wounded place. I say this not to minimise the impact of a current hurtful event, but to put it in the attachment context of your overall relational experience throughout your life. It is inevitable that our past experiences impact how we respond to attachment threats in the present. It would be foolish to not learn from past experiences – the protective parts of ourselves want us to be on the lookout for similar trauma in future relationships!

It is adaptive to be on the lookout for potential hurt, this is how we keep ourselves safe. Opening your heart to another is already a risky thing to do, but if you have been hurt in close relationships before, it makes such sense why you would be especially on-guard for similar hurt. Any harsh experience of broken trust will have left its mark on your psyche – for it not to would be foolish. While sensible and understandable, experiences like this can colour your presence with your current partner, making you more needy for reassurance or distrustful and wary. This could make you hyper-sensitive to signs of possible hurt or betrayal and make you more likely to guard your heart from fully being open. We know that people who have witnessed one parent break the other's trust in an extramarital affair can withhold emotionally in their adult relationships for fear of being hurt in the same way. Paradoxically, they can be at a higher risk of replicating the same behaviour in their close relationships.[8] However it manifests, the hurt suffered leaves a legacy of watchfulness, and sometimes, proactive hurtful acts under the guise of "I'll never be hurt like that again."

As humans who bond, we simply can't avoid the reality that the things we experienced early in life that we shouldn't have – like abuse, cruelty, betrayal, violated boundaries – leave an emotional imprint. They become signposts for our emotional world warning us to protect ourselves from similar hurt in the future. The things we might have missed out on but longed for – like love, kindness, compassion, encouragement, safety – remain as voids needing to be filled. We remain hungry for these unmet needs. A small, fragile, but hopeful part seeks to make up for these missing ingredients that all humans crave. These raw experiences of *enduring* or *going without* become attachment wounds that we carry carefully and vigilantly. Our emotions serve as a signalling system, and they flare when our wounds get bumped, telling us that we need to pay attention to what matters, and ensuring that we take action to protect ourselves from further harm.

Consequently, the wounds we carry impact how we navigate close relationships – how we protect ourselves, how we might come to be hurtful to those we love, and how we respond to relational hurt. They leave scars and can instil guarding behaviours in us that impact or even jeopardise the creation of healthy relationships.

Here are some examples of experiences in early, close relationships that can leave a legacy of attachment trauma:

- *Caregivers who are neglectful, dismissive, or abandoning.* When an attachment figure is neglectful of a child's basic needs, or dismissive of their emotional expression, including their worries, fears, or doubts, they learn that their needs are not important and that no one will care about them. When attachment figures are abandoning, they teach a child that no one will be there for them when they need them, that they are on their own.
- *Parental figures who are frightening or intimidating.* Experiencing an attachment figure as frightening is completely traumatising and disorganising to a child's nervous system. It will instil a fear of seeking contact comfort as well as an awful isolation in that child. With no safety in the attachment bond, the child is left alone to manage. They will become fearful of inviting more mistreatment and will do all they can to avoid this. This obliterates the child's faith in others as safe.
- *Caregivers who are disapproving, critical, or shaming.* These experiences crush a child's fragile sense of self-worth and shame them to their core. Children with parental figures such as this will recoil from attention, shying away from being noticed, and will often learn to hide themselves for fear of further judgement or disapproval. The feeling of rejection by those who should be most accepting leaves an enduring imprint on a child's self-identity.
- *Parental figures who are controlling, smothering, or intrusive.* Attachment figures such as this leave no room for a child to develop autonomy and mastery. They teach a child to prioritise the needs of others and to dismiss their own feelings, thoughts, and needs. This can leave a child doubting who they are and feeling that they can only express themselves in secret. They learn that they must hide and self-manage their needs.
- *Caregivers who are deceptive.* When an attachment figure distorts the truth, lies to a child, or asks them to lie for them, the foundation of the attachment bond is broken. A child is placed in an untenable position where they must supress what they know and instead follow what they are told. It shakes their faith in the attachment figure's judgement and leadership and teaches them powerful lessons about others' trustworthiness and reliability. This leaves a child questioning what is real and who to trust.
- *Parental figures who are frightened, overwhelmed, or suffering.* Caregivers who are themselves anxious, hurting, not coping, and afraid are unable to provide a secure base for a child to develop into healthy autonomy and to trust in their ability to manage what life throws at them. This leaves a child either under-functioning through lack of resilience, leaving them to face life anxious and uncertain, or over-functioning through a need to "parent" their parent, robbing them of the freedom

of childhood and forcing them to take on an adult role too soon. Either way, children in this predicament miss out on the comfort of having a stronger, wiser other to turn to.

- *Caregivers who violate boundaries.* Parental figures who violate physical and emotional boundaries teach a child that their body, their needs, and their feelings are irrelevant – they must appease others and prioritise the other's needs over their own. This immeasurably impacts a child's sense of self-worth, their capacity for self-awareness, and their ability to feel safe in relationships. It stunts the normal and healthy process of being able to set boundaries, to say no, and to ask for what you need.

These examples of destructive caregiving have a profound impact on a person's attachment strategies, as well as their model of self and other, and on how they manage their emotions and navigate interpersonal relationships throughout their life. Remember, we are exploring this to make sense of "old" wounds that might be there for you and that might be bumped and awakened by this attachment injury, not to "blame" or scapegoat your earliest caregivers. I want to stress that less-than-optimal parenting is often a by-product of trauma in the parent. People generally have their reasons for being hurtful and usually they do not set out to be harmful. My intention is not to "parent-blame" or to find excuses for hurtful actions (either in your parent, your partner's parents, or in each other), but rather, to make sense of the lessons you learned about relationships in your most meaningful early connections, and how these lessons might be feeding into the current attachment injury you are facing. In Figure 5.1, I invite you each to take some time alone to reflect on the impact of your earliest attachment relationships and how echoes from the past could be showing up in relation to the current attachment injury.

"Old" pain versus "new" pain

So much tenderness surrounds historically painful places, and if the current attachment injury awakens them, then you are dealing with the current injury *and* you are dealing with what it arouses from the past. This current attachment injury might be conceptually different from relational hurts you have endured at other times in your life, but echoes of past pain are likely to come to the fore when you are suffering. They are bound to need your care and attention as part of the recovery process. Some of this can be done with your partner, but when it comes to past pain, much of this work will need to be done on your own.

It makes perfect sense that past relational injuries leave scars that can flare in subsequent relationships. If you have experienced past hurts and betrayals from those closest to you, these old wounds are bound to be activated by a current attachment injury. Regardless of the time that might have passed,

The Impact of the Past

This sheet will help you to reflect on your earliest attachment relationships & what they taught you to expect from others & about your own self-worth. It will help you think about how hurtful events from the past might be flared by the current attachment injury.

What did you learn about close relationships growing up?

Did you learn that turning to others in times of need was a good or a bad idea & why? Can you think of examples?

Model of Other

What did you learn about your worthiness of love & care?

In your earliest relationships, what did you learn about your worthiness of love & care? How did you learn this?

Model of Self

Echoes from the past showing up in the current injury

What did you endure or go without (remnants of pain) in the past that could be flared by the current attachment injury?

Clare Rosoman 2024

Figure 5.1 Impact of the past.

emotion knows no chronology and the hurt from the past can come alive in the present as if it has happened anew.[9] This is especially the case when the current attachment injury taps right into the heart of an earlier attachment wound – after all, pain born in-relationship comes alive in-relationship.

When anyone is swamped with current distress, it can be difficult to tease out how much of the pain is a measure of the current hurt and how much is an echo from the past. Only you can decipher this – no other person could ever claim to know this. In fact, it could be extremely invalidating to have your current pain dismissed as stemming from an earlier wound and therefore less important. That could render the current hurt insignificant and leave your pain unacknowledged. Likewise, a supposedly resolved wound or one so far in the background to be relegated as insignificant can take you by surprise by coming to life again in the context of a new hurt, revealing itself to be *far* more raw than you thought. Current pain can flare old pain. This does not make either less significant, but the cumulative affect can be immense. *Knowing your pain and tending to it is the precursor to being able to turn to your partner for repair or being present to help your partner to repair.*

Separating past and present pain

Where possible, separating out past hurt from present hurt can be helpful. For instance, if you had an abusive parent, it can be helpful to separate out the fear you felt as a child in their presence from the unease you feel as an adult when your partner shows heated emotions. Noting the differences between these two attachment experiences can be extremely helpful and reassuring. It reminds you that you are in a different situation now, that your partner is not your parent, and that you have more agency as an adult than you once did as a child. This separation of the past from the present can help you to regain your balance when old wounds flare. It can help you to see that you may have developed watchfulness as a survival strategy that can be quick to set off sirens and alarms in situations that appear dangerous – but that aren't actually as dangerous as the ones you faced earlier in life. While these coping tools once ensured your survival, they might no longer be needed now. We develop our coping strategies for good reason, and we don't give them up easily or without being absolutely sure of safety. Bringing awareness to the moments when protective coping strategies flare can allow you to slow the process, to separate past from present, and to engage your own sense of choice and agency in the present moment.

Linking past and present pain

On another but related note, it can also be helpful to find the common threads that link past hurts to current hurts. This means finding the attachment significance that links seemingly different triggers from the past to the present attachment injury. For instance, watching your parents fight and your mother walk out leaves a wound that will understandably be flared by your partner's raised voice. This fear of the worst happening has been earned through the bitter experience of conflict leading to loss and so will underpin your responses to conflict forevermore. It is impossible to unlink these two attachment-related fears, but sometimes, it may not be clear that the echo from the past is driving your protective behaviours in the present. No wonder heated emotion sends you reeling – you have lived the worst consequences of that! For another example, growing up in a house where things were hidden creates a unique sensitivity for an adult with a partner who shuts down and says everything is fine. Again, these two attachment-related experiences might be entirely different, but they will be linked in the hurt partner's felt-sense. They share a common fear of concealment causing damage in relationships and a mistrust of what is outwardly shown. No wonder you think the worst when your partner appears not to be sharing! Taking a moment to explore what might be behind your surface reactions and linking past relational hurts to the current moments of tension between you and your partner can make sense of reactions that can otherwise feel nonsensical.

I invite you to reflect on the hurts you endured in your earliest attachment relationships, in your subsequent adult relationships, as well as in your current relationship, and see if you can find differences between them *and* the common thread that links them. This is a process of building self-awareness about your attachment scars and wounds. What we are willing to explore, we can become acquainted with, and what we are acquainted with, we can befriend. While it can feel extremely difficult to face our emotional scars, it is also very freeing to finally face them, to speak about how we got them, and to process the emotion that comes with those scars. This is the best way that I know of to process pain, to care for the parts that hurt within you, and to seek repair where needed.

Revisiting painful emotions and experiences might feel counterproductive to some people who believe it is best to leave the past in the past. However, in my experience as a therapist, when the past keeps popping up and impacting the present, there is something important there that needs attending to. To continue to ignore it will leave it unprocessed, likely to be awakened at every opportunity, and will mean that you potentially miss a chance to learn from this hardship. The past stays more easily in the past when it has been noted, processed, and understood. This process helps past trauma become woven into the narrative of your life – to become part of your story – rather than bursting out unprocessed when triggered and derailing the plot.

For some past injuries, it might not be possible to seek repair or even to gain acknowledgement from another. This may be the case for hurts caused by attachment figures who are no longer in your life or who might

Getting to Know Your Pain

This sheet will help you to reflect on your attachment-related pain from past hurts & from the present attachment injury. Whether you are the hurt or the hurtful partner, take a moment to reflect on the meaning of these past & present events.

What hurts most about this current attachment injury?

What is the most painful aspect of this attachment injury for you? Can you feel, acknowledge & make room for that?	What is at the core of the attachment-related pain for you - the part that speaks to the security of the bond?

How does this current injury echo past injuries you have faced?

How is the current injury similar in attachment significance to past hurts in close relationships?	How is the current injury different from past experiences of hurt?

Common Attachment Threads

What remnants of pain from the past need soothing now? Is this something that your partner can provide? If not, who might?	What do you need your partner to hear & acknowledge as part of repairing the current attachment injury?

Clare Rosoman 2024

Figure 5.2 Getting to know your pain.

be unwilling or unable to repair with you. However, just knowing this means that *you* can take care of these raw places and accurately attribute pain where it belongs.

For the current attachment injury, using Figure 5.2, I ask you and your partner to take some time (individually) to think about the most hurtful part of this injury for you. What is at the core of the attachment-related pain for you? How has this injury redefined your bond with your partner? Try to be with your pain, to make space for it, and to honour the importance of your experience. This will help you to distil its central message. What of your pain is from the past and what is from the current attachment injury? In what ways does this injury echo past hurts? In what way is it different? What are the common threads that give it its attachment meaning for you?

This is a process of clearly apportioning blame for pain to the accurate source and is the beginning of getting clearer about what you need for good repair. I know that you and your partner need to repair your attachment injury, but we will do a much better job of that if we know exactly what we are repairing and exactly where the soothing balm needs to be applied. This means, whether you are the hurt or hurtful partner, getting clear about the pain and about taking an appropriate amount of responsibility for it. It's no good asking your partner to make amends for past pain that they had no hand in, such as, holding your partner accountable for the impact of your parents' hurtful actions. It's no good asking your partner to forgive actions that are stemming from past pain such as a history of trauma because your mother was overbearing. However, sharing your discoveries about your past pain and its impact on the present can be ultimately bonding. It can help you to better understand your past pain *and* your present pain. You will then be clearer about what you need from your partner to soothe the current pain, and what parts of you still hurt from the past – parts that need some care and attention directly from you.

Self-protective behaviours

The ways you learned to cope with difficult relationships and traumatic life experiences in earlier phases of your life will have become protective coping strategies. These much-needed tools for navigating a dangerous world and dangerous relationships were your survival tools. They kept you safe, helped you to avoid further hurt, and might have even kept you alive. Two of my colleagues, Leanne Campbell and James Hawkins, describe these coping strategies as "earned protections."[10] This description honours a person's need to acquire protective strategies when immersed in socially harmful environments, particularly early in life. Where staying small or getting loud was a requirement to avoid further abuse or to prevent rejection, where mistrust saved your life, where withholding vulnerability was needed to subsist, these were necessary protections. They helped you to survive during hard times and they will come to the fore when you need them now. For many people, the world remains unsafe in some spheres, even as an adult. This is the case for those regularly exposed to minority stress and discrimination and for those who have detrimental attachment figures in their lives. These earned protections will still be necessary for their security and survival.

Sometimes the things that keep us the safest can also keep us alone. When you must develop protective strategies to prevent others from having access to you, you can get so good at walling yourself off that you can find it hard to let anyone close – even those worthiest of your trust. Protections might keep others out, but they also keep you shut-in, alone. This isolation might feel safest when connection with others has caused you harm, but as humans, we don't tend to do well in isolation. In Figure 5.3, take a moment to think about the hurts you have endured in relationships throughout your life and the ways you have tried to protect yourself from future hurt. What do you notice about how you protect yourself from relational hurt and where you learned to do that? How did that way of coping protect you? Does it ever have a negative impact on your closest relationships? Does it ever work against what you are longing for in your relationships? For many people, they notice that their protections are often at odds with their desire to let certain, special people close.

Protective strategies acquired from past relational trauma will inevitably show up in your relationship now. While there to keep you safe from hurt, they can cause hurt to others or to the bond between you and those most important to you. These behaviours can occur because of developmental trauma and leave you susceptible to breaking your partner's trust or to compounding injuries if you are hurt in your current relationship. While protective on some levels, on others, they can lead to hurtful actions or breaches of trust, and they can certainly impact a person's capacity for healing from an attachment injury.

Some examples are:

- Finding fault in your partner as a way to justify not becoming too close to them.
- Withholding information from your partner as a way of pushing them away and preventing them from becoming too close to you.
- Telling your partner what they want to hear to avoid disappointing them or to prevent potential conflict.
- Withholding emotionally so that your partner never sees the "real" you.
- Controlling your partner out of fear of them leaving.
- Not telling the truth or withholding certain information to prevent judgement or conflict.
- Escalating your emotional signals to demand that an unresponsive partner pays better attention.

Protective Coping Strategies

This sheet will help you to reflect on your earned protective strategies & how they might impact the healing of the present attachment injury. Whether you are the hurt or the hurtful partner, take a moment to reflect on how you show up in this relationship.

Earned protections

How did you learn to protect yourself in close relationships? Why did you have to learn this?	How has this way of coping protected you throughout your life?

Current protection

What are you currently protecting yourself from feeling or experiencing?	How are you protecting yourself now? What do you tell yourself & what do you do?

Impact of protections

How is this way of protecting yourself from hurt impacting the repair of this injury?	If you weren't protecting yourself in this way, what could you experience with your partner?

Clare Rosoman 2024

Figure 5.3 Protective coping strategies.

- Criticising your partner as a way of "levelling the playing field" when your own inadequacies are at risk of exposure.
- Pointing out things your partner is doing that upset you in a way that is critical and blaming of them to push them away or to see if they care about you.
- Questioning your partner and doubting their authenticity.
- Pulling them close then pushing them away – sending confusing signals.
- Hiding things from them.
- Holding your partner accountable for things that happened to you in earlier relationships.
- Escalating your demands of your partner when they seem disengaged, distracted, or withdrawn to see if they care about you and the relationship.
- Forcing your partner to choose between you and someone else important to them as a test of their loyalty.
- Becoming threatening towards the other or the relationship to make them back down from their position in a conflict.
- Sending unclear signals about what you want and then being disappointed or angry when your partner does not meet them.
- Seeking approval or reassurance of your worth from others at the expense of your primary relationship.

As you can see in these examples, the function of the protection is to minimise hurt to the self. Each strategy aims to prevent too much risk of contact, exposure, or hurt in a relationship. The protective strategy while protecting one aspect of the self, often creates damage to other aspects of the self, such as the longing to have a healthy and happy relationship. These ways of managing fear of relational hurt ravage the relational bond by infusing it with unclear signals, heightened emotion, and hurt feelings. This damages the security of the attachment bond between partners and can sometimes cause so much damage that they can even create an attachment injury. Even if protective strategies such as those above weren't responsible for the current injury you are facing, they will certainly create blocks to recovery and healing. The need to stay safe will often fiercely compete with, and often outweigh, the need to be close. If closeness involves the risk of hurt, it makes perfect sense why a person would opt for distance from another. When you have been hurt, this is never more so the case. When you have caused hurt, this can amplify your fear of causing more damage or being hurt in turn.

Caring for your hurt

Naturally, protective coping strategies will come alive in the context of the current attachment injury. When such an important relationship with someone who means so much to you is in jeopardy and old attachment wounds are flared, this will summon your strongest and most faithful protective coping strategies. Your need to protect yourself will probably involve pushing the other away which can add to a sense of isolation and distress for you both. When protecting ourselves, we tend to send unclear signals, to be more defensive, and to be less flexible in our responses. We tend to overreact rather than underreact, to err on the side of caution, and to be closed to letting the other impact us. This makes sense, but, it will get in the way of healing. Healing this attachment injury will require being open to the other, letting them impact you, being more flexible in your responses, and to taking in another perspective. It will also require you sharing your heart openly, rather than from behind your protective shield. To allow this work to be possible, your protective coping strategies need to be slightly lowered to fully see, hear, and feel the other, and for them to be able to see, hear, and feel you. This feels so risky when there is so much pain present.

The dilemma for most people in attempting to repair an attachment injury is how to lower their protective shield when they feel so desperately hurt and are so afraid of witnessing the other's pain. I want you to know that being able to repair an attachment injury of this nature *will* involve a conscious lowering of your protective coping strategies and the sending of signals of vulnerability to the other, so that you can find your way back to each other and restore the security in your bond. Without being able to choose when to lower your shield a little, the two of you will be unable to share and soothe your pain and to repair your bond. Our aim is to help you to develop adaptive flexibility, where you can choose when you need your protections and when it is safe enough to lower them.

To do this, you need to firstly start by knowing your pain more. This means knowing what hurts you, what sets off your attachment sirens and alarms, and being able to know when your protective coping mode kicks in. Being able to step out from behind your protective coping strategies involves being able to identify that you are using a protection and being able to explore why that might be. When you can become curious about your emotional world, you can then notice more about your reactions and the wisdom in them. You can then find the meaning in them, and bring soothing and care to the parts that hurt. This is important work that sets the scene for being able to clearly share your pain with your partner in a way that they can hear and take in and being able to provide the same for them in return. We are going to work on the sharing part as we progress through this book, but for now, I encourage you to use Figure 5.4 to reflect on your protective strategies and on what you are needing, firstly from yourself to regulate and soothe the parts that hurt, to prepare you for lowering your shield and sharing your pain in Chapters 7 and 8.

Caring for Your Hurt

This sheet will help you to reflect on what you do when using your protective strategies & to explore the pain behind the protection. Whether you are the hurt or the hurtful partner, this sheet will help you to better care for yourself when hurts come alive.

How do you know when you are in your protective coping mode?

What do you say or do?	What do you tell yourself?	What do you feel?

What is behind your protections?

What have you come to learn about the pain behind the protection?

Caring for your hurt

What do you need when this pain comes alive? How can you better care for yourself in these moments?

▶ To share it with someone who can hold it gently

▶ To offer compassion to the parts that hurt

▶ To spend time doing something you enjoy

▶ To find the meaning in the pain

Clare Rosoman 2024

Figure 5.4 Caring for your hurt.

Now that you have explored the deeper hurts that might be evoked by the current attachment injury and found their differences and common threads, you have done the hard work to prepare you for sharing with your partner. Knowing and being with your own pain and being aware of your protections are invaluable in attachment injury repair. The balance this work will give you will allow you to share clearly and to remain present to your partner's experience. Read on to Chapter 6 for complex attachment injuries or progress to Chapter 7 to commence the attachment injury resolution process.

Notes

1 Bowlby, J. (1969/1982). *Attachment and loss: Volume 1 attachment.* New York, NY: Basic Books.
2 Mikulincer, M., & Shaver, P.R. (2004). Security-based self-representations in adulthood: Contents and processes. In W.S. Rholes & J.A. Simpson (Eds.). *Adult attachment: Theory, research and clinical implications* (pp. 159–195). New York: Guilford Press.
3 Woldarsky, C., & Greenberg, L. (2014). Interpersonal forgiveness in emotion-focused couples' therapy: Relating process to outcome. *Journal of Marital and Family Therapy,* 40(1), 49–67.
4 Cozolino, L. (2014). *The neuroscience of human relationships: Attachment and the developing social brain* (2nd ed.). New York: W.W. Norton & Company, Inc.
5 Lewis, T., Amini, F., & Lannon, R. (2000). *A general theory of love.* New York: Vintage Books.
6 Mikulincer, M., & Shaver, P.R. (2020). Enhancing the "Broaden and Build" cycle of attachment security in adulthood: From the laboratory to relational contexts and societal systems. *International Journal of Environmental Research and Public Health,* 17, 2054.
7 B. van der Kolk. (2015). *The body keeps the score: Mind, brain & body in the transformation of trauma.* New York: Penguin Books.
8 Weiser, D.A, Weigel, D.J., Evans, W.P., & Lalasz, C.B. (2015). Family background and propensity to engage in infidelity. *Journal of Family Issues,* 38, 15. https://doi.org/10.1177/0192513X15581660.
9 Rheem, K.D., & Rosoman, C. (2023). *An emotionally focused workbook for relationship loss: Healing heartbreak session by session.* New York: Routledge.
10 Campbell, T.L., & Hawkins, J. (2022). *Healing relationship injuries with the attachment injury resolution model – cultural considerations.* Online workshop presentation, March 2022.

Chapter 6

Making sense of complex injuries

Now that we are ready to dive into the attachment injury repair process, I am aware that sometimes, hurts in relationships are bidirectional and complex. There is not always a clear "hurt" and "hurtful" partner. This can make the process of attachment injury repair uncertain – who is the one receiving care and who is making amends? What if both people have hurt each other in different or similar ways? What if there was an injury that pre-dates the current one? What happens to these past issues? Do they receive airtime or are they no longer important? What if there have been subsequent hurts? Which injury do we look at first? Whose pain do we prioritise and how do we ensure that both partners' experiences are attended to?

In this chapter, we will attempt to find the answers to these important questions. We will pause to look at some of the ways that partners can become entangled in complex patterns of hurt and we will outline a path to repair, tailored to fit for you and your partner, and the specific relational hurts you have endured. To do this, I will identify examples of complex hurts, such as dual injuries (where partners are equally hurt), eclipsing injuries (where one partner's hurt overshadows the other's), retaliation injuries (where one partner's hurtful act follows a hurt issued by the other), and erosion injuries (smaller hurts that don't completely break trust but erode it over time in a cumulative manner). When the trust is broken in multiple and complex ways, we need to modify or adapt the approach to healing. We will look at how to approach this work to accommodate intricate layers of hurt to gain a clear path forward for repair.

Sometimes, there is an obvious and agreed-upon attachment injury where one party has transgressed and needs to make a repair. If this is the case in your relationship, it will be clear how to commence the attachment injury resolution process because it will be clear who is the "hurt" partner and who is the "hurtful" partner. If this sounds like you and your partner, you can choose to proceed to Chapter 7, now. However, for the vast majority of people, relational hurts are complex and multi-faceted.

DOI: 10.4324/9781003466499-9

If the hurts you have endured in your relationship are of this nature, rest assured that this is normal, and that repair is still achievable. To ensure the best outcome, we need to take some time to understand the attachment injuries that you are facing and to map out a path forward that is agreed on by you both and that feels fair and achievable. In all likelihood, this will involve untangling each partner's experience of betrayal and hurt and taking time to process each hurt one-by one. Before we can do that, let's take some time to understand the nature of complex, bidirectional attachment injuries.

Dual injuries

In some relationships, partners have *both* violated promises and let the other down, leaving each partner feeling wronged and shattering the trust between them. These hurts can co-occur and can involve different or similar wrongdoings. As a result, partners can individually feel that they are the injured party and that the other needs to make a repair with them. This can lead to stalemates and even to a "competition" for who is the more aggrieved party. Obviously, this situation will impair the resolution of the attachment injury and can even set partners on a negative spiral of escalating accusations. If each maintains their stance that the other is at fault, there will be no safety to lower their protective shields or to reconnect through shared vulnerability.

Sonia and Emma whom we met in Chapter 3 were both hurting and doubting their ability to repair their five-year lesbian, monogamous relationship. If you recall, Sonia had been secretly taking prescription pain medication and denying Emma's concerns about her withdrawal, drowsiness, and personality changes. This was revealed when she had a car accident while under the influence of her pain medication, which brought about police involvement and potentially threatened her livelihood. The secrecy of these actions and the potential threat to their income ruptured Emma's trust in Sonia, especially given the duration of Sonia's denial of there being any issues. Unbeknownst to Emma, Sonia was managing significant hurt of her own after discovering an email chain between Emma and a co-worker that was clearly emotionally intimate. Emma had been confiding in a colleague about her relationship with Sonia and her feelings of distance and confusion. These conversations had become much more emotionally intimate and, along with doubts about her feelings for Sonia, Emma had disclosed feelings of love for this other person.

During their fights about Sonia's prescription medication use, Sonia revealed that she had read the emails between Emma and her co-worker. Emma defended her need to seek support seeing that Sonia had been so emotionally unavailable, and Sonia protested this breach of trust. Sonia was understandably concerned about Emma's commitment to their relationship and Emma was concerned that Sonia was not trustworthy. Both injuries were substantial and needed repair for Emma and Sonia to have a future, but it was unclear how to manage these two significant body-blows to their relationship at once. Neither felt that they could trust the word or intention of the other, both remained defensive and self-protective, further damaging their bond, and leaving their pain unheard and unsoothed.

Eclipsing injuries

It is very common and completely understandable that an attachment injury rocks a relationship to its core, the hurtful event taking centre stage. Other smaller issues, niggles, and concerns usually pale into insignificance in the face of such a rupture to the bedrock of the relationship. Partners become absorbed in the urgency of the fallout of the attachment injury and prioritise attending to the pain of the hurt partner. This is totally reasonable and required; however, the nasty side effect is that smaller or less central matters are often relegated to the background. Other concerns are tabled for "later" and can be very difficult to raise given the pressing nature of the injury at hand. This is particularly the case when a hurtful partner has a grievance that is unrelated to the attachment injury or that pre-dates it. Given their involvement in the breach of trust, partners who have broken the other's trust can often feel they do not have the right to ask for their concerns to be heard. In this way, the enormity of the attachment injury eclipses other less seen, harder to share, or longstanding hurts that might be part of a relationship's history, or of either partner's experience.

Susan and Paul, a monogamous couple, whom we met in Chapter 3, were reeling from the discovery of Paul's affair. This was such a huge rupture to the fabric of their relationship that they were unsure if it was even possible to come back from something so dire. Susan felt immensely hurt and rejected – she was raging at his betrayal – after all she had sacrificed for their marriage and family! Paul knew that he had made a huge mistake and wanted to save his marriage but felt overwhelmed by Susan's pain. He was unsure if he could ever earn back her trust and repair their bond. Susan bombarded Paul with questions about the affair to attempt to make sense of it and to feel that nothing was hidden from her. Understandably, she was tormented by Paul's betrayal and scared of what it meant for their future. It was all she could think about, there were reminders everywhere she looked, all their conversations ended up coming back to this injury. Her pain was so great and Paul's breach of their bond so disastrous. Susan's need for repair was urgent and legitimate. It was reasonable that her experience took up all the space in the relationship.

The trouble with this common dynamic is that underlying issues for Paul that might have contributed to a breach of trust in their relationship were going unheard. Paul did not feel entitled to share his longstanding hurt over feeling the sting of Susan's criticism or her lack of support. He had learned to bottle these concerns, withdrawing into himself and distancing from Susan. Historically, Susan would complain about Paul's lack of presence with her and their family, becoming at times caustically critical. Paul would attempt to manage these moments by brushing off her concerns and defending himself. When that was unsuccessful, he would become compliant – apologising, and promising to be more connected to Susan and the family. Paul kept his need for Susan's support and reassurance to himself. Over time, he felt more and more hurt by her criticism, and increasingly resentful over carrying the family's financial stress alone. Given the current situation between them and his grave mistakes, he felt that his hurt might never be acknowledged. How could he possibly ask for reparations for such a minor issue considering his current transgressions? Without being able to process these concerns for Paul, Paul and Susan might never be able to fully repair the attachment injury or have the opportunity to strengthen their relationship moving forward.

Retaliation injuries

Another complicating factor when there has been an attachment injury is that hurt partners can lash out in retaliation in the most destructive ways. This can involve abusive behaviour, shaming behaviours, or even attachment injuries in return. Obviously, this is destructive to the individual partners and to the relationship, making repair impossible. Retaliatory actions will never create a context for repair and will only serve to further damage the fragile remaining threads of connection. This is not just the domain of wronged partners either. Hurtful partners can act in retaliatory ways when confronted with the shame of their actions, lashing out at the other to "level the playing field." Sometimes, people can feel justified that their hurtful acts are warranted given the original attachment injury. Even if this is the case, if you want to restore your connection, you will never be able to do so in a war zone. Remember, if you are intent on hurting each other, it will be impossible to regrow trust, love, and care. Retaliatory actions completely preclude repair.

Callum and Casey, who we met in Chapters 2 and 3, had an open relationship with clear ground rules around other partners and sexual safety. They had chosen not to tell their families about their open relationship status because they knew that it would not be met with acceptance and understanding. Both had parents with traditional relationship values, and they felt that they would not be embracing of Casey and Callum's choice to have an open relationship. When Callum discovered that Casey had continued a relationship with another partner after telling him it had ended, he was hurt. However, when he discovered that she had had unprotected sex with that partner as well, he was devastated. How she could break their agreement and put his health at risk was beyond his imagination. It shattered his view of her as safe, as his person, and as his partner. One night shortly after this discovery, Callum's hurt spiralled, and he impulsively revealed to Casey's family that she had slept with another person. Given that her family thought they had a traditional, monogamous relationship, Casey was harshly judged as a "cheater" and Callum received the utmost of support. This was hugely hurtful to Casey because she was met with recrimination and rejection by her family when she couldn't fully defend herself. On top of this, she then felt forced to explain the intricacy of the relationship agreements she had in place with Callum and risked further judgment and rejection from her family. This retaliatory action had grave consequences for Casey and Callum. Not only were they dealing with the original attachment injury, they were also dealing with the fallout of Callum's detrimental actions.

Erosion injuries

In some relationships, there has been no single, specific event that has toppled the walls of the relationship, clearly identifiable as an attachment injury. However, you might very much feel the fallout of broken trust and accumulated hurt. Perhaps, there has been a backlog of smaller disappointments, moments of misattunement, or of ruptured trust, that have damaged the fabric of the attachment bond more and more over time. This might be due to repetitive injuries that happen each time partners have a particularly bad fight, making it increasingly difficult to reweave the bond after ruptures. Or it could be from partners not revealing their concerns resulting in ongoing hurts with a lack of repair. There might be an event that represented the "last straw" or there might not. Erosion injuries are cumulative injuries that slowly erode trust and connection over time. Any single event in this litany of smaller "cuts" might not meet the definition of an attachment injury by itself, but the consequence can be a "death by a thousand cuts" for the relational bond. Each event plays its role in wearing away the bond a little more each time. In a cumulative manner, it can become harder to repair each smaller rupture and the bond can become thinner and weaker over time. To repair these ruptures and to prevent ongoing damage into the future, we need to gain clarity about the issues that are quietly devastating to the bond between partners. We need to address and repair each one and make changes so that they do not continue to undermine the foundation of your relationship moving forward.

Matt and Dina, whom we met in Chapter 3, had a history of bad fights where vastly hurtful things were said to each other – things that rocked the foundation of their trust and emotional safety. During one particularly heated moment, Matt made damaging and dismissive comments about Dina's lifelong struggle with eating and her body image, saying, "I never wanted to be with someone with an eating disorder." She experienced this as acutely painful and her view of Matt as her safe place was shattered. Dina attacked Matt's struggle to find stable employment saying, "Well, I never wanted to be with an unemployed loser." This sent Matt reeling and evoked old wounds around never earning his father's approval as a child and subsequent feelings of failure. Both hit so low in these heated moments that their bond was severely frayed. Each time they touched into these painful hurts they would explode into another fight where more hurtful things were said. Each fight further shredded their bond over time, making repair more and more elusive. With every rupture, it was more difficult to repair the broken threads. Their bond was losing its stretch and becoming frayed and brittle.

Now that we have looked at some of the ways that hurts can become complex and bidirectional, use Figure 6.1 to explore the complex nature of the injury or injuries to your bond that will need attention in the repair process.

Adjusting the repair process to accommodate complex injuries

When there is complexity in the attachment injury, we need to spend some time looking at the layers of hurt for each partner. Ultimately, we need to make a plan of action so that each hurt can be attended to as part of the resolution process. For some people, this might look like making a list of injuries and working their way through each, one-by-one. For others, it might involve working through the most pressing issue and then re-evaluating the need to process additional hurts that may have been left unresolved. How to know which one to look at first depends on the nature of the injury and each partner's needs. Sometimes, there is a call for give and take, or alternating whose grievance is looked at.

In my experience, working with people as they rebuild trust after an attachment injury, we usually need to start with the most present or urgent threat to the relationship – the issue that has the most attachment significance and poses the biggest threat to the relationship security. Usually, the outcome of resolving this primary attachment injury will impact how partners go on to resolve other historical, or less-pressing, matters. Some concerns feel less troubling when the central attachment injury is resolved, and the bond feels more secure. Other hurts will feel more relevant and

Complexity of the Attachment Injury

This sheet will help you to name the complexities of the attachment injury you are facing in your relationship. For many people, relational hurts are complex & multi-faceted. Identifying the elements of broken trust between you & your partner will help us to map out a path towards healing.

Which type of complex injury are you facing?

Dual Injury	Eclipsing Injury	Retaliation Injury	Erosion Injury
Partners have both violated promises & let the other down, leaving each partner feeling wronged & shattering the trust between them. These hurts can co-occur & can involve different or similar wrongdoings. Partners can each feel that they are the injured party & that the other needs to make a repair with them.	Partners become absorbed in the fall-out of the attachment injury & prioritise attending to the pain of the hurt partner. Other smaller issues, niggles & concerns do not get airtime. This is particularly the case when a hurtful partner has a grievance that is unrelated to the attachment injury or that pre-dates it.	Either partner can lash out in retaliation after an attachment injury. This can involve abusive behaviour, shaming behaviours, or subsequent attachment injuries. Retaliatory actions are destructive to the relationship & to each partner & only serve to further damage the fragile remaining threads of connection.	There might not be a clearly defined attachment injury, but there have been an accumulation of smaller disappointments, hurts, moments of misattunement, or of ruptured trust, that have damaged the fabric of the attachment bond more & more over time eroding it in a cumulative manner.

Layers of hurt in your relationship

If you are not dealing with one clear incident of hurt & the attachment injury between you is more complex, take some time to list the nature of the hurts you have each experienced.

Clare Rosoman 2024

Figure 6.1 Complexity of the attachment injury.

possible to address once there is some progress made in achieving a positive resolution of the key attachment injury. As partners feel heard and met in their pain, and as their trust starts to re-grow, it can feel far safer to address additional tender spots in the relationship. Each resolution compounds this good work by providing subsequent opportunities for connection, empathy, and understanding. These tough moments can strengthen the security of the bond further still by revising long-held assumptions, correcting misunderstandings, and allowing partners to attend to each other in new ways. Each corrective experience partners have weaves more threads into their connection, making it stronger and more flexible.

To plan for this corrective work, Figure 6.2 can help you to list which hurts are most vital to be addressed for each of you. You are likely to each have different injuries that need to be repaired. Take some time to individually reflect on what is most painful for you and which hurts need to be tended to. List them with the most important at the top. It's okay if you only have one and it's okay if you have more than one. This is about giving you some space to share what *you* really need to be addressed in the reparative process – what needs to be heard to allow you to move forward. If there are more than two people involved, you can use an additional sheet. There is space for three concerns each, but feel free to make this fewer. If you have more than three key hurts, I would caution you to narrow down to the essential injuries that you need tackled to avoid the process feeling overwhelming for your partner. This will force you to distil your pain to the core of what has felt most upsetting and is most in need of acknowledgement and repair.

Next, see if the two of you can agree on an order to address each person's hurts as we commence the attachment injury resolution process next chapter. Again, in Figure 6.2, there is space for six issues to be listed, but you might not need all of these. When choosing an order to focus on each point, compromise might be needed as well as trust that there will be room for both of your experiences. Our aim is for both of you to feel heard and understood in the repair process. I would suggest starting with the most urgent injury – the one that most threatens the current security of the relationship. As you resolve this key concern, it will provide a strong platform for addressing subsequent hurts. Some partners like to take turns so that they each know that their hurt will be addressed next. *Taking turns in this way will mean that the role of "hurt" and "hurtful" partner will change depending on whose issue is being processed. When working with one partner's hurt, they will be in the role of the "hurt" partner and the other in the role of the "hurtful" partner. Roles will then be swapped as you move to another attachment injury from the list. I prefer to think of this process as involving a "sharing" and a "witnessing" partner as pain is shared and held in the attachment injury resolution process.*

Attachment Injury Repair Priority list

Finding a collaborative way forward when there have been complex injuries

Key hurts needing to be addressed for Partner 1:

1.
2.
3.

Key hurts needing to be addressed for Partner 2:

1.
2.
3.

Collaborative Priority List for Attachment Injury Repair

Taking into account both partners' needs, can you agree on a priority list for hurts that need to be worked through as part of the attachment injury resolution process? List below:

1.
2.
3.
4.
5.
6.

Clare Rosoman 2024

Figure 6.2 Attachment injury repair priority list.

Removing barriers from the repair process

Hopefully, you have now gained a clearer understanding of the complexity of your attachment injury and the unique hurts that inhabit each of you. I hope you now feel that you have a priority list for addressing the particular issues that are impacting you both. However, before we commence the attachment injury resolution process in Chapter 7, I want to spend a moment emphasising some additional factors that can complicate and even prevent the process of repair. In this book so far, we explored how emotional reactivity can flare and block healing (the negative relational cycle) in Chapter 4, and we looked at how each person's own past-trauma experiences can be triggered by an attachment injury in Chapter 5. Now, I want to bring your attention to some different factors that can impact healing. These are related to a person's ideas and beliefs about recovery from an attachment injury. How you make sense of a betrayal such as the one you are facing, the beliefs and expectations you hold about the likelihood of repair, and the expectations you carry for the future of the relationship can significantly influence how open and engaged you can be in a process of repair.

What I am questioning here is how deeper issues within either or both parties can block the healing and influence the outcome of the repair process. Deep-seated beliefs can complicate the recovery from an attachment injury, even if the attachment injury is not as complex as some of the examples we have looked at earlier in this chapter. In fact, it might not be the complex nature of dual injuries or retaliation injuries, but the aftermath of the injury that complicates the healing. It might be the ambivalence that arises, the shattered dreams, the changed view of yourself, and of the other that adds complexity to the healing process.

Following an attachment injury, both hurt and hurtful partners have told me that they have concerns about the possibility of being able to repair this breach of trust, what it says about their commitment to each other, what it will mean for the future, and the fear of being hurt again, among others. These reasonable worries are bound to arise with the reverberation of an attachment injury. How tightly we hold on to these worries is often informed by a lifetime of experience and from the societal messages we receive about relationships. How absolute we are in our convictions will impact how flexible we can be when working through an attachment injury. Nothing upends your world and shatters your assumptions like a betrayal from one you trust implicitly. Nothing challenges your view of yourself like causing pain to one you love. To heal, to forgive, and to regrow your bond, it will involve challenging some of the assumptions you might be holding onto about relationships. The more flexible in your beliefs you can be, the more effectively you can adapt to this new reality in your relationship.

Letting go of the idealised relationship

Firstly, I invite you to ask yourself to reflect on your beliefs about this breach of trust. What would you say to a friend facing this same injury? Asking yourself to think about your learnings throughout your life about betrayal can help you to identify your expectations and assumptions. For instance, if you hold a belief that once broken, trust will never fully regrow, you might have a harder time of recovering from broken trust. If you have an all-or-nothing view of love and loyalty – that if someone hurts you, they cannot possibly love you – then you might grapple with accommodating a hurtful act into the narrative of your relationship with your partner. In my experience, the more black-and-white someone's thoughts are about their partner's or their own hurtful acts, the more difficult it is to repair. The more rigidly you hold on to an idealised view of love and connection, the more it will be challenged by an attachment injury, and the harder it will be to accept the imperfection of this rupture. For many, healing involves abandoning the view of the relationship as "innocent" and accepting that it is no longer as perfect and unsullied as it once was. Healing involves forgiveness of your partner and yourself for your contribution to the injury and its outcome and being prepared to revise your image of the relationship. In a way this is a more "mature" form of love.[1] This does not mean accepting a less-than relationship, but it means expanding your frame to include the reality of a relationship with perfectly imperfect partners who will misstep and hurt each other at times, but who also put in the work to repair and to strengthen it. Just as the Japanese art form of Kintsugi involves putting broken pottery pieces back together with gold, some say that repairing your relationship after a rupture is the "gold" that makes it even more beautiful for having weathered hardship.

Letting go of the idealised view of the relationship allows you to enter a new phase together that is more real and honest. It is my hope that this next chapter in your story together is one that allows you to each be authentic, to have learned more about each other, and to be clearer about what you need to flourish. This involves on some level, letting go of your previously held view of your partner, and of yourself. It means owning your role in the attachment injury and being willing to actively participate in the repair process – to peel back the layers and let your vulnerability be witnessed by the other. Accepting your partner's humanity, seeing them as less-than-perfect, can provide a powerful release from the strictures of unrealistic or romanticised views. You deserve this same freedom. Committing to an attachment injury resolution process is a mature and courageous step *into* your new relationship and away from old patterns.

Working with ambivalence

After an attachment injury, whether you are the one who has been hurt or the one who has caused hurt, it is completely normal to question whether it is worth staying. Feeling ambivalent about the relationship and uncertain about your commitment to it is *totally normal*. Why wouldn't you question if it is worth salvaging the wreckage when it is lying broken, beached on the shore? Some people don't dare utter these words and others yell it loudly, but almost everyone feels ambivalence in some way. Ambivalence can feel like a natural consequence of the attachment injury. However, some people have told me that to doubt their commitment to the relationship feels like a mark of dishonour – as though they are being disloyal, weak, or cowardly in questioning their desire to stay the course. Being uncertain about something as important as your relationship is bound to happen when it is rocked by a betrayal. In whatever way you are experiencing or have experienced ambivalence, I want to make space for it. It is a natural part of the process of acknowledging hurt, but we don't want it to negatively impact the healing.

I see ambivalence as a pragmatic solution to pain. If you have been burned, it makes sense to pull away from the source of the heat. When the source is something that matters gravely to you, of course, you will be in a dilemma between approach and withdrawal. Both feel risky, neither feels right. This a holding place to allow you to protect yourself from ongoing pain and to consider your options. I would urge you to not make decisions based on your ambivalence because of its protective function. Decisions based on ambivalence are likely to protect you from hurt, but they can also limit the possibility of repair. Staying in your relationship and repairing pain involves risk, and there is no way to do that whilst completely protecting yourself.

Ambivalence can limit attachment injury repair if it means that you cannot open your heart to the other. Holding part of yourself back is understandable, but if your heart is closed and you have one foot out the door, then it does not matter what your partner says or does, their attempts to reach you will be futile. This is of course, detrimental to the repair process, not to mention demoralising to you both. Ambivalence can also mean that you mistrust your partner's good intentions, that you view them through a suspicious lens, and doubt the sincerity or permanence of any positive changes they might make. Again, this wariness is hard-won, but it will block the possibility for change. You might find yourself questioning your partner's or your own reasons for staying, which can also undermine the repair process – casting acts of commitment in a dubious light. This guardedness is sensible, and while protective, it undermines growth and the rebuilding of trust. It can be frightening to trust positive changes in case it sets you up for future hurt or disappointment. I want to acknowledge the role of fear in healing. The role of ambivalence and self-protection is to manage threat and to reduce fear. Once you can see the function in your ambivalence, then it can be dismantled.

Ask yourself how your ambivalence might be impacting how present you can be to the repair process. If you are still engaged in actions that would breach your partner's trust, should they discover it, you are not engaged in a healing process. If you are making active plans to leave and to dissolve the relationship, you are not going to be very open to repair with your partner. If you are staying only because you are afraid to be on your own, you are not going to be able to open your heart to the other. If your key aim is to protect your self-image or to defend your integrity, then you are not going to be able to attend to your partner's vulnerability. If you only want guarantees against future hurt before you can risk revealing yourself and sharing with your partner, then you are approaching the process in reverse. Ambivalence and self-protection are like kryptonite to the attachment injury resolution process. You can't heal if you don't open your heart to the other and you can't grow if you don't listen to the lesson.

Setting the intention for repair

You have put so much emotional labour into understanding the attachment significance of this attachment injury and reflected on your role in its impact. You have unpacked your negative cycle, owned your reactivity, and explored your past trauma. In this chapter, we have looked at complexity in attachment injuries and formulated a priority list for tackling the ruptures to your attachment bond. We have named and explored some potential blocks to the repair process. Now, it is time to set your intention for the healing process.

Committing to the Attachment Injury Resolution Model is a critical life decision. It is one that no one starts out on with a 100% confidence in a positive outcome. Whether you are repairing with a view to rebuilding the trust in your relationship – to stay committed to each other – or whether you are repairing to honour what you have had and to consciously separate or redefine your relationship, this is an act of love on your relationship's behalf. It takes courage to work through emotional pain together and to confront that which is most difficult to face. The presence and bravery required epitomise the value you place on this relationship.

For the healing process to be effective, it involves all party's commitment and their willingness to be open. Sometimes, it can help to picture yourself in six months or a year or even five years, reflecting on where you want to be and what small changes would be needed from you both to get there.

If you were able to work through this body-blow to your relationship, to resolve the hurt, and to rebuild the trust, what would your relationship look like? This vision can sustain you as you step into uncertain waters and it can help you to pull yourself out of the spiral of hopelessness that can so easily threaten to pull you under. Can you each commit to this relationship and to repairing your bond? Can you share the mutual risk of further hurt? Can you do this together with no guarantee of the outcome? If you can both answer "yes" to these questions, then you are ready for the next chapter. With this attachment injury, you have a special opportunity, delivered to you in an unpleasant package, that can teach you profound lessons about yourself and your partner, and can change your relationship for the better. Those who "cut-and-run" miss out on that potential growth.

As we come to the end of this chapter and approach the repair work in earnest in Chapter 7, I ask you each to set your intention for healing. Using Figure 6.3 individually (you will each need a form), contemplate your reasons for committing to this work and why you value this relationship. Consider the assumptions or beliefs that could possibly block you from being open to your partner. Ask yourself how you can be intentional about acknowledging them and setting them gently aside. Can you commit to opening your heart and letting your partner impact you? Can you reveal your vulnerabilities? Can you let yourself be truly seen? Can you acknowledge what you want from the repair process and what you are we willing to bring?

Checklist for attachment injury repair

What a lot of work you have put into preparing for the attachment injury resolution process! I appreciate your patience and the effort that goes into reflecting deeply on your own reactions and the unique meaning of this attachment injury for you and your partner. I want to reassure you that the bulk of the work is in the preparation. Many people stumble at these preliminary hurdles and are unable to proceed to the repair process in earnest. Many become blocked in their own reactivity or their need to preserve their self-image. Many avoid the tough task of truly looking at yourself and your actions, at truly facing up to mistakes and their consequences. The fact that you are still reading at this point speaks volumes about your commitment to your relationship and to your personal grit.

I feel that I need to offer a word of warning about proceeding into the deeper repair work without being sufficiently "de-escalated." When I use the term *de-escalated*, I am referring to a marker for change that EFT therapists use to ascertain whether there is enough safety between partners to step into the deeper emotional waters required to restructure your

Setting the Intention for Repair

Committing to the attachment injury resolution process

Your commitment to the relationship

What are your personal reasons for committing to resolving this attachment injury?

What is it that you value about this relationship & about your partner?

Your commitment to healing

What are the assumptions or beliefs that you hold that could block you from being open to this repair work?

✓ Acknowledge assumptions & set them aside

✓ Open your heart to the other - let them impact you

✓ Be vulnerable - let the other truly see you

Your contribution to the process of repair

What would you like to gain from the repair process?

What are you willing to bring to the repair process?

Clare Rosoman 2024

Figure 6.3 Setting the intention for repair.

attachment bond.[2] If partners are still becoming caught in their reactive cycle and saying or doing hurtful things to each other, there is simply not enough safety and stability in the system to move into a healing space. Healing requires mutual vulnerability and mutual risk. No sensible human will risk showing their tender, vulnerable emotions if the other appears cold, critical, explosive, hostile, or dysregulated.

Before you consider the next steps in the Attachment Injury Resolution Model, I ask you to reflect on the following questions:

1 Can you and your partner identify your negative cycle and step out of it by deliberately changing habitual patterns of reactivity, such as by taking a time-out?
2 Can you both notice and catch your own reactive emotions and take steps to consciously manage them, individually?
3 Are you each a little less self-protective and better able to hear and feel the other?
4 Have you gained a deeper understanding of your own reactions to your hurt and the meaning of this attachment injury for you?
5 Have you gained some new insights from your partner about the meaning of the attachment injury for them?
6 Are you committed to a process of change and growth – in yourself – not just in your partner and your relationship?
7 Are you committed to this relationship and to healing from this attachment injury, even if that means confronting uncomfortable encounters and painful emotions?

Your answers to these important questions determine your readiness to move into the next stage of the Attachment Injury Resolution Model. I am assuming that you can answer "yes" or "mostly yes" to these questions and that you are feeling prepared for the next steps! Restoring the security in your bond is a pure and beautiful process when well-prepared for.

Let's take a moment to celebrate all your work and to review the steps that you have completed so far. These steps form the groundwork for the next steps of the recovery process. Using Figure 6.4, check that you have completed the following tasks and have the required ingredients for attachment injury resolution. Figure 6.5 summarises the goals of Phase 1 of the Attachment Injury Resolution Model that you have now worked your way through. Then, it's time to lean in and restructure your attachment bond.

Preparation Checklist
for Attachment Injury Repair
Celebrating progress & readiness for the attachment injury resolution process

- ☐ Become aware of the attachment significance of broken trust on loving bonds & the nature & impact of the current rupture (Chapters 1 & 2)

- ☐ Read the overview of the attachment injury resolution process (Figure 3.1) to familiarise yourself

- ☐ Take on board & act on your three key tasks to create a context for healing (Figures 4.1 & 4.2)

- ☐ Identify the negative relational cycle that blocks healing & reflect on your own reactivity (Figures 4.3, 4.4 & 4.5)

- ☐ Take time to explore on the impact of the past on this injury for you (Figures 5.1 & 5.2)

- ☐ Identify your protective coping strategies & how you can better care for your pain (Figures 5.3 & 5.4)

- ☐ Explore & understand the complexity of the attachment injury & its impact on each of you (Figure 6.1)

- ☐ Create a shared attachment injury repair priority list that you are both happy with (Figure 6.2)

- ☐ Set your intentions for repair outlining your commitment to the resolution process (Figure 6.3)

Clare Rosoman 2024

Figure 6.4 Preparation checklist for attachment injury repair.

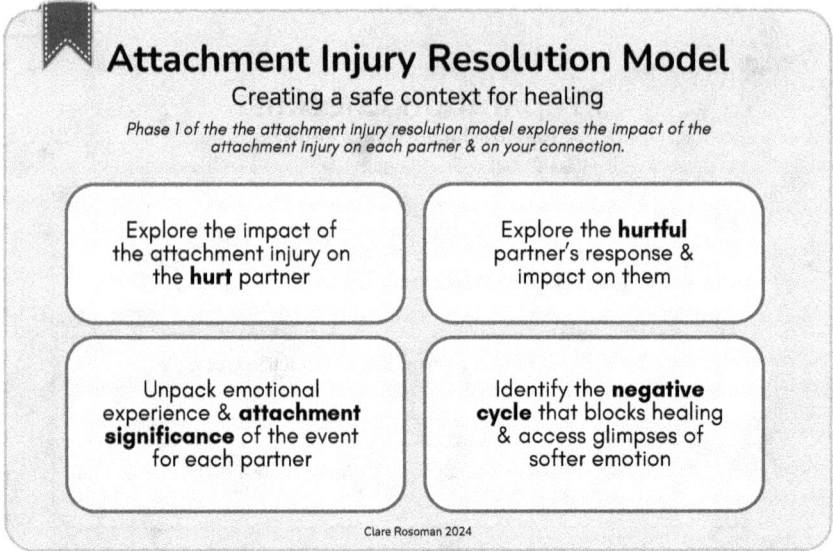

Attachment Injury Resolution Model
Creating a safe context for healing

Phase 1 of the the attachment injury resolution model explores the impact of the attachment injury on each partner & on your connection.

Explore the impact of the attachment injury on the **hurt** partner

Explore the **hurtful** partner's response & impact on them

Unpack emotional experience & **attachment significance** of the event for each partner

Identify the **negative cycle** that blocks healing & access glimpses of softer emotion

Clare Rosoman 2024

Figure 6.5 Phase 1 of the Attachment Injury Resolution Model.

Notes

1 Abrahms-Springs, J. (2020). *After the affair: Healing the pain and rebuilding trust when a partner has been unfaithful* (3rd ed.). New York: Harper.
2 Johnson, S.M. (2004). *The practice of emotionally focused couple therapy: Creating connections* (2nd ed.). New York: Brunner/Mazel.

Part III

Healing

Repairing the bond and re-establishing security

Chapter 7

Working through the injury for the hurt partner

Now that we have established safety, understood the meaning of the attachment injury and its impact for each partner, and can see and exit the negative cycle that has been blocking recovery, we can begin the healing process in earnest. You have reflected on the role of past trauma, the complex nature of some attachment injuries, and the beliefs or assumptions that can block healing. At the end of the last chapter, you set your intentions for the reparation of this attachment injury. Your hard work so far completes Phase 1 of the Attachment Injury Resolution Model. We can now put that wonderful groundwork to good use as we enter Phase 2. Chapters 7 and 8 will guide you through the processes required for Phase 2, and Chapter 9 will take you through Phase 3. These next three chapters will support you in processing emotion, sharing pain vulnerably, and with restoring security in your loving bond once more.

In this chapter, *our focus is solely on the hurt partner*. If you are the hurtful or witnessing partner, you might like to read this chapter to understand the work that your partner will be undertaking, or you can move on to Chapter 8 where our focus is on the hurtful partner and their role in the attachment injury resolution model. In this chapter, we will be helping the hurt partner to explore and process the impact of the attachment injury so that they can share with their partner in new, more vulnerable ways. This means connecting with the impact of the injury, the essence of the hurt, and integrating the elements of the experience to share with the other.[1] This is a challenging process where painful emotions such as hurt, fear, sadness, and anger are bound to show up in spades. We will arm the hurt partner with tools for processing big feelings so that they can work through their pain and can send clear signals to the other – signals that pull for understanding and care rather than defensiveness. This represents a powerful new step for the hurt partner to reach into the depths of their pain and to share it with the other openly and without their protective shield in place. This is a monumental task given that, following a breach of trust, the other now appears dangerous – it is a leap of faith.

DOI: 10.4324/9781003466499-11

Before we start this work, I want you, the hurt partner – the one who will be sharing your pain – to know exactly what is expected of you in the attachment injury resolution process. It is important for your sense of predictability, agency, and safety that the process is clearly outlined and that you know exactly what you are embarking on. Figure 7.1 provides an overview of the tasks required for hurt, or put more accurately, "sharing" partners. If you and your partner have complex, bidirectional injuries, you will each take turns in the role of the hurt/sharing partner and in the role of the hurtful/witnessing partner and might need to repeat this process as you work through several separate hurts.

Assembling and ordering your emotions

Before any human can share a clear message of pain or need to another, they need to firstly be aware of their emotions and, secondly, able to befriend them. The best preparation you can do for healing this rupture is to spend some time processing and exploring your pain. As you look at Figure 7.1 and imagine encountering your most primary and vulnerable feelings about this attachment injury, how do you feel? As you imagine turning and sharing these tender experiences with your partner, what happens inside for you? These questions aim to evoke your curiosity about your inner world – your feelings, thoughts, and reactions. For many people, the idea

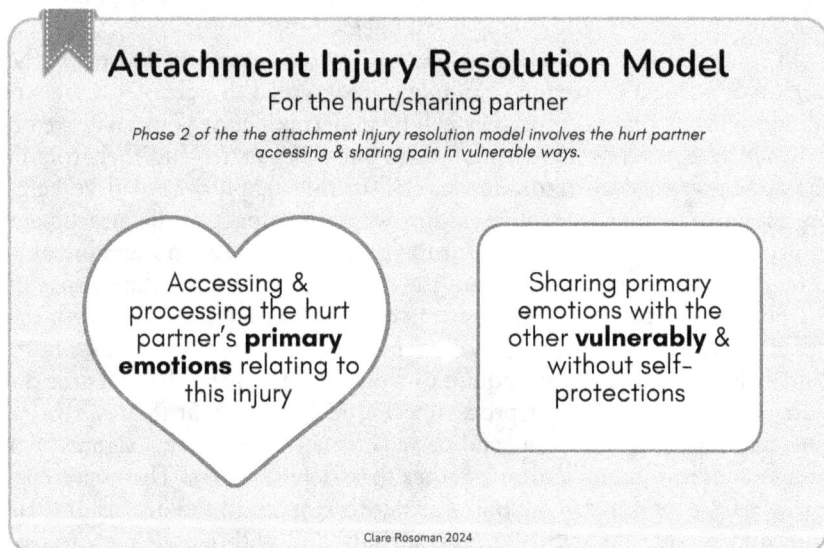

Attachment Injury Resolution Model
For the hurt/sharing partner
Phase 2 of the the attachment injury resolution model involves the hurt partner accessing & sharing pain in vulnerable ways.

Accessing & processing the hurt partner's **primary emotions** relating to this injury

Sharing primary emotions with the other **vulnerably** & without self-protections

Clare Rosoman 2024

Figure 7.1 Attachment injury resolution model – for the hurt/sharing partner.

of paying attention to painful emotion feels foreign and even pointless. What good could it possibly do to dwell on painful emotions? Well, it can do a *lot* of good, actually. Embedded in your most painful and tender emotions is the bonding agent that will repair your bond – if your partner can meet you with theirs in return. I want to acknowledge that the idea of sharing your most vulnerable experiences with another is scary for all, and for some, it is downright terrifying. However, we know that this is an important part of the repair process. Being able to connect with your emotional world and make sense of what you find there is a valuable skill for all humans, not just when we want to repair an attachment rupture with our special other. *Before we look at sharing anything with your partner, I want to help you to order and distil your inner world, so that your signals, when sent, will be crystal clear and straight from the heart – so that they can land right where they need to.*

How comfortable you are with touching your inner pain and sharing it with others will be impacted by your experiences in close relationships and what you have learned through these experiences. As you explored in Chapter 5, you might have had positive experiences of sharing emotion and felt that they were well-received, or you might have had negative experiences of your emotions being dismissed or even ridiculed by others. Naturally, these experiences will inform this part of the process for you and will impact your willingness to attempt it. I encourage you to acknowledge all that you have learned about sharing in relationships and to be kind to yourself as you contemplate taking the risk of sharing your pain with your partner. Being able to share clearly starts with being able to tune into your inner world, so let's work on that first.

To guide you through this process, I want to share some wisdom from Emotionally Focused Therapy (EFT), and specifically, how this model of therapy assists people to distil and make sense of their emotional experiences. EFT helps people to tune into their emotional world and to order and assemble the pieces of their inner experience into a coherent whole. The process of paying attention to your emotional experience helps it to become known, distinct, and clear. It becomes more familiar and easier to be with. Tuning-in like this – with curiosity – allows the wisdom embedded in your experience to be discovered and honoured.[2] It helps you to encounter yourself in new ways and to attune to your needs more effectively. The result of this is that you can send clearer signals about your needs to your loved ones, making it more likely that they will be responded to positively. The more you know yourself, the more you can pull others close to you.

After an attachment injury, when your most precious relationship is under threat, you might shy away from closeness with your partner. You are bound to experience a myriad of emotional reactions and your signals might have been scrambled as the two of you have become tangled in a negative cycle. This is very common following a rupture in trust. As we have looked at earlier in this book, being aware of your reactivity and being able to make sense of your inner world are vital when navigating tough relational moments. I want to help you to practice the skill of ordering your emotional experience to prepare you for being able to share the most important aspects of this injury with your partner in clear, non-reactive ways. In EFT, we call this "emotion assembly"[3] and it is an important method for becoming acquainted with your inner world. To assemble emotion, we use Magda Arnold's elements of emotion,[4] to curiously pay attention to each facet of your emotional experience and to tune into its message. It is as though we are gathering all the fragmented pieces of your feelings and reactions to this injury, all together in a tidy ball, so that they can later be shared with clarity.

To "assemble" your emotion, I suggest firstly noticing the physical sensations that arise as you think about the attachment injury. This injury will be a trigger for alarm in your nervous system – it is a threat to your safe reality. Notice how you feel in your body when there is a reminder of this event. Is there a sensation that arrives in your belly, head, hands, chest, or elsewhere? Do you notice heat, coldness, tightness, heaviness, fluttery sensations, nausea, pain, tension, stillness, or movement? If so, where do you feel it? Is it changing or static? Moving or still? Heavy or light? I am inviting you to bring mindful awareness to your inner experience and to engage your curiosity as you explore it without judgement. Breathe slowly and smoothly as you pay attention to your inner sensations and consciously allow them to be there. Feel yourself soften around them – making room for them. Now, notice your thoughts. What do you tell yourself about this event? About yourself, your partner, your relationship, the future, the past? As you ponder these thoughts, what happens to the physical sensations that show up for you? Do they stay the same or do they alter? Observing them from a working distance; what changes do you notice in them? And finally, what do you normally do to cope when these feelings or thoughts are present for you? How do you manage the painful aspects of this experience? Notice the connection between feelings, thoughts, and behaviours. Does this way of coping or protecting help you or does it come with challenges? Figure 7.2 will guide you to ponder these questions. Notice how you feel after curiously observing your inner responses to reminders of this attachment injury.

As you move further into this process, knowing that to resolve this injury you need to share your pain with your partner can be a very scary prospect indeed. When we are in self-protection mode, it goes against all our instincts to make ourselves vulnerable. You can use the same principles of emotion assembly to make sense of, and to order your experience, as you imagine sharing these tender emotions with your partner. As you acknowledge that you need to share your pain vulnerably with your partner, what happens for you? As you picture yourself turning to your partner and letting them see your pain, how do you feel inside? What sensations come

Emotion Assembly
Tuning into your emotional world

This sheet will help you to reflect on the elements of your emotional experience & to find the order & wisdom embedded within. Using the attachment injury as the "relational trigger" what happens inside for you?

Noticing how you FEEL - physical sensations

What sensations show up when you think about this attachment injury?
What happens in your body?

- Where do you feel it?
- What do you feel?
- Is it changing or static?
- Heavy or light?
- Moving or still?
- Make room for it
- Observe without judgement

Noticing your THOUGHTS - meaning-making

What do you tell yourself about this attachment injury, about your partner, yourself, your relationship, the future, the past?

Look out for **Model of Other** themes

Look out for **Model of Self** themes

Noticing what you DO - coping strategies

What do you DO when these painful reminders & emotions show up?
How do you try to manage the painful aspects of this experience?

Does this help or does it come with challenges?

Clare Rosoman 2024

Figure 7.2 Emotion assembly.

alive for you? Where do you feel them? Can you make room for them? What do you say to yourself? How does this impact how you feel or what you do to cope? How do you imagine protecting yourself or managing intense emotion as you share your pain with your partner? And how might this affect the outcome? These questions hone your attention to your inner world and the exquisite logic of human emotion.

I hope that you can meet your pain with care and kindness. I hope that you can allow your understandable human reactions to exist without judgement and can bring curious and kind awareness to them. As you can do this, they become more familiar and easier to be with. Emotion assembly will be invaluable in preparing you to share your experience clearly and vulnerably with your partner.

Matt and Dina, whom we met in Chapters 3 and 6, had an explosive cycle where each would say and do things that triggered alarms for the other and caused further hurt and wariness. It was important for them to each be able to slow and order their own inner emotional experience before sharing it with each other, so that they could send clear signals from the essence of their pain rather than scrambled signals that contained barbs. Being able to make sense of their inner worlds meant that they could bring care and clarity to their experience which then helped them to be careful with each other's tender feelings. This helped them to step out of their negative cycle and to step into the repair process with more vulnerability and less fear of escalation.

Finding the meaning in your experience

For the next tool to ready yourself to share your hurt with your partner in ways that will contribute to the repair of the attachment injury, we need to understand the unique meaning of this event for you. How it upended your world and changed your view of everything. Sharing the meaning of this event, and the impact it has had on you, is a crucial ingredient in attachment injury resolution. It is necessary for your partner to understand the impact of this event on you and it is important for you to be heard and acknowledged. If you recall, in Chapter 5, we explored the meaning of this attachment injury – how it changed your view of your relationship, yourself, and your partner. The attachment significance of an event such as the one you are facing is monumental. If the relationship didn't matter to you, this event would be far less meaningful or even insignificant.

If this hurt also awakens echoes of past relational hurts and traumas, then it is likely to have an additional layer of attachment meaning for you. If it compounds negative experiences in relationships, or is a repetitive injury in this relationship, then of course it has far more potency to destroy loving connection. A betrayal of trust in an attachment relationship teaches a person a powerful lesson about the other and sometimes about themselves. As we have discussed in earlier chapters, our sense of identity and worth is shaped and altered in our closest relationships. The meaning that you make about this attachment injury will be informed by years of experiences in prior relationships throughout your life, as well as your cumulative experiences in this relationship.

As you were slowly and curiously observing your emotion in the earlier emotion assembly exercise, I wondered what you noticed about the thoughts that came up for you relating to the attachment injury? How did this injury shake your safe world? How did it impact your feelings about your partner, and your relationship? How has it impacted your view of yourself? How did this injury redefine your view of the present, the past, and the future? What are the tough lessons you have learned from this event that you are hoping your partner can correct or heal? *This is your attachment protest!* This is the part that has been jolted and needs to be heard. An attachment injury cannot be healed alone. This pain needs to be shared and your protest witnessed. You need to be met and soothed by your partner. Often there is an attachment protest and plea for correction in these messages, such as "Please reassure me that I can trust you again, this event taught me that I can't, but I want to be able to, can you help me with that?" As my colleague, Dr Kathryn Rheem says, sharing like this represents a person reaching out to their partner with their pain in their outstretched hand, asking them to share their pain, and to help them with it.[5] Only the one who has hurt you can heal this part of the injury. I ask you to consider how you could share the attachment meaning of this injury with your partner and how they could help you with this as you move forward and heal together.

We met Susan and Paul in Chapters 3 and 6. Susan was angry at Paul for breaking her trust and having an affair with a co-worker, her pain was clear, and Paul was devastated knowing that he had inflicted this upon her. However, when Susan could vulnerably share with him how his actions had shattered her view of them as an impenetrable, formidable team, how she felt that her sacrifice for the family and for him was disregarded – that she felt completely abandoned by him and left alone in the world – then it really hit him. He came to understand how his actions had signalled to her that they were no longer as one. He had stepped away from her and from their team, leaving her all alone. This impacted him far more than her rage or her threats to leave. The thought of his person feeling so rejected broke his heart. Seeing her pain register for Paul was immensely validating for Susan. It reassured her that he truly understood the impact of his actions and was remorseful for causing her harm.

Deepening vulnerability

For the final tool in your attachment injury resolution tool kit, we need to access your core vulnerability. Argh I hear you groan, not vulnerability, anything but that! Being vulnerable when your trust has been broken is agonising and can even feel misguided. You might ask yourself why you must be vulnerable when you're the one who was hurt – shouldn't they be the one to be vulnerable first? While understandable, avoiding vulnerability just doesn't work. For repair of this injury, it is going to require you *both* being willing to be vulnerable. If you stay behind your protective wall, your partner won't be able to reach you and to impact you. Resolution requires you to share in the pain together, rather than apart. I know that it feels risky, but I imagine that, if you are still reading, this relationship means so much to you that you cannot simply walk away. I know from experience, that it is impossible to stay in a relationship and to repair a rupture of trust if one or both partners keep their protective shields up. It blocks the healing because healing can only happen when hearts connect – when people can meet in vulnerability.

Meeting in vulnerability means allowing your most raw and tender primary emotions to be felt and revealed to your partner. Sharing in this way spreads the load of the emotional pain, making it relational rather than individual. It is time for you to carry this pain together rather than suffering separately. Reaching out and sharing the most painful parts of your experience will allow your partner to step forward and to help you with it. Rest assured, they have a whole chapter on how to do that in Chapter 8! This is the only way I know to repair bonds and to help partners to grow from suffering. Remember, this way of repairing attachment injuries is evidence-based, which is immensely reassuring.[6]

When I talk about accessing your vulnerability, I mean taking the elevator down into your emotional world, beneath protective surface emotions, and into the softest, darkest corners – the places that feel most tender. The parts of you that rarely see the light of day and you may not visit very often, if at all. Most of us spend our lives avoiding certain aspects of our emotional worlds where pain and shame live, constructing our world instead to hide from or to compensate for those places. This might be seen in someone overworking to compensate for feeling not smart enough, someone going out of their way to help others out of a fear of not being lovable enough, or someone exuding confidence to hide their crippling self-doubt. These tender places where we nurse our doubts about our worth are the hardest to be with, and yet, can be the seat of the greatest growth. If we can lean into our most vulnerable, most wobbly, and uncertain places within us and learn to embrace them, we grow tremendously. Better still, if we can share them with trusted others, under the soothing balm of their acceptance, these wounds within us can heal. We can be released from patterns of compensation and unhealthy coping that hold us back, we can more authentically connect with ourselves, our special others, and our lives.

An attachment injury will often bring us closer to these vulnerable, painful places than any other life experience can. These tender spots where we doubt our lovability and our trust in others often have their origins in the painful messages we receive in relationships with those whom we trust. Our vulnerabilities are usually created in an attachment context, so it makes perfect sense that they will come alive when we are hurt by someone we love. To heal from this injury, you need to take the brave step of sharing your vulnerability with your partner. Our aim is for you to have a corrective experience that repairs the rupture and allows you both to move forward, stronger for this breach.

To deepen your contact with your most vulnerable, most primary emotions, I invite you to ask yourself some key questions. Figure 7.3 will guide you through this process. What hurts most about this attachment injury? What painful places does it scrape against inside you? What old wounds does it awaken? What is most painful for you to touch? When was the moment that the injury happened, when the floor fell out from underneath you? Was there a "never again" moment where you decided that you could no longer turn to your partner and trust their word? What was that like for you? How have you carried that pain? What is the hardest part about this pain for you? What is the most difficult part to share, to let your partner see?

Staying with your experience, to contact it yourself, will be so difficult, but I want you to know that this pain needs to be heard, to be witnessed. Acknowledging it to yourself is a huge first step. Staying with the pain, making room for it, expanding it, allowing it, naming it, acknowledging it, distilling it to its core message, is powerful work towards healing. Now it is ready to share, and it needs to be witnessed by your partner.

Sonia and Emma, whom we met in Chapters 3 and 6, had been growing more distant as Sonia's work and caring for her mother consumed her time, and Emma gave up on her attempts to reach her. When Sonia's secret prescription medication dependence came to light, it was only Emma's sharing of her deep loneliness and her fear of losing Sonia that penetrated her protective defences. Sonia was moved by Emma's vulnerable plea for connection and her deep sorrow at losing her connection with Sonia. She began to see that behind Emma's anger was fear of losing their bond. Emma's vulnerable sharing of her childhood abandonment resonated with Sonia as she made sense of the depth of Emma's pain in feeling shut out by Sonia. When Sonia wept and tremulously shared how hurt she had been to learn of Emma's bond with a co-worker, Emma was powerfully impacted. She had wondered if she mattered at all to Sonia, but her reach reassured Emma of her importance to her. Vulnerability was the catalyst to Emma and Sonia finding their way back to each other.

Accessing Vulnerability - Hurt Partner

Hurt or sharing partner bravely exploring their deepest, most primary emotions

This sheet will help you to deepen the most vulnerable & primary aspects of your emotional experience relating to this attachment injury. This work will prepare you to share with your partner in new ways.

What is the most painful part of this injury for you?

What hurts most about this breach of trust?

What old wounds does it awaken?

What has it been like for you, living with this pain?

Can you describe the moment that the injury happened, when the floor fell out from underneath you? How did that feel? How have you carried that pain?

Can you imagine sharing this pain with your partner?

What is the most difficult part of this experience to share, to let your partner see?

What are you most afraid could happen if you share this with your partner?

Clare Rosoman 2024

Figure 7.3 Accessing vulnerability in the sharing partner.

Sharing pain vulnerably with your partner

Following your reflections in Figure 7.3, it is now time for you to *share the attachment significance of this attachment injury, along with your vulnerable feelings, with your partner*. This a crucial step in the Attachment Injury Resolution Model. No matter how well prepared you are, it is still extremely difficult to share your heart with someone who has hurt you so deeply. Find a time when you are both ready to be present with each other, and there are no distractions, and take the brave step of sharing your heart. I encourage you to be aware of the self-protections that will swoop in to try to save you. While well-intentioned, these coping strategies will take you out of vulnerability. Notice the tell-tale signs of the protections and coping strategies you identified in Chapter 5 (Figure 5.3) coming to the fore. They are there to keep you safe from risk, but risk you must, if you want to repair your bond. You need to let your partner see your pain, to share it with them, and to allow healing. This can only happen in a context of mutual vulnerability and mutual risk, and only with open hearts.

Tips for sharing your pain

1 *Breathe and stay grounded.* Stay in touch with and aware of your body sensations, the feelings that show up, the thoughts that are running through your mind, and how you are coping in the moment. Treat yourself with kindness and remember the reasons you are taking this brave risk. Your relationship matters too much not to. Your self-growth matters too much not to. How you share will impact how you are received.
2 *Stay on-track.* Remain connected to the essence of the message that you want your partner to hear and be impacted by, returning to that place if you get off-track. Be clear about the attachment impact that this injury has had on *you* and try to only speak for yourself and not for your partner. Avoid slipping into assuming your partner's thoughts or intent, knowing that they will have ample opportunity to share their experience directly.
3 *Stay vulnerable.* If you can share the most vulnerable parts of your experience, you are providing the most potent agent for healing your bond. So long as your partner can meet you in vulnerability, you are doing your absolute utmost to give your relationship the best chance of repair. Notice the temptation to put your protective shield up. This is natural, but, will be a barrier to connection. Ask yourself – am I sharing from my pain or from my protections right now? Return to the most vulnerable, most painful part of your experience and let your partner see that. If you can, finding your partner's eyes can really help vulnerability to flow for you both. Not everyone is comfortable with this, but it can be extremely helpful for bonding connection.

Sharing/hurt partner reaches vulnerably

This sheet will help the hurt/sharing partner to organise their thoughts & feelings as they share their experience of this attachment injury with their partner in the Attachment Injury Resolution Model.

Tips for the sharing partner

Stay grounded	Stay on-track	Stay vulnerable
Breathe...Stay in touch with & aware of your body sensations, the feelings that show up, the thoughts that are running through your mind & how you are coping in the moment. Treat yourself with kindness & remember the reasons you are taking this brave risk. How you share will impact how you are received.	Remain connected to the essence of the message that you want your partner to hear & be impacted by. Return to that place if you get off-track. Be clear about the attachment impact that this injury has had on you & try only to speak on your behalf & not for your partner.	Share the most vulnerable parts of your experience. If your partner can meet you in vulnerability, then you are both giving your relationship all the ingredients needed for repair. Notice the temptation to put your protective shield up. This is natural but will be a barrier to connection.

Can you share the impact of this attachment injury with your partner?

Using your discoveries from previous exercises, can you let your partner know how this injury has impacted you on an emotional level? What do you most need them to understand?

Clare Rosoman 2024

Figure 7.4 Sharing/hurt partner reaches vulnerably.

Figure 7.4 will guide you in how to share your vulnerable feelings and the impact of this injury on you.

In the next chapter, the hurtful or witnessing partner will be supported to respond to this vulnerable reach with accessibility, responsiveness, and engagement – the building blocks of secure attachment and the crucial ingredients for repair.

Notes

1 Zuccarini, D., Johnson, S.M., Dalgleish, T.L., & Makinen, J.A. (2013). Forgiveness and reconciliation in emotionally focused therapy for couples: The client change process and therapist interventions. *Journal of Marital and Family Therapy*, 39(2), 148–162.
2 Johnson, S.M., & Campbell, T.L. (2022). *A primer on emotionally focused individual therapy: Cultivating fitness and growth in every client*. London: Routledge.
3 Johnson, S.M. (2019). *Attachment theory in practice: Emotionally focused therapy (EFT) with individuals, couples and families*. New York: The Guilford Press.
4 Arnold, M.B. (1960). *Emotion and personality*. New York: Columbia University Press.
5 Rheem, K., & Olden, J. (2021). The EFT Cafe. *Stage Two Attachment Injury Repair*. www.theeftcafe.com.
6 Makinen, J.A., & Johnson, S. (2006). Resolving attachment injuries in couples using emotionally focused therapy: Steps toward forgiveness and reconciliation. *Journal of Consulting and Clinical Psychology*, 74, 1055–1064.

Chapter 8

Reconciling the injury for the hurtful partner

In this chapter, we help the hurtful partner to witness the pain from the hurt partner while maintaining their emotional balance. The hurtful partner is encouraged to hold the other's pain – to attend, to witness, and to acknowledge it. It is so very difficult to confront the impact of your own actions, knowing that you caused harm to someone you care about. The hurtful partner will be supported in this place, to see and gently lower their protective shield, and to respond to the hurt partner from a place of compassion and care. When the hurtful partner can remain present and attuned to the other's pain and let it impact them, they break the feeling of isolation for the hurt partner. In fact, they are *each* no longer alone and absorbed in their private pain, they can now share the load of this hurt together. This represents a key shift in the pattern between them that restructures their bond as secure once more. Partners sharing in mutually vulnerable, emotionally accessible ways forms the glue that repairs the ruptured bond. Reconciliation, the restoration of trust, and a softer emotional connection evolve as a direct result of this process.[1]

Our last chapter focused on the hurt (sharing) partner, so in this chapter, *our focus is solely on the hurtful, or, what I like to think of as the "witnessing" partner*. This chapter continues the work of Phase 2 of the Attachment Injury Resolution Model (see Figure 3.1 for a reference), which involves being present to your partner's pain, so that you can respond in emotionally accessible ways. It means standing steady in the face of big emotions, even if you encounter floods of your own emotions. We will help you to heal this rupture using your most valuable resource – your presence. Your presence is crucial to the restoration of trust, so we will firstly focus on how to meet your partner in their pain and, secondly, on how to respond in ways that build security. How to be accessible, responsive, and engaged – the building blocks of secure attachment.

Before we start this work, I want you, the hurtful or witnessing partner – the one who will be holding your partner's pain – to know exactly what is expected of you in the attachment injury resolution process. As I have said

DOI: 10.4324/9781003466499-12

Attachment Injury Resolution Model
For the hurtful/witnessing partner

Phase 2 of the the attachment injury resolution model involves the hurtful partner attending to the pain of the hurt partner in non-defensive ways.

Accessing & processing the hurtful partner's **primary emotional** responses

Sharing how they are **impacted** by the other's pain – expressing responsibility, remorse & apology

Clare Rosoman 2024

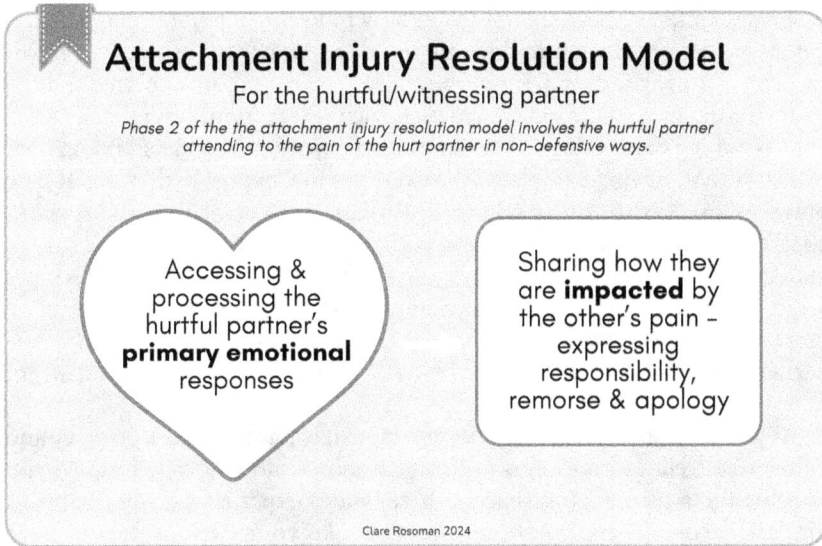

Figure 8.1 Attachment Injury Resolution Model – for the hurtful/witnessing partner.

before, I wouldn't ask anyone to engage with something without knowing what the process involves, having their own agency to choose their path, and knowing what will be expected of them. To provide this perspective, Figure 8.1 presents an overview of the tasks required for the hurtful or witnessing partner when attending to their partner's pain in the Attachment Injury Resolution Model. Just note that if you and your partner have complex, bidirectional injuries, you will each take turns in the role of the hurtful/witnessing partner and in the role of the hurt/sharing partner, and will need to repeat this process as you work through each separate hurt.

Assembling and ordering your emotions

Standing steady in the face of the other's pain is a tall order for anyone. Unless you are a robot, it is bound to evoke strong emotions in you. If the relationship matters and your partner matters, then it will flare upsetting emotions that have you reaching for your protective coping strategies. As the supportive partner in the repair process, you have two key tasks; *the first is to attune to your partner's pain and the second is to respond non-defensively, in ways that restore your partner's faith in you as their safe attachment figure.* We know that your reaction to your partner's experience, as the one who has caused pain, is vital to the repair process, so managing what comes up for you and keeping your balance is our first key priority.

In this section, we are going to look at how to keep your emotional balance. Before we do that, I want to offer a word of assurance that successful repair involves *both* partners putting in the effort. You cannot be expected to hold steady in the face of unbridled, reactive, vicious emotion, or verbal attacks. I am assuming that your partner has put hard work into understanding their pain and that, having completed the exercises in Chapter 7, they are able to bravely share it with you in vulnerable ways. If they can achieve this remarkable feat, then it will be possible for you to lean into their experience and to take in their message, but your response is pivotal in whether this becomes a healing moment or another rupture that sets you both back. I want to prepare you to receive their reach well! I want to ensure that you can be the partner you want to be and that the two of you can repair this attachment injury.

As you imagine witnessing your partner sharing their most primary and vulnerable feelings about this attachment injury, how do you feel? As you imagine them turning and sharing these tender experiences, what happens inside for you? These questions aim to evoke your curiosity about your inner world – your feelings, thoughts, and reactions. For many people, the idea of paying attention to painful emotion feels unfamiliar and even futile. Given that your partner is going to need you to tolerate and attune to their emotions, and that many of your own are likely to show up in the process, being able to keep your emotional balance is an important skill. It is one that we all benefit from as humans and as creatures who bond. Just as I did in Chapter 7 (with the hurt partner), I want to share some wisdom from Emotionally Focused Therapy (EFT) and specifically, how this model of therapy helps people to order and make sense of their emotional experiences. I apologise if this is repetitive for those who have already read Chapter 7, but being able to tune into our emotional world and to make sense of our experience is just so important for all of us, that I feel I need to reiterate it here! In EFT, we help people to pay attention to their emotional experience – to slow down and to observe their inner world, piece by piece, moment by moment. Far from being futile, this helps it to become known, distinct, and clear. Paying curious attention to your inner world and to your emotions allows you to find and benefit from the wisdom embedded in your experience.[2] It helps you to encounter yourself in new ways and to notice your needs, which unsurprisingly helps you to attend to other people's emotions and needs differently as well. The result of this is that your relationships improve, you can better attune and respond to others' emotions, and you can send clearer signals about your needs to your loved ones.

After an attachment injury such as the one you are facing, your relationship could really benefit from emotional attunement. Care, presence, and understanding are part of the soothing balm that will heal the attachment wound. *In short, being able to attend to your partner's emotion depends on your ability to manage your own.* After an attachment injury, emotions between partners can run high and your signals might have become jumbled as the two of you became embroiled in a negative interactional cycle. This is so common following a breach of trust. As we have looked at earlier in this book, being aware of your emotional reactivity and being able to make sense of your inner world is vital when navigating tough relational moments. I want to help you to practice the skill of ordering your emotional experience to prepare you for being able to attend to your partner's pain as they vulnerably share the impact of this injury with you. In EFT, we call this "emotion assembly,"[3] which is an important method for observing and finding the order in your inner world.

To practice the skill of "assembling" your emotion, I suggest firstly noticing the physical sensations that arise as you picture your partner sharing their hurt with you. Imagine that they are now able to share in vulnerable, soft ways, rather than reactive, blaming, or shaming ways. Their pain will be a trigger for alarm in your nervous system – it is likely to throw you off-balance. Notice how you feel in your body when there is a reminder of this event or when you see your partner's pain, when you see evidence of the hurt you have had a hand in. Is there a sensation that arrives in your belly, head, hands, chest, or elsewhere? Do you notice heat, coldness, tightness, heaviness, fluttery sensations, nausea, pain, tension, stillness, or movement? If so, where do you feel it? Is it changing or static? Moving or still? Heavy or light? I am inviting you to bring mindful awareness to your inner experience and to engage your curiosity as you explore it without judgement. Breathe slowly and steadily as you pay attention to the sensations of your feelings and consciously allow them to be there. Feel yourself soften around them – making room for them. Now, notice your thoughts. What do you tell yourself about this event? About yourself, your partner, your relationship, the future, the past? As you ponder these thoughts, what happens to the physical sensations that show up for you? Do they stay the same or do they alter? Observing them from a working distance; what changes do you notice in them? And finally, what do you normally do to cope when these feelings or thoughts are present for you? How do you manage the painful aspects of this experience? Notice the connection between feelings, thoughts, and behaviours. Does this way of coping or protecting help, or does it come with challenges? Figure 8.2 will guide you to ponder these questions. Notice how you feel after curiously observing your inner responses to reminders of this attachment injury and your partner's pain.

As I said to the hurt partner in the previous chapter, I hope that you can meet your pain with care and kindness. You deserve this. We all have the capacity to hurt the ones we love, and we still deserve kindness and

Emotion Assembly

Tuning into your emotional world

This sheet will help you to reflect on the elements of your emotional experience & to find the order & wisdom embedded within. Using the attachment injury as the "relational trigger" what happens inside for you?

Noticing how you FEEL - physical sensations

What sensations show up when you think about this attachment injury? What happens in your body?

- Where do you feel it?
- What do you feel?
- Is it changing or static?
- Heavy or light?
- Moving or still?
- Make room for it
- Observe without judgement

Noticing your THOUGHTS - meaning-making

What do you tell yourself about this attachment injury, about your partner, yourself, your relationship, the future, the past?

Look out for **Model of Other** themes

Look out for **Model of Self** themes

Noticing what you DO - coping strategies

What do you DO when these painful reminders & emotions show up? How do you try to manage the painful aspects of this experience?

Does this help or does it come with challenges?

Clare Rosoman 2024

Figure 8.2 Emotion assembly.

understanding. Your willingness to enter into a repair process such as this speaks volumes about who you are and what this relationship means to you. I hope that you can allow your understandable human reactions to exist without judgement and can bring curious and kind awareness to them. As you do this, they will become more familiar and easier to be with. Emotion assembly will be invaluable in preparing you to hold space for your partner as they risk opening their heart to you. *Remember that your key goal in this part of the Attachment Injury Resolution Model is to be there for your partner.* If you make it "about you" your partner will feel dropped, right when they need to feel safely caught! Try to hold that in mind as you attune to their experience. Take note of your own reactions *and* keep your focus on your role – to witness and hold the other's pain.

Taking in the other's pain non-defensively

By this stage in your reading, you are fully aware that your response is critical in determining whether your hurt partner is left feeling held or dropped. Your role in the resolution of this attachment injury is pivotal – your response, or lack of response, establishes whether you and your partner have a moment of repair or another painful moment of disconnection. After an attachment injury, there are often so many moments of disconnection that the bond can become terribly frayed and unable to withstand many more. The stakes are so high. For most people in this situation, their natural urge is to move away from the other's pain by deflecting or rationalising or minimising or using any method to cope known to them. This is logical and all about coping in the moment – trying to gain emotional balance in the best way you know how. When something hurts, we protect ourselves. We turn away from the pain and instead turn inwards. We attempt to recapture our balance by managing the source of the pain. In this case, source of the pain is your partner. I want to help you to notice this urge and to consciously turn towards your partner's pain.

I am hoping that by this point in the attachment injury resolution process, your partner is not going to be firing reactive emotion towards you. If that is happening, then you are both not ready for this part of the process and need to go back to Chapter 4 to do some more work on stabilisation. Assuming that your partner is doing a great job of reaching to you vulnerably with their pain in their outstretched hand,[4] it will be easier to stay present and to lower your defences. However, witnessing their raw, real, pain can bring the urge to hide, or to defend, or to turn away to the fore. Let's look at noticing your defences, because they are probably the biggest threat to repair in this part of the process.

Your partner's message may be very difficult to hear, their disappointment in you and their hurt agonising to withstand. Of course, you will want to move away from their heat, but this will only make things worse.

You need a new way of managing the pain and that involves leaning *into* it, rather than turning away. When we are in self-protection mode, it goes against all our instincts to lean towards something painful and threatening. It is really challenging to attend to the other – especially when they are angry with you or disillusioned in you. However, this is what I am asking you to reconcile – that you must move *towards* the pain to resolve it. You must go against your instincts, your habitual ways of coping with emotional pain.

Callum and Casey, whom we met in Chapters 3 and 6, had an open relationship and their bond was shattered by a broken agreement around other partners. Casey kept a relationship with another partner secret and had unprotected sex with that person, violating the agreed boundaries of her relationship with Callum. Callum was deeply hurt by Casey's actions and was scared about potentially being exposed to a sexually transmitted disease. He worked hard on managing his reactivity and, as they moved more deeply into the repair process, he was able to vulnerably share his pain and fear with Casey. It was so hard for her to witness his tender emotions without cascading into her own shame and marshalling her self-protective urge to defend herself. Casey learned to notice the sensation of her shame and to make space for it without it taking over. She focused on listening to Callum and attuning to the pain in his eyes so that she could hear and understand his message. She wanted him to feel met by her. Her presence in this way soothed the protest in Callum – he felt understood – he knew that she was there with him and not hurrying to a solution or defending herself. He could see that she cared about his pain, and this reassured him that he mattered to her.

How do you imagine protecting yourself or managing intense emotion as you witness your partner's pain? How will you monitor your own emotions and the urge to defend? How do you think your partner will interpret any attempts on your part to turn away, to minimise, or to rationalise? How might this impact your partner when they are so vulnerable? What do you think they need from you in that moment? These questions hone your attention to your "job" in this part of the Attachment Injury Resolution Model. When your partner takes the risk to show you their heart, your principal role is to meet them where they are and to let them feel your presence. They will not be able to feel your love and care if you move into a protective space, that is, if you defend yourself, rationalise, explain, shutdown, turn away etc.

Being present to your partner's pain involves lowering your protective shield and unwaveringly witnessing their pain. It means staying with it, taking it in, and letting it *move* you. Let yourself be impacted by your partner. When you can allow your partner's experience to touch your heart, it will register in your body, and it will show on your face and in your eyes. I realise that this is not for the faint of heart! Fully feeling another's pain without turning away is incredibly difficult. But this emotional labour is imperative to your partner feeling met in their pain and trusting that their experience matters to you. It is the most direct way to reassure them that you feel it along with them. Look at your partner as they share, look into their eyes, notice their body posture, the little gestures of distress that you can see such as tension, redness in the face, tightness in their voice, the jiggle of a foot. Notice the ways they attempt to seek comfort like rubbing their arms, squeezing their fingers, wringing a tissue. Listen to their tone of voice thickening with supressed tears or becoming small and quiet. Notice how exposed they are when they risk showing you the most vulnerable parts of their inner world. Tune into their emotions more than their words. Really allow yourself to confront the pain that you had a hand in. Let yourself be moved by your partner's pain and let that show on your face, and in your words, and your gestures. Your partner *needs* to see their pain reflected on your face and in your eyes before they can trust that you fully understand the impact of this attachment injury for them. *They will not be able to move forward and to let go without this recognition.*

In order to deepen your contact with your partner's emotional experience, I invite you to ask yourself some key questions. Figure 8.3 will guide you through this process. What hurts most about this attachment injury for your partner? What have you learned about their experience that you didn't know before? What parts of their experience are the most difficult for you to hear? Can you let their pain impact you? How do you feel inside as you witness their pain? What is most painful for you to stay with?

Sharing your response to the other's pain

Witnessing in this way is likely to bring up the most painful, rarely visited, vulnerable places within you. Most of us have parts of our emotional worlds where pain and shame live, that we avoid going near and try to hide from. This might be seen in someone overachieving to compensate for feelings of inadequacy, or, someone avoiding connection with others to guard against a fear of rejection. These tender spots where we doubt our self-worth and our "goodness" often have their origins in painful messages we receive in relationships with those who we trust. When we've hurt someone that we love and are held accountable for our actions, it can bring to life the most frightening messages from the past. It can make the fear of being rejected and abandoned seem very real. Fear of the outcome can paralyse a person and block them from attuning to the other, swamping them in the worst-case scenario, and hijacking their ability to connect. Fear can tell you that your partner will never forget this, that they will hold it against you forever, that they will never trust you, and they'll always view

Accessing Vulnerability - Hurtful Partner

Witnessing pain & holding space

This sheet will help you to witness & hold your partner's pain as they vulnerably share the impact of the attachment injury with you. This work will prepare you to repair with your partner & strengthen your bond.

Can you let your partner's pain touch you?

What is like to hear about their hurt, to see it on your partner's face & to let it touch you?

Do you notice the urge to protect yourself from your partner's pain? Can you lean in?

What have you learned about your partner's experience?

What have you learned about their experience that you didn't know before?

How does your partner's pain impact you emotionally?

Can you connect with your vulnerable feelings?

As you witness their pain & understand their experience more, what does it bring up for you? How can you manage your own emotions, so that you can continue to be there for your partner?

Clare Rosoman 2024

Figure 8.3 Accessing vulnerability in the witnessing partner.

you with those disappointed eyes. Fear can warn you that if your partner sees your flaws, they won't want you, especially now that you have caused them so much pain.

It is understandable that these fears will lurk there for most people when they have contributed to broken trust in a relationship. However, if those fears block you from being present to your partner in the repair process, they can become self-fulfilling prophecies. They can completely sabotage the healing process. Likewise, shame about your sense of "okay-ness" can create a barrier to repair because it makes a person want to hide away – to slink off on their own. When we feel that we have been exposed as bad, as flawed, or as broken, it can compound a crawling sense of unworthiness that can make you want to hide yourself away to prevent the inevitable rejection that you know is coming. However tempting this is, your partner needs you right now. They are still engaged in the process of repair – they haven't given up on you or your relationship. They need you to hold firm and not to allow fear or shame to derail you. They need to feel your heart in this moment – to feel that you are there and that you care about their pain. When you can show up for them, even though it is very hard, then your partner can begin to trust that you will not hurt them again. They can trust your investment in them and the relationship when they see you commit to the process. Instead of allowing your fear and shame to take you out of reach, you can use it to let your partner know how much this relationship means. When your partner hears how scared you are of losing them, how mad you are at yourself for causing pain, it actually reassures them that you are taking this seriously and that you are holding yourself accountable. It gives them confidence that you are going to learn from this and that their heart is safe with you moving forwards.

This is supported by the research into forgiveness which shows that hurt partners need to see their pain register on the face of the hurtful partner in order to let go. They need to know that they have been felt by the other and that their pain matters to them. They need to see that you deeply regret causing pain.[5] It has also been shown that expressions of shame promote forgiveness. In an interesting study looking at couples who had suffered an attachment injury, hurt partners were more likely to accept a repair attempt if hurtful partners showed that they took accountability for the hurtful act in a non-defensive manner and displayed evidence of this injury having disturbed them deeply, causing them to reflect on themselves. The researchers concluded that the hurt partner softened their protective stance after witnessing the hurtful partner grappling with their shame over causing pain. This level of emotional labour seemed to reassure hurt partners that the injury was being given weight, and that considerable effort had gone into resolving the causes for it and the consequences of it.[6]

I need to acknowledge that it is so brave and so courageous to engage with your partner and your own tender emotions in this way. Resolution requires to you share in the pain together, rather than apart. It is far more difficult to witness pain and to attend to it with presence and care than it is to stay behind your protective wall or to leave the relationship. It says so much about who you are, what your partner means to you, and how important this relationship is, that you are willing to take this brave step. Not only is attending to your partner's pain in this way effective in repairing ruptured attachment bonds,[7] sharing your inner turmoil with your partner can provide a powerful remedy to fear and shame. The fear of being rejected and the shame of not being enough begin to melt away and to transform when you are an active part of the healing process. Just as your partner is boldly sharing with you, when you share your fears and doubts you are allowing the two of you to grow stronger, together.

Having witnessed your partner's pain and confronted the most tender and difficult to touch depths within you, what is it that you want your partner to know? What does your heart want their heart to know? How has their pain impacted you? Do you feel empathy for their experience? Remorse for impacting them so profoundly? Sorrow for being hurtful? Clearly signalling to your partner that you are moved by their pain – "it hurts me to know that I hurt you" – is a crucial ingredient to repair. It says to the hurt partner that their pain matters to you, that they matter to you, and that you can prioritise attending to their suffering over and above your own comfort.

Can you take responsibility for causing them pain, even if it is not entirely simple and clear-cut? Is there some part of the shared experience that you can be accountable for? Can you own your role in the breach of trust and the impact it had on your partner and on your bond? Can you let them know about your feelings of remorse and shame? Can you offer an apology?

As you consider sharing these important reflections, here are some tips to keep you on-track as you respond to your partner's vulnerability and, where appropriate, offer an apology.

Tips for responding to the other's pain

1 *Breathe and stay grounded.* Stay in touch with and aware of your body sensations, the feelings that show up, the thoughts that are running through your mind, and how you are coping in the moment. Treat yourself with kindness and remember the reasons you are hanging in there to witness your partner's pain. Your relationship matters too much not to. Your self-growth matters too much not to. How you respond to your

partner's pain will impact whether they feel met by you or abandoned by you in this time of need.

2 *Stay focused.* Remain connected to the essence of the message that your partner is sending, listen for their attachment protest, their longing, their pain. Tune into the attachment impact that this injury has had on *them* and try to avoid being distracted by the impact it had on you. Resist the urge to explain, to provide context, to defend, deflect, or to minimise. These attempts to save-face will only prove to your partner that defending yourself is more important to you than attending to their pain.

3 *Stay vulnerable.* Your partner is taking a huge risk with you. Stay connected to your role as the holder of their experience. This is a huge responsibility and how you rise to the challenge will determine whether you connect or disconnect – rupture or repair. Notice the temptation to put your protective shield up or to move away from their pain. When your partner reaches to you vulnerably, with their pain in their outstretched hand, you need to meet them there with your own vulnerability. Let their pain move you. Notice how you respond to their pain, let them see it on your face and in your eyes. Know that when you do this, you are giving your relationship the best chance of repair.

Figure 8.4 will guide you with tips for how to attend to and respond to your partner's pain as they risk sharing it with you.

Tips for an effective apology

If it feels important for you to acknowledge, to take responsibility for, and to apologise for hurt that you have caused your partner, here are some tips for an effective restorative reach.

1 *Put your partner first.* The most effective way to repair a relationship after a rupture is to let the other know that you care more about attending to their pain than about defending yourself. Now is not the time to defend yourself. Separate your intent from your impact. You might not have intended to cause pain or harm, but the impact on your partner was painful and harmful to them and to your bond. The impact on your partner needs attending to as a matter of priority. You will have time later to provide contextual information.

2 *Speak from the heart.* Let your partner know how you feel, knowing that you caused them hurt. Show them that you are impacted by their suffering and that it hurts you to witness their pain. Compared to the time surrounding the injury, your apology needs to be as loud as your silence was, as present as your absence was, and as emotionally engaged as your distance was. Even the best words have no meaning if they

Hurtful/witnessing partner responds with care

This sheet will help the hurtful/witnessing partner to respond to their partner's pain in ways that honour the connection & rebuild the bond in the attachment injury resolution model.

Tips for the witnessing partner

Stay grounded	Stay focused	Stay vulnerable
Breathe...Stay in touch with & aware of your body sensations, the feelings that show up, the thoughts that are running through your mind & how you are coping in the moment. Remember, how you respond to your partner's pain will impact whether they feel met by you or abandoned by you. Be there for them.	Remain connected to the message that your partner is sending, listen for their attachment protest, their longing, their pain. Tune into the impact of this injury & try to avoid being distracted by the impact it had on you. Resist the urge to explain, to provide context, to defend, deflect, or to minimise.	Stay connected to your role as the holder of your partner's experience. Notice the temptation to put your protective shield up or to move away from their pain. Meet them in their vulnerability with your own. Notice how you respond to their pain, let them see it register on your face & in your eyes.

What do you want your partner to know?

Using your discoveries from previous exercises, can you let your partner know that their pain matters to you? How it feels for you to witness their hurt? Can you let them know that you hear, that you understand & that you care? Can you offer repair through acknowledgement &/or apology?

Clare Rosoman 2024

Figure 8.4 Witnessing/hurtful partner responds with care.

not are accompanied by alive, present, vulnerable emotion. Let yours show and your words will have more healing power.

3 *Take responsibility.* Own your role in those hurtful acts and the resultant damage to the attachment bond. Acknowledging the specific details provides evidence that you have heard and understood the impact of this attachment injury on your partner and on the bond between you. Reassure them that you can see how you came to be hurtful and that you will work on not repeating that behaviour or creating those circumstances again.

4 *Learn from it.* Show your partner that you are putting in the emotional labour to understand how you came to be hurtful and to learn from this event so that it is never repeated and so that you can create change and growth in your relationship moving forward. This will give your partner confidence that you take this extremely seriously and that you will not only make amends, but you will also make changes moving forward. Hurt people need reassurance that they won't be hurt in the same way repeatedly. Only then can their trust regrow. We will do more of this work in the next chapter.

Figure 8.5 lists these tips in case you need to refer to it.

By now you have practiced observing and assembling your own emotional reactions that are flared when witnessing your partner's pain, you

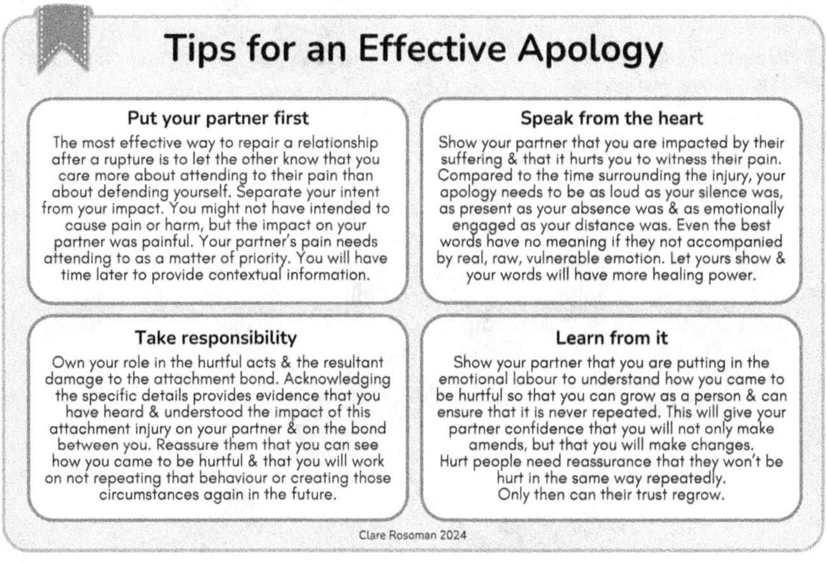

Tips for an Effective Apology

Put your partner first
The most effective way to repair a relationship after a rupture is to let the other know that you care more about attending to their pain than about defending yourself. Separate your intent from your impact. You might not have intended to cause pain or harm, but the impact on your partner was painful. Your partner's pain needs attending to as a matter of priority. You will have time later to provide contextual information.

Speak from the heart
Show your partner that you are impacted by their suffering & that it hurts you to witness their pain. Compared to the time surrounding the injury, your apology needs to be as loud as your silence was, as present as your absence was & as emotionally engaged as your distance was. Even the best words have no meaning if they not accompanied by real, raw, vulnerable emotion. Let yours show & your words will have more healing power.

Take responsibility
Own your role in the hurtful acts & the resultant damage to the attachment bond. Acknowledging the specific details provides evidence that you have heard & understood the impact of this attachment injury on your partner & on the bond between you. Reassure them that you can see how you came to be hurtful & that you will work on not repeating that behaviour or creating those circumstances again in the future.

Learn from it
Show your partner that you are putting in the emotional labour to understand how you came to be hurtful so that you can grow as a person & can ensure that it is never repeated. This will give your partner confidence that you will not only make amends, but that you will make changes. Hurt people need reassurance that they won't be hurt in the same way repeatedly. Only then can their trust regrow.

Clare Rosoman 2024

Figure 8.5 Tips for an effective apology.

have become aware of your protective, coping strategies that take you out of connection, and you have committed to attending to your partner's pain – even if it is so very difficult to do. That is how important this relationship is to you. You have reached out to your partner and responded to their pain from an engaged and responsive position. You have vulnerably let them see that their pain moves you, and that you feel it too, knowing you have caused pain to someone so precious. You may have even made some active reparative steps through expressing remorse or offering an apology, where appropriate. This is amazing work! Through this process, I imagine that you have learned a lot about yourself and how you came to be hurtful. Next chapter, you will have a chance to share this with your partner as you complete the final part of the attachment injury resolution process.

Endnotes

1 Zuccarini, D., Johnson, S.M., Dalgleish, T.L., & Makinen, J.A. (2013). Forgiveness and reconciliation in emotionally focused therapy for couples: The client change process and therapist interventions. *Journal of Marital and Family Therapy*, 39(2), 148–162.
2 Johnson, S.M., & Campbell, T.L. (2022). *A primer on emotionally focused individual therapy: Cultivating fitness and growth in every client.* London: Routledge.
3 Johnson, S.M. (2019). *Attachment theory in practice: Emotionally focused therapy (EFT) with individuals, couples and families.* New York: The Guilford Press.
4 Rheem, K., & Olden, J. (2021). The EFT Cafe. *Stage Two Attachment Injury Repair.* www.theeftcafe.com.
5 Zuccarini, D., Johnson, S.M., Dalgleish, T.L., & Makinen, J.A. (2013). Forgiveness and reconciliation in emotionally focused therapy for couples: The client change process and therapist interventions. *Journal of Marital and Family Therapy*, 39(2), 148–162.
6 Woldarsky Meneses, C., & Greenberg, L.S. (2014). Interpersonal forgiveness in emotion-focused couples' therapy: Relating process to outcome. *Journal of Marital and Family Therapy*, 40(1), 49–67.
7 Makinen, J.A., & Johnson, S. (2006). Resolving attachment injuries in couples using emotionally focused therapy: Steps toward forgiveness and reconciliation. *Journal of Consulting and Clinical Psychology*, 74, 1055–1064.

Chapter 9

Antidote bonding for both partners

When the partner who caused hurt can keep their balance in the face of their own emotions and attend to the other's raw vulnerability, this represents an enormous shift in the relational pattern. It opens the door to healing and draws upon your inner resources as individuals, and your attachment resources as a team, to repair this fracture in trust. You should both be congratulated on your hard work in Chapters 7 and 8. It is a testament to your strength and courage that you have arrived in this place. While Chapter 7 focused on the hurt partner and Chapter 8 focused on the hurtful partner, this chapter focuses on you *both* as it guides you through the final tasks of the Attachment Injury Resolution Model to achieve "antidote bonding." Phase 3 of the Attachment Injury Resolution Model powerfully restructures the attachment bond as secure and represents the fractured "bone" of the bond being healed – consequently becoming stronger in the broken place.

For this crucial part of the process, partners take the risk of identifying and asking the other for what they need to heal. This is no small undertaking, and it epitomises the shift from individual, self-protective coping, to relational coping. This means turning to the other for reassurance and support, rather than coping alone. When a person vulnerably asks another for what they need, they are risking enormously. This reach is a leap of faith, and when safely caught by the other, it restores the security of the loving bond. This accomplishment provides evidence of the other's accessibility, responsiveness, and engagement, which are, as we have said, the building blocks to secure attachment. After a breach of trust, partners usually avoid relying on the other for fear of further hurt or disappointment. When hurt partners can ask for reassurance and hurtful partners can ask for understanding and forgiveness, and they are received supportively, the bond is restructured. When needs are met with acceptance, it not only restores the attachment security in the relationship, it also provides an "antidote" against future damage.

As you can see in Figure 9.1, to do this important work, the hurt partner will be empowered to take in the other's reparative signals, to identify what

DOI: 10.4324/9781003466499-13

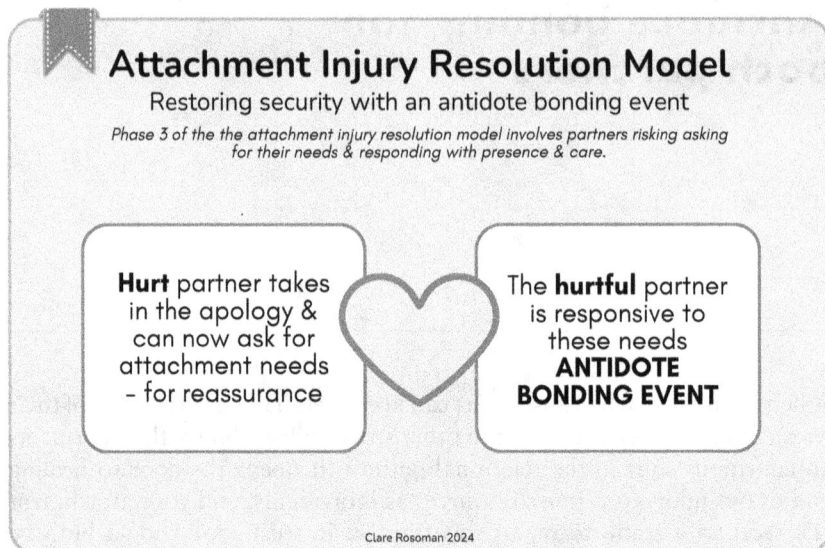

Attachment Injury Resolution Model
Restoring security with an antidote bonding event
Phase 3 of the the attachment injury resolution model involves partners risking asking for their needs & responding with presence & care.

Hurt partner takes in the apology & can now ask for attachment needs – for reassurance

The **hurtful** partner is responsive to these needs **ANTIDOTE BONDING EVENT**

Clare Rosoman 2024

Figure 9.1 **Phase 3** of the attachment injury resolution model.

it is that they need from their partner to feel safe again, and to share these needs. When they share softly and vulnerably, this pulls for the partner to respond in new and reassuring ways.[1] The hurtful partner will be encouraged to hear and meet these needs, and to experience the sense of agency that comes with being an active participant in the repair process. In addition to this work, the hurtful partner will be supported in making sense of how they came to be hurtful, to reflect on what they have learned about themselves from this attachment injury, and to share this with the other. Providing context and showing evidence of learning and growth from this unfortunate event are important ways that trust can regrow in this relationship.

The tasks in this chapter involve emotional labour from you both but will allow you to heal together. Opening your hearts to each other and turning to each other for help is the antidote to the pain of betrayal for the hurt partner and to the helplessness in the hurtful partner. When pain can be healed in-relationship, it restores trust for the hurt partner and ameliorates the shame for the hurtful partner.

Task 1 for the hurt partner: taking in the hurtful partner's response

Dear hurt partner, you have bravely shared the depths of your pain in the service of repair. It is my sincere hope that you have been met by your partner with compassion and understanding. Now, there are two more important tasks for you to complete to fully repair your precious attachment bond. The first is to let your partner's response impact you and the second is to ask for your needs. We will look at them separately, starting with taking in your partner's response to your pain. In Chapter 8, your partner worked hard to prepare themselves to attend to the pain they know they caused you. I hope that your vulnerable sharing of the impact of the attachment injury was attended to by your partner with openness and non-defensiveness. I hope that they were moved by your pain and able to stay present, engaged, and responsive to you. Goodness, you need to be met in this place and not dropped again. I sincerely hope you felt that. I hope that you feel less alone in your pain and that you felt your partner's nurturance. If you did, I ask you for a moment to reflect on how you knew that your partner felt you, that they were with you, and that they were moved by your emotion. Did you see it in their eyes, in their gestures, could you hear it in their voice or in their words? If you did, the crucial question I have for you is: were you able to take it in? If they offered an apology or expressed heartfelt remorse at causing you anguish, I hope that you were able to open your heart to that and to let it take hold. I hope that a small part of you can accept their reach and soften towards it, even though there might be a very wary part residing there still. Your task, hurt partner, is to let your partner's compassion and care wash over you, to take it in, and to receive it.

Many people who have been hurt struggle with receiving care and empathy from the one who hurt them. The protective part of them warns them against trusting it and cautions them to stay guarded. This is totally understandable. However, I hope that in time and with some repetition, you can begin to trust in the veracity of your partner's support. You might need to have several instances of taking your pain to your partner and being received with care before you can trust in the legitimacy of this new way of interacting together. Of course you do. Each time you can connect over this attachment injury in new, vulnerable ways, you are cementing in a new pattern, a new cycle. It takes time to trust a new pattern – anything new feels scary and untrustworthy until it becomes familiar, predictable, and reliable.

Usually, these moments of being met in your pain are not enough in isolation to repair a ruptured bond. You will need many of these moments, and that is totally okay. Engaged conversations like these build on each other as more threads are woven back into your connection. As Shirley Glass says, when trust has been broken, it cannot simply turn back on like flicking a switch, but rather it goes from dark to light, like gradually turning on a dimmer switch.[2] I urge hurtful/witnessing partners to hear this and to rest assured, that each time they witness their partner's pain with compassion, they are providing more evidence of this new pattern for the other to trust in. You are helping to turn that dimmer switch. However, it will most likely need revisiting many times. Each time there is a new trigger, each time there is a reminder like a meaningful date or significant event that brings with it reminders of the dark time in your relationship. The more the hurtful partner can be patient and remain accessible and responsive and the hurt partner can remain open to sharing and open to receiving comfort, the more your trust will regrow, and your new pattern will become bankable.

Figure 9.2 will help you to explore and articulate what it is like for you to accept care from your partner. This will prepare you for what comes next, asking for your partner's help in meeting your needs.

Task 2 for the hurt partner: asking for what you need

And now, hurt partner, your final task involves courageously turning to your partner and asking for your needs to be met. I know that this is asking an enormous amount when you have been so hurt and let down, but risking in this way creates a powerful context for healing. When you open your heart to the other and vulnerably ask them to help you, when you ask for what you need from them to move forwards with a little less pain, you are giving them the opportunity to join you. You create an opening for them to step forward into the relationship space and to actively take part in healing the broken trust. You provide them with the formula for healing your heart.

To help you with this process, here are some things to think about and Figure 9.3 will guide you to share your needs with your partner.

1 *Speak from the heart.* What is it that your, poor bruised heart needs to heal? What does the smallest, most vulnerable part of you need from your partner? What are you crying out for? What do you need to hear or to see that would soothe the hurting places within you? Take a moment to focus on your pain and to consider allowing your partner to apply some healing balm, right on the sore spots. Remember to stay in touch with your most vulnerable feelings, knowing that they contain the wisdom that informs you about your deepest needs. Notice and set aside the temptation to put your battle-gear on, instead staying focused on what you need, deep down, and sharing this vulnerably. This may be recognition of your pain, acknowledgement of all you have been through, an understanding of your partner's suffering to break your isolation, or something else. What you need is individual to you and is important in this process.

2 *Keep it achievable.* Concentrate on asking for things that your partner can actually give you. They cannot turn back time and undo this hurtful

Hurt Partner Takes in Care

Hurt or sharing partner risks opening their heart to accept the other's care & remorse

In the early part of Phase 3 of the Attachment Injury Resolution Model, the hurt partner risks accepting the others' care & support. This sheet will help you to explore what this is like for you.

What was it like to share your pain with the other?

How was it for you to share your pain with your partner? How did you feel inside?

How did your partner respond to your vulnerability?

Did you feel that your partner heard & understood? Did you feel that they were moved by your pain? How did they show this?	How did your partner's care, support, remorse & apology (if needed) impact you emotionally? Was it heartfelt?

Can you accept your partner's support or their apology?

Could you take in your partner's offering of care? If so, why? If not, what was missing?	What was the most helpful or healing thing your partner did? What do you need more of?

Clare Rosoman 2024

Figure 9.2 Hurt partner takes in care.

Hurt/sharing partner asks for their needs

This sheet will help the hurt/sharing partner to ask for what they need from the other to help them to heal & to rebuild security in the bond as the final part of the Attachment Injury Resolution Model.

Tips for the sharing partner

Speak from the heart	Keep it achievable	Focus on attachment
Take a moment to focus on your pain & to consider allowing your partner to apply some healing balm, right on the sore spots. Remember to stay in touch with your most vulnerable feelings, knowing that they contain the wisdom that informs you about your deepest needs.	Concentrate on asking for things that your partner can actually give you. Think about what you need from them that would offer you some healing. Our aim is to help you identify what you need from your partner that would allow you to move forward with a little less fear.	Think about your bond with your partner & what you need from them to confirm that you are a team again & that you can depend on your partner once more. These factors relate to a feeling of attachment security & that is what we want to restore following this injury.

What do you need from your partner?

What do you need to hear or to see that would soothe the hurt places within you? What do you need from your partner to move forward with less pain & fear? What would restore your faith in the relationship & in your partner?

Clare Rosoman 2024

Figure 9.3 Sharing/hurt partner asks for their needs.

event, nor can they always provide a satisfactory explanation for their actions. Instead, think about what you need to understand about their experience or what was happening for them at the time and their motivations (they will be reflecting on this later in this chapter). Think about what you need from them that would offer you some healing. Our aim is to help you identify what you need from your partner that would allow you to move forward with a little less fear. Some fear is inevitable following an attachment injury, after all, you have experienced the loss of the innocence of this relationship. Take a moment to consider how your partner can help you with your fear – how they could help your trust to regrow. Understandably, most hurt people need some assurance that they will not be hurt in the same way in the future. Depending on the nature of the attachment injury, your partner may or may not be able to offer this much-needed assurance. Think about what you need that would help you to hold your fear a little more lightly – how could they help you with that?

3 *Focus on attachment*. Think about your bond with your partner and what you need from the other to confirm that it is mutually important and protected, that you are a team again, and that you can depend on your partner once more. These factors relate to a feeling of attachment security and that is what we want to restore following this injury. In a secure relationship, you know that your partner cherishes you, they are there when you need them, and they will support and encourage you. Security gives you confidence that you will both hold the other's heart gently and that you will protect the specialness of this attachment bond. When you reflect on these features of security, what do you need more of from your partner? What are you crying out for on an attachment level? What do you need to hear that would restore your faith in the relationship, in your partner's reliability as an attachment figure, and in your confidence that you matter to them?

Antidote bonding event

As you know, how the hurt partner's needs are responded to determines whether this is a restorative, bonding event, or another in a long line of misses. The onus is on the hurt partner to share vulnerably, in non-blaming ways, and on the hurtful partner to respond to those needs with accessibility, responsiveness, and engagement. This is the "ARE" of secure attachment[3] and it sends a powerful attachment message right to the hurt partner's heart that says, "You can turn to me, I will meet you in your pain, your needs matter, soothing you is more important than my own comfort." This is extremely potent in re-establishing trust. Your presence and care repair the damage done by your absence, your dismissal, your carelessness, or your hurt. I cannot state this strongly enough. I have seen the power of this moment over and over again with the beautiful, heroic people I have worked with as they restore the security in their attachment bonds. When the hurt partner reaches and risks asking for their needs, and the hurtful partner unwaveringly attends to them, amazing things happen. The willingness of the witnessing partner to withstand their own discomfort for the sake of assisting their partner provides potent evidence of their care, and of their ability to put the partner's needs first. The sacrifice of their own comfort in this moment proves to the hurt partner that they are trustworthy and value the other more than meeting their own needs.

This seems to be the case even when the hurt partner's needs can only partially be met. Being heard and acknowledged is soothing as a function of the connection, even if it is not possible to offer a tidy solution to all the things they are crying out for. Even if there are still messy factors relating to this injury. As we have explored in earlier sections of this book, often the attachment injury involved the hurtful partner disregarding the needs of the other. I think that this is why this moment in the repair process is so profound – it unwinds the impact of the injury, even if we can't unwind time and erase the event itself. It provides proof that the partner who caused pain is attentive and persistent in providing repair. That they will put their partner's needs for care and support first.

Sonia and Emma, a lesbian, monogamous couple we met in Chapters 3, 6, and 7 had dual injuries. Emma was hurt by Sonia's hidden prescription medication dependence and Sonia was hurt by Emma's emotional connection with a co-worker. They took turns in the role of sharing and witnessing partner as each had the opportunity to express the impact of the other's betrayal while being heard and cared for by the other. When they addressed Sonia's hurt over Emma's emotional attachment to her co-worker, it was powerful for Emma to hear about her pain and her fear of losing their relationship. Emma had truly felt that Sonia didn't value or need their emotional connection, and she was rocked to hear of Sonia's heartrending pain because of Emma's duplicity. When Sonia vulnerably shared her agony at reading the emails between Emma and her co-worker, and hearing Emma profess love for the other person, Emma had to work hard to stay present to her pain. How she wanted to defend herself and to explain! She knew that if she did that, Sonia would feel dismissed and their cycle would recur, only creating more distance between them. Instead of defending, Emma was able to lean into Sonia's pain, to see the heartbreak in her eyes, and to let it impact her. Only when she could let Sonia see her torment at knowing that she broke Sonia's trust in such a profound way, did Sonia feel soothed. Seeing her pain reflected back in Emma's eyes offered her some assurance that Emma truly understood, that she mattered to her, and that she would not hurt her like that again. When Emma backed this up with a heartfelt apology, Sonia could feel its authenticity – she could begin to open her heart and to trust it. This powerful exchange empowered Sonia to bravely ask for what she needed – to know that Emma's relationship with her co-worker had ceased and to understand her reasons for breaking Sonia's trust. This reach from Sonia was palpably vulnerable and alive with possibility for reassurance rather than recrimination. Emma rose to the challenge by non-defensively offering confirmation that the relationship was over and by explaining her motivations and what she had come to learn from this mistake. Emma's openness and responsiveness to Sonia's pain and her needs provided evidence of her commitment to the relationship and went a long way to restoring Sonia's trust in her.

In Figure 9.4, the partner who caused hurt can organise their thoughts and feelings to ready themselves to respond to their partner's needs in ways that provide a container for their experience and can begin to restore their faith in the connection.

Task 1 for the hurtful partner: learning from this event

For partners who have caused pain or broken trust, there is an opportunity in this wretched situation, to grow and expand personally. In Chapter 2, we looked at some of the reasons why good people can become hurtful to those they love, and in Chapter 5, we looked at the role of past trauma in contributing to hurtful actions and to the processing of an attachment injury. In Chapter 8, you attended to your partner's pain and reflected on your role in this rupture in your relationship. My hope is that, by working through this book and honestly reflecting on your actions and your possible motivations, you are becoming clearer about the contextual factors that led to this breach of trust and what this means for the future. I hope that you are clearer about what caused you to step away from your values or to violate a promise – whether it came from impulsivity and thoughtlessness, a denial of the significance of your actions, a need to hide part of yourself, a desire to meet your needs in covert ways, a form of lashing out, unhelpful emotion-regulation strategies, or an unacknowledged destructive impulse (to name just a few).

I hope that, while holding your humanity gently and remembering that we all make mistakes, you can take a candid look at your actions and learn from them. This is how we grow. If you don't learn, you don't change. When something upends your world and threatens all you know, then it has the capacity to teach you the most important and valuable lessons in life. Humans facing difficult situations are capable of positive change, of not just surviving a difficult experience and returning to normal functioning, but of growing *beyond* their normal functioning. This is the concept

Hurtful/witnessing partner responds to the other's needs

This sheet will help the hurtful/witnessing partner to respond to the other's needs in an accessible, responsive & engaged way. Their presence & care is crucial in repairing the attachment injury.

Creating an antidote bonding event

When someone who has been hurt, vulnerably asks the other for what they need in order to heal, they are asking enormously. This reach is a leap of faith. When safely caught by the other, it restores the security of the loving bond. This is extremely potent in re-establishing trust. When hurt partners can ask for reassurance & they are received supportively, the bond is restructured.

The hurtful or witnessing partner's presence & care can repair some of the damage done by the attachment injury. This accomplishment provides evidence of the other's accessibility, responsiveness & engagement, which are the building blocks to secure attachment.

When needs are met with acceptance, it not only restores the attachment security in the relationship, it provides an "antidote" against future damage.

Responding to your partner's needs

How do you feel as you hear your partner share their needs with you? How can you make sure that they feel heard, cared for & understood? Write your ideas here:

Actively addressing your partner's needs

Can you take steps to address your partner's needs? For instance, by answering their questions honestly, attending to future planning, providing information openly, letting them know they matter, taking practical action. List what you can do to address their needs here:

Clare Rosoman 2024

Figure 9.4 Hurtful/witnessing partner responds to the other's needs.

of post-traumatic growth.[4] While you might not necessarily have faced a life-threatening trauma, the threat of the loss of an important relationship is a form of relational trauma that brings into question everything you thought you knew. It shakes your world. Awful, yes, but also full of rich learning opportunities if you let it.

The work of self-reflection and learning will certainly benefit you as a human. However, it is also extremely powerful for repairing attachment bonds. Your partner has been hurt by you, this injury has blown your secure connection apart, but your partner is looking for ways to repair. If they are still engaged in this process, you can help them by sharing what you have discovered about yourself on account of this attachment injury. Seeing that you have struggled to make sense of how you came to be hurtful will offer them reassurance that you are putting in the work on your relationship's behalf. Offering them your thoughts and reflections provides them with evidence of self-examination as well as providing an alternative narrative for your actions to the one they might be carrying. Usually, hurt partners hold a very negative and wary explanation for their hurtful partner's actions – things like "they just don't care, they are selfish, they want their cake and to eat it too, they are disloyal, they are a liar, they are untrustworthy" etc. Your partner does not want these awful attributions to be true. They desperately need an alternative explanation that they can live with and trust in. I imagine that you need that too.

Using Figure 9.5, can you take some time to write down what you have discovered about yourself in this process? Get curious and think about what you'd like to share with your partner. What was it like for you knowing you caused pain? How have you carried that pain? How have you tried to cope with that? What is the hardest part about this injury for you? What have you come to learn about yourself and your motivations for this hurtful act? Does this tell you something about your unmet needs, your lack of self-awareness, or your inability to express your needs, your desire to take care of your needs on your own, to hide a part of yourself, to manage your emotions in destructive ways? What is the most difficult part to share, to let your partner see? What reassurance can you offer them about your growth?

Task 2 for the hurtful partner: asking for your needs

For the partner who has caused hurt to share their learning and growth in this way, this demonstrates commitment to the relationship and to self-growth. As part of that growth, I invite you to reflect on whether there is anything that you want your partner to know or that you need from them. While your role in the attachment repair process is almost entirely focused on witnessing and attending to your partner's pain, rubbing on

Personal Reflections on this Injury

Witnessing /hurt partner sharing what they have learned from this event

This sheet will help partners who have been hurtful to reflect on what they have learned from this attachment injury. These reflections will be pivotal in growing from the rupture & re-building security in your bond.

Impact

How have you carried the burden of knowing you caused hurt? What has that been like?

What is the hardest part about this injury for you? How have you coped with that?

Self-awareness

What have you learned about yourself & your reasons or motivations for the hurtful acts or events?

Lack of self-awareness
Thoughtlessness
Unmet needs
Addiction
Impulsivity
Self-sabotage
Covert decision-making
Avoidance
Fear of rejection
Loneliness
Poor coping
Approval-seeking
Entitlement

Growth

What do you want your partner to know about why this happened & what you have learned from it? What reassurance can you offer them about your growth?

Clare Rosoman 2024

Figure 9.5 Personal reflections on this attachment injury – hurtful partner.

that soothing balm, there is room for you to ask for what you need too. You might need their understanding, their forgiveness, or their grace. You might need reassurance from them that they are still committed to this relationship and that your heart is safe with them. You might need certain things to change in the relationship moving forward, as a consequence of this injury and all that you have learned about yourself and your needs. Now is your chance to vulnerably ask.

For this process to be helpful and healing, it is important that you ask for your needs from a position of vulnerability and while holding the current attachment injury in mind. Just as your partner was instructed, I encourage you to think about what you need on an emotional level, what you need to restore the security in your bond, and how your partner could release you from some of your pain and guilt moving forward. I caution you from raising a plethora of additional concerns about the relationship or your partner while you are in such a fragile state of repair. This would be like running on the broken leg before it has rebuilt its strength. There will be time for processing other issues once you are in a more stable place together. Right now, think about what you can offer your partner and what you need from them to help you to both contribute to the restoration of security in your bond as your first priority.

Figure 9.6 gives you a space to explore your needs along with some tips to keep you on-track.

Forgiveness and letting go

Now for a final word in this chapter, I want to help you both to reconcile the pain, regret, guilt, fear, and sadness that have come with this attachment injury and to consider letting go. This can be a tall order and it might be too soon to even consider, but I'd love to at least plant the seed. Ultimately, when it does feel right, I want this for you both so that you can move forward together in new ways, rather than being held back by the past. It is possible for you to each grow as people and for your relationship to grow from this suffering. It is possible for suffering and growth to co-exist.

Forgiveness is an interesting concept that can feel right for some and uncertain for others. In this context, where you are both making valiant and honest attempts to repair damage, I see forgiveness and moving on as a way of choosing happiness over righteousness. As Sue Johnson says, "You can be right, or you can be close, but you can't be both." Yes, harms may have been delivered, and they need to be thoroughly attended to, but dwelling on those mistakes will only erode your connection and prevent the restoration of trust. As long as you hold onto your righteousness, you will create a barrier to connection. Needing to be right means that

Hurtful/witnessing partner asks for their needs

This sheet will help the hurtful/witnessing partner to ask for what they need from the other to help them to heal & to rebuild security in the bond as the final part of the Attachment Injury Resolution Model.

Tips for the hurtful partner

Consider your needs

Take moment to consider if there is anything that you want your partner to know or that you need from them. While your role in the attachment repair process has been focused on witnessing & attending to your partner's pain, there is room for you to ask for what you need too.

Stay vulnerable

For this process to be helpful & healing, it is important that you ask for your needs from a position of vulnerability & whilst holding the current attachment injury in mind. Think about what you need on an emotional level, what you need to restore the security in your bond & to move forward.

Keep it focused

I caution you from raising a plethora of additional concerns about the relationship or your partner whilst you are in such a fragile state of repair. There will be time for processing other issues once you are in a more stable place together. Restoring your bond is the first priority.

What do you need from your partner?

What do you need to hear or to see from your partner that would soothe your fear & guilt? How could they help you to move forward with optimism?

Clare Rosoman 2024

Figure 9.6 Hurtful/witnessing partner asks for their needs.

your partner must be wrong. This becomes a threat to closeness because it invites defensiveness. It prevents you from finding a comfortable place where each person's humanity and imperfection can be held lightly.

The reconciliation process involves an acceptance of what has happened, an acceptance of each person's humanity, and a level of grace for each other's flaws and missteps. If you find yourself becoming stuck here and, despite your attempts to repair the damage that you or your partner have caused, you still feel unable to accept and to let go of those transgressions, you might need more time and more personal reflection on what it is that you need and how your partner could help you with that. It can take time to work through this process and you might not be ready yet. There might still be parts of this injury that have not been adequately addressed for your fears to be cushioned. That is totally okay.

Forgiveness is not a pre-requisite for healing, but it does help. As social beings, we tend to prefer to heal interpersonal ruptures rather than live with a grudge, but that does not mean that this is the only way to come to terms with what has happened.[5] Forgiveness is an intentional strategy that interrupts patterns of avoidance and revenge, decreases negative thoughts and behaviours towards someone who has wronged you, and promotes relationship cohesion.[6] Forgiveness does not mean excusing or dismissing bad behaviour or ignoring the devastating impact of another's actions. Forgiving someone is an evocative process that involves a deliberate and intentional attempt to understand the hurtful event, to take into account the other person's perspective, and to understand the context in which they were hurtful. This is why it is so important for the partner who has been hurtful to share their experience (not excuses) and what they have learned from this event. When the hurt partner can hear this and make a concerted effort to understand and empathise with the other, then this can alter any negative opinions they might be holding about the other's actions.[7] As you know, this can be a challenging process, but the benefits of forgiveness can be profound. Forgiveness is associated with positive physical and mental health outcomes including reduced stress, lower resting heart rate, and greater life satisfaction, as well as having a positive impact on relationship functioning.[8]

How easily you can achieve forgiveness and whether this is even a goal for you depends on many factors related to the relationship, the nature of the hurt, your experiences with previous hurts, and how successful the repair attempts have been. However, your *attachment strategies* can also play a role. Research has shown us that people with secure attachment strategies tend to find forgiving transgressions easier because they hold more positive views of others and are more likely to interpret their behaviour neutrally.[9] People with anxious attachment strategies can struggle more with forgiveness because they are likely to feel more intense levels of distress, to dwell on these hurts, and to attribute negative meaning to the other's actions.[10] This can make it difficult to process the hurt in a new light. And for people with avoidant attachment strategies, working through hurts and achieving forgiveness go against their usual tendency of sidestepping or suppressing their vulnerable emotions. While they are less likely to ruminate over hurtful events than those with anxious attachment strategies, their lack of connection to their emotional world might preclude them from accessing or sharing their pain, and from finding empathy for the other's perspective, which can stifle forgiveness.

When someone has been hurt and they have felt that their pain has been heard and acknowledged, there is usually a reduction in their need to protest the injury, and they can be more open to the other's experience. Being able to find empathy for the other's experience seems to be instrumental in achieving a sense of forgiveness. When you can understand the other person's experience, it enables you to modify the assumptions you had previously held about their motives or who they are, and it makes forgiving more likely. It has been shown that those with a greater ability to empathise with their partner were more likely to forgive, and those who struggled to let go of negative interpretations about their partner's intentions were less likely to forgive.[11] When we empathise with a partner who has hurt us, our desire for reprisal often reduces. Seeing their humanity and acknowledging that good people can make dire mistakes lessens our righteously indignant need for reckoning. So, in this way, forgiveness relies on being able to take in the other's perspective and to form an alternative explanation for the hurtful person's intent and actions. This too enables you to regrow your trust in them and rebuild the security in your bond.

It is important to note that, whether you have been hurtful or you have been hurt, *you both* deserve this generosity. As Alice Miller says, "You are never as guilty as you feel, or as innocent as you'd like to believe." I implore you to look at your own actions through the same kind and empathic lens so that you might be able to give yourself the gift of empathy and understanding that comes with forgiveness. I have not met a single person who is not harbouring some shameful or guilty feelings about their actions in their relationships. Being able to see hurtful acts in a new light forms part of the "work" of recovering from this negative event in a way that will lead to growth rather than stuckness. Having an expanded view of hurtful acts and developing empathy and understanding for yourself and your partner will set you free from negative patterns and allow you to build a stronger bond together. Forgiveness will encourage you to grow as people and transcend the hardship you have faced, stronger and wiser for it. The hard work that you put into repairing this rupture in trust truly will leave your relationship stronger in the broken place.

Notes

1 Johnson, S.M., & Brubacher, L.L. (2016). Deepening attachment emotion in emotionally focused couple therapy (EFT). In G. Weeks, S. Fife & C. Peterson (Eds.). *Techniques for the couple therapist: Essential interventions* (pp. 155–160). New York, NY: Routledge.

2 Glass, S.P. (2003). *Not just friends: Rebuilding trust and recovering your sanity after infidelity*. New York: Free Press.

3 Johnson, S.M. (2008). *Hold me tight: Seven conversations for a lifetime of love*. New York, NY: Little, Brown.

4 Tedeschi, R.G., & Calhoun, L.G. (2004). Posttraumatic growth: Conceptual foundations and empirical evidence. *Psychological Inquiry*, 15(1), 1–18.

5 Abrahms, J.A. (2004). *How can i forgive you? The courage to forgive, The freedom not to*. New York: Harper Collins.

6 Guzmán-González, M., Wlodarczyk, A., Contreras, P., Rivera-Ottenberger, D., & Garrido, L. (2019). Romantic attachment and adjustment to separation: The role of forgiveness of the former partner. *Journal of Child and Family Studies*, 28, 3011–3021.

7 Kimmes, J.G., & Durtschi, J.A. (2016). Forgiveness in romantic relationships: The roles of attachment, empathy and attributions. *Journal of Marital and Family Therapy*, 42(4), 645–658.

8 Hirst, S.L., Hepper, E.G., & Tenenbaum, H.R. (2019). Attachment dimensions and forgiveness of others: A meta-analysis. *Journal of Social & Personal Relationships*, 36, 11–12. https://doi.org/10.1177/0265407519841716.

9 Guzmán-González, M., Wlodarczyk, A., Contreras, P., Rivera-Ottenberger, D., & Garrido, L. (2019). Romantic attachment and adjustment to separation: The role of forgiveness of the former partner. *Journal of Child and Family Studies*, 28, 3011–3021.

10 Hirst, S.L., Hepper, E.G., & Tenenbaum, H.R. (2019). Attachment dimensions and forgiveness of others: A meta-analysis. *Journal of Social & Personal Relationships*, 36, 11–12. https://doi.org/10.1177/0265407519841716.

11 Kimmes, J.G., & Durtschi, J.A. (2016). Forgiveness in romantic relationships: The roles of attachment, empathy and attributions. *Journal of Marital and Family Therapy*, 42(4), 645–658.

Part IV

Growth

Stronger in the broken place

Chapter 10

Earning security

In this chapter, we review the powerful healing work that you have accomplished in Part III as you worked through the Attachment Injury Resolution Model, and we will build on it. We will look at how to establish and maintain a new, positive interactional cycle where clear signals make it easier for partners to meet each other's needs. Now, the fear and pain in the hurt partner can be shared when it flares, and the hurtful partner can see a road to reconnection and their role in it. There will inevitably be times when reminders of this attachment injury will come alive, and old wounds are bumped. This chapter looks at how to manage these flares in ways that continue to build the security of the bond, rather than weaken it. This foundation gives us room to look at other hurts that might be related or unrelated to the attachment injury and to practice "cementing in" this new positive interactional cycle.

Just as a broken limb needs to regain the strength in the surrounding tissue, your relationship bond needs to be strengthened by practicing the moves of this new cycle until it becomes habitual, and your bond is strong and secure. We take some time in this chapter to explore the negative cycle that might have pre-dated this attachment injury and the unmet needs that could have been festering for either or both partners. We build on the good work that went into repairing this attachment injury by looking at how to continue to build security and trust moving forward, and, we look at common traps that people can fall into when recovering from an attachment injury and how to avoid them. This chapter also looks at the impact of an attachment injury on romantic partners' sexual connection and how to reconnect sexually when the attachment injury has impacted this important area of the relationship. This work is all about building on the gains you have made so far and continuing this amazing work to ensure that it lasts into the future.

DOI: 10.4324/9781003466499-15

Ongoing healing conversations

For most people, repairing an attachment injury is not completed with only one meaningful conversation. This stands to reason because there are usually layers of hurt that need to be visited and there well may be injuries for each partner that need addressing one by one. If you refer to the exercise you did in Chapter 6 (Figure 6.2 – Attachment injury repair priority list), where you listed the hurts that needed to be addressed for you both, have you been able to talk about each one on that list? If not, I'd encourage you to take each person's concern and work through the steps of Phases 2 and 3 (listed below), so that you can hopefully experience some resolution on each issue. Some issues may have naturally resolved as the primary attachment injury was repaired and others will become more prominent or feel more manageable after this initial work. You might have additional items to add to that list now. That is perfectly fine and represents the organic nature of healing – it can change flexibly to meet your needs. This process of combing through the concerns and hurts that you each hold provides an opportunity to practice the steps of a new and far healthier pattern of communication. I have listed the steps again as a reference and I urge you both to use all that you have learned so far to address the layers of hurt present for you both surrounding this injury.

Phase 1:
- Notice the negative cycle and take time to reflect on what each partner is feeling underneath their surface reactions. Exit the negative cycle by tuning into the pain that is showing up and acknowledging the attachment impact of the injury for one or both partners.

Phase 2:
- Hurt partner accesses and touches their vulnerability and shares this vulnerably with the hurtful partner.
- Hurtful partner takes in their pain and lets it impact them. They share the impact and offer care, remorse, and an apology if required.

Phase 3:
- Hurt partner accepts care from the other and allows it to touch their heart. They can now ask for what they need from the other to restore their trust.
- Hurtful partner acknowledges these needs and meets them where possible, by offering reassurance that the other will not be repeatedly hurt in this way (antidote bonding).
- Cherry-on-top: Hurtful partner reflects on their role in this injury and what they have learned from it. They can now offer reassurance of their growth and can ask for forgiveness and understanding.

Each time you follow this process to resolve the hurts that have occurred in this relationship, you are strengthening your bond. You are helping the broken bone to strongly knit together. Interestingly, the ends of a broken bone need to touch or at least be close to each other for the osteoblasts (the bone cells) to reach out and find each other. They need to be close enough for the growth factor to have any effect. When they join, they knit together, reconnecting the two broken ends. This is what your tender hearts are doing as you reach out to each other and share your pain and fear. This act brings you closer and allows the attachment bond to do its work. Just as the growth factor propels the bone cells to repair the break, the attachment bond helps you to find your way back to each other after a rupture. Just as the bones can knit together, so too can your hearts.

There may be many injuries to repair or only one or two. Some might require a handful of conversations and others many more to resolve the hurt and to rebuild the trust. There is no timeframe or limit on how the repair process unfolds. If you can follow these steps each time, you will be supporting the regrowth of your attachment bond and hopefully benefitting as a result. You will know when each injury is healed because you will feel lighter, the issue will no longer feel as present or distressing, and you will feel a little closer to your partner. For most people, repetition is important for fully processing the residual effects of a breach in trust and for developing confidence in the changes.

Each interaction in this healing manner builds on the one before it and lessens the need to return to these painful topics. However, it is important to note that until someone has had their pain sufficiently witnessed, they *will* keep bringing it up. It will have a way of surfacing whenever there are reminders, and its effects will continue to be felt. Repetition is the nervous system's way of alerting you to a potential threat. If the same issue repeatedly is raised, then my best guess would be that there is an aspect of that original injury that either hasn't been accessed and shared by the hurt partner or there is an aspect of their pain that has not been fully heard and acknowledged by the hurtful partner. People don't repeat for no reason, it means that something hasn't been fully resolved. If that part of the hurt person's experience lives on unsoothed and unprocessed, it will activate their defences and undermine attempts to rebuild the connection. If this is happening to you or your partner, I would encourage you to dive a little more deeply into the painful parts of this experience and to find the pieces that have been missed. You might need to work with a therapist to help you if you find yourself stuck.

Once you have worked through all the hurts listed for each partner on your priority list, there is still one more factor to consider. That is, preparing for reminders or "flare-ups" of a previously resolved attachment injury. I think of these moments as the echoes of the injury – moments when the pain surfaces for one or both partners and they become activated and on high alert. They are a normal part of the recovery process and do not indicate a setback. How you navigate these times is essential to the maintenance of your healing. These echoes might include direct reminders of the event such as an affair partner attempting to make contact, or they can include more subtle triggers such as one partner changing the passcode on their phone. There might be certain dates that have special significance such as the anniversary of the injury or previously held special dates that now have changed meaning such as the discovery of a betrayal on a birthday. Certain places, items, or sensations can become imbued with meaning, triggering intense memories of the attachment injury. This is completely normal and not a sign of incomplete healing. The more you can prepare for any potential difficult spots you might encounter in future the better.

Ask yourself and your partner to reflect on potential reminders of this attachment injury so that you can be prepared for them. If you can be aware of triggers and reminders ahead of time, then you can make a plan to tackle them – together. Figure 10.1 will help you with this. Each time you can turn to your partner and let them know that you have bumped into a reminder of the event, and they can offer you comfort, you have triumphed as a team! That truly makes your bond stronger in the broken place. This protective action is just like the bony callous that forms around the break in a bone. This callous protects the bone cells as they do their work and remains in place once the break is healed, making it stronger where it once was weak.

Addressing relationship concerns separate from the attachment injury

Once you have worked through the key hurts and breaches of trust that have rocked your relationship, you will no doubt have experienced a new way of being together. You are now becoming clearer about your inner world and better able to let your partner in and to ask for what you need. You are resolving hurts together instead of separately. I imagine that this is quite different for you both. Turning to the other for help with your pain is often new and foreign, but as you do this and offer the same in return, you are creating a new interactional pattern – a new cycle. This is a secure cycle where you know that your partner will be there when you need them, that they care about you, and that they are your teammate in life. We want to ensure that these wonderful changes, the security you are building in your bond, are locked in for the long term.

For many people, this new way of reaching to each other, leading with vulnerability and sending clear signals of need, is completely different compared to how they interacted before the attachment injury. This is the potential "silver lining" of having survived such a relational trauma. What doesn't

Managing Reminders of the Event

Planning ahead to manage flares after an attachment injury

This sheet will help you to identify potential reminders or "echoes" of this resolved attachment injury. Making a plan to manage these triggers together will strengthen your attachment security.

Potential echoes of the attachment injury

Partner 1

What reminders of this attachment injury are you likely to encounter moving forwards? Are there any particular things that you might find upsetting or that you would like your partner to know?

Partner 2

What reminders of this attachment injury are you likely to encounter moving forwards? Are there any particular things that you might find upsetting or that you would like your partner to know?

Managing these echoes as a team

Partner 1

How could you let your partner know when you are reminded of this event? How could they help you with this? What do you need from them to reassure you?

Partner 2

How could you let your partner know when you are reminded of this event? How could they help you with this? What do you need from them to reassure you?

Clare Rosoman 2024

Figure 10.1 Managing reminders of a hurtful event.

break you as a unit certainly can make you stronger. If you had a negative relational cycle before the attachment injury, you are not alone. This is very common and might have even contributed to the injury in some way by creating distance between you, creating unclear signals, or building resentment. A negative pattern or cycle is a repetitive, recursive loop that partners become caught in when things become tense between them. If you recall in Chapter 3, we looked at typical negative cycles that many people become embroiled in. These negative cycles have a way of worsening the disconnection as each partner feels unheard and misinterpreted. The more each copes in the way that makes sense for them, the more they send alarming signals to the other. Partners tend to pursue for connection or to withdraw from connection, depending on their attachment strategy (anxious or avoidant) and the way they do that is triggering for the other. Pursuers often look critical and explosive to withdrawers; hence they want to step out of range. Withdrawers often look uncaring and disengaged to pursuers; hence they push for evidence of care. Both sets of signals scare the life out of the other and contribute to the disconnection and erosion of the attachment bond.

There is no better time than now to examine the cycle that might have been in residence before this attachment injury set off a bomb in your relationship. For some, this is clear and obvious, and for others, it might be more subtle and require some open consideration. Following an attachment injury, you can find yourselves in an amplified version of a pre-existing cycle, so it is simple to identify, or you might find that the negative cycle following the injury was completely different to the cycle that was there, even if quietly, before the breach of trust. I ask you to reflect on the pre-existing cycle by thinking about how you used to raise concerns with each other and manage conflict.

Who was the one who initiated these conversations and how? Who was the peacekeeper who preferred not to talk about potentially contentious things, and how did they manage that? How did you manage disagreements? How were feelings expressed or not expressed? How were you left feeling after a tense moment? How did you resolve these differences? Did one comply but not fully agree? Did one feel reassured for a while but then the issue would resurface? How did you each feel about your relationship and your partner after a trip though the cycle? Were you left stung by harsh words, doubting their love for you, mistrusting their words, feeling unheard or unacknowledged, feeling controlled or suppressed, wondering if you should be together? These questions will prompt reflection on the pre-existing cycle and alert you to issues separate from the attachment injury (or related to it) that still need addressing. If there was a pre-existing negative cycle at play before this attachment injury, then it will undermine the foundations of the wonderful work you have done together in this book unless you identify and tackle it. Write down the features of your cycle that pre-dated the attachment injury in Figure 10.2.

Cycle that Pre-dated the Attachment Injury

Identifying the relational cycle that existed before an attachment injury

This sheet will help you to identify the elements of the negative relational cycle that might have been present before an attachment injury. It might be different to the cycle that followed the injury.

Partner 1

What do you do? What do you show your partner?

What do you tell yourself? What is the meaning you make?

Surface emotion that you show:

What are your primary, vulnerable emotions that are harder to show?

What are your deepest, attachment needs?

Partner 2

What do you do? What do you show your partner?

What do you tell yourself? What is the meaning you make?

Surface emotion that you show:

What are your primary, vulnerable emotions that are harder to show?

What are your deepest, attachment needs?

Clare Rosoman 2024

Figure 10.2 The cycle that pre-dated the attachment injury.

You might remember Paul and Susan from earlier chapters. They were a monogamous couple struggling with the aftermath of Paul's affair. Understandably, this was devastating to their connection and Susan's pain was front and centre as they worked through the Attachment Injury Resolution Model. Paul was able to stand steady, despite his fear of losing Susan and his family, to witness and attend to her pain. He resisted becoming defensive or justifying his actions and Susan managed to lower her protective armour and to vulnerably share her desolation and hurt. She shared her raw disbelief that her partner and best friend could betray her trust in such a monumental way and threaten all they had built together. She reached into the depths of her pain and shared her fears of not being enough for Paul, of feeling discarded by him, and of feeling broken. Paul's anguish in response to her disclosures and his heartfelt apology went a long way in reassuring Susan that she mattered to him and that he understood. He expressed how much he deeply regretted his actions and how angry he was at himself for causing so much devastation and destruction to all that he holds dear. The more he was present to Susan's pain and held himself accountable for hurting her and for stepping away from his values, the more she could trust the veracity of his word. As Paul saw his impact on Susan and that he could attend to her and help her to heal, a little of his shame resolved, and their bond began to repair.

This was fantastic progress for Susan and Paul; they felt a renewed sense of optimism for their relationship and were closer than ever. They planned to renew their vows and to take a second honeymoon. However, for this work to be built on a strong and stable platform, they still needed to address the cycle that pre-dated Paul's affair. Before the attachment injury, Paul and Susan had a pursue-withdraw cycle where Susan would complain about Paul's lack of presence with her and with their family, becoming at times demanding. She missed their fun times together and worried about the growing distance between them, this alarm came across in her delivery. Unfortunately, her attempts to reach him landed harshly with Paul and he would cope by brushing off her concerns or defending himself. When that did not reassure Susan, she would escalate her message in a further attempt to be heard. Paul, feeling criticised and stung, would resort to becoming compliant, apologising, and promising to do more with Susan and the family. Paul did this to keep the peace, but he kept his distress over feeling criticised by Susan, and his growing resentment about carrying the financial stress of the family, to himself. He simply bottled these concerns, withdrawing and distancing from Susan, which, of course, triggered her alarm and confirmed her worry that he was disengaged. The more she protested in the way that made sense to her, the more she pushed him away, and the more he coped in the way that made sense to him, the more he triggered her alarm. This was a negative cycle that was quietly but surely eroding their bond.

The consequence of this was that Paul never shared his hurt over Susan's harsh words or his need for her support and reassurance. She didn't seem safe to approach when she seemed so disappointed in him! Sadly, this robbed Susan of the opportunity to be there for him, thereby correcting this assumption. The more Paul kept his concerns to himself, the more alone they both felt. Resolving the attachment injury clearly reassured Susan that she mattered to Paul and bound them together once more. However, unless Paul could take the risk to talk about how he felt in their old cycle, it risked being perpetuated. If he continued to "hide and comply" without follow-through, he would only activate Susan's alarms again. Unless Susan could talk about her need for togetherness in soft ways, she risked protesting harshly again. It was now crucial for them to identify the "old" cycle and for them both to expose and share their hurts and needs, so that they could heal and move forward in new ways.

Working through historical issues and unpacking a cycle that pre-dated the attachment injury is vital work for ensuring that these wonderful changes are cemented in. We can think of this as ongoing physiotherapy to support the newly healed broken bone. All the structures around this break need strengthening so that the bones are well supported moving forward.

Cementing in the new cycle

The work of observing and catching an "old" cycle is extremely useful in locking down the new positive cycle. It might seem counterintuitive to "rake over old ground" by looking back at old fights and tough spots, but this is actually great "physiotherapy" for your newly repaired bond.

Ask yourself whether there is anything that you are avoiding talking about for fear of how it might go. This is an invaluable question for finding opportunities to practice the new steps of your positive cycle. There might be certain topics that you both carefully avoid raising or old hurts that seem inconsequential now. There might be smaller issues that used to send you hurtling into the old, negative cycle. Revisiting these sensitive topics that might be separate from or related to the attachment injury provides an opportunity to cement in the new cycle as well as making sure that there aren't any festering concerns that can undermine your progress in the future.

As part of this process, I encourage you both to reflect on the unexpressed or unmet needs that you can identify as you observe your historical relationship issues. What were you needing in those tough moments? Was it reassurance that you are cared for, liked, and cherished? Was it that you are safe from hurt, rejection, or loss? Was it that you are wanted, that you are accepted as you are, that you are enough? These are common attachment needs that all humans will resonate with on some level. Ask yourself which ones apply to you or could be better described to encapsulate what you were crying out for from your partner in your "old" cycle. For some, these unmet needs are clear, and for others, you might only be able to identify the unmet attachment longings that were there for you with the benefit of hindsight. One of the advantages of working through an attachment injury is that it takes you closer to your pain *and* to your attachment needs. You get clearer about what you want and don't want in your loving bond. Now is the time to share this with your partner. This will help you to move forwards in ways that prioritise each person's needs rather than repeating old patterns that only serve to threaten your bond.

Each time you can connect in a new way over past hurts, you are cementing in your new interactional pattern or cycle. This new pattern replaces the "old" cycle that you were caught in after the injury and becomes your norm – your secure attachment bond. Many find that once they can do this, they can solve practical issues or historical stuck spots that used to trip them up in the past. As Sue Johnson says, "with security, comes flexibility." Because the new cycle honours both people's needs and is not plagued with defensiveness and wariness, there tends to be much more give and take. This means that partners can come up with creative solutions to problems and can be more flexible in their responses. We only become rigid and unmoving when we are under threat. When we feel safe, we can bend and flex with our partner for the good of the relationship – there is a good amount of stretch in the fibres of the bond. Now might be a good time in your recovery to think about any practical issues that you can solve as a team.

Let's revise what a healthy cycle looks like to provide a quick reference guide to raising relationship concerns. Figure 10.3 lists the steps of the new cycle as a reference.

Steps of the new cycle

1 *Notice your own reactivity.* Look out for your habitual coping strategies that pop up when your relationship feels wobbly (usually either anxious pursuit or avoidant withdrawal). Give yourself space to slow down and to look for your vulnerable, primary emotions (pain, fear, shame, sadness, anger). Stay with them for a moment to get acquainted and to let them move you closer to your values and needs. Tune into the message in them and gain clarity about the pain and the need.

2 *Send softer signals.* Turn to your partner for help with this. Do this vulnerably and by sending clear signals ("I am feeling..."). Give them space to respond and the grace to manage their inner world, just as you are.

The Steps of the Positive Cycle

1. Notice your reactivity	2. Send softer signals	2. Respond with care
Look out for your habitual coping strategies that pop up when your relationship feels wobbly (usually either anxious pursuit or avoidant withdrawal). Give yourself space to slow down & to look for your vulnerable, primary emotions (pain, fear, shame, sadness, anger). Stay with them for a moment to get acquainted & to let them move you closer to your values & needs. Tune into the message in them & gain clarity about the pain & the need.	Turn to your partner for help with this. Do this vulnerably & by sending clear signals (I am feeling...). Give them space to respond & the grace to manage their inner world, just as you are. They might need a moment to regain their balance. If needed, ask your partner for their support or for help – ask for your needs (Can you help me by...?). This is an attachment-based reach, appealing to their desire to care for you, rather than a list of demands.	Knowing that your person is there when you need them, that they will respond with care & that you matter to them are crucial ingredients for secure attachment. Make sure that you hold this in mind as you respond to your partner's vulnerability. Be your partner's safe place, especially when they feel small, sad, scared, or vulnerable (safe-haven). Help & encourage your partner, especially when they feel uncertain or discouraged (secure-base).

Clare Rosoman 2024

Figure 10.3 The steps of the new cycle.

They might need a moment to regain their balance. If needed, ask your partner for their support or for help – ask for your needs ("Can you help me by...?"). This is an attachment-based reach, appealing to their desire to care for you, rather than a list of demands.

3 *Respond with engagement and care.* Knowing that your person is there when you need them, that they will respond with care, and that you matter to them are the crucial ingredients for secure attachment. Make sure that you hold these tenets in mind as you respond to your partner's vulnerability. Be each other's safe place to land, especially when they feel small, sad, scared, or vulnerable (safe haven). Help and encourage each other. Be each other's number one supporter, especially when they feel uncertain or discouraged (secure base).

Building trust in your relationship

Every time you and your partner can actively engage in the new cycle, you are building your trust in each other to be accessible, responsive, and engaged. When your partner experiences you as open to them and as careful in how you raise concerns, they see you as non-threatening. You build the other's trust in your responses and intentions. They begin to trust that you are never intentionally hurtful, that they are safe with you. If your responses are predictable and reliable, this creates immense safety, which is especially important after an attachment injury. When you can share your vulnerabilities with your partner, just as they can with you, then the risk is shared between you. You each hold the other's heart gently. Trust is built in these small moments when hearts meet and are held in gentle acceptance.

Trust is built in a million small ways such as when you keep a promise, when you say what you mean and mean what you say, when you remember something important that your partner is facing and you ask them about it, or when you are transparent about your feelings, thoughts, and the details of your life. Trust is mutual, so the more you are open, the more your partner will be as well. The more you give your partner the benefit of the doubt, and trust their good intentions, the more you accept them as they are and allow there to be differences between you, the more you can both be authentic in this relationship, and trust in the other's support.

If we think about the function of a secure attachment figure, it is a special someone who offers a safe haven of comfort when we feel vulnerable and a secure base to launch from when we feel uncertain. You can build the trust and security in your bond by ensuring that you provide these important functions for each other. The safe haven of a loving attachment figure is like a big pair of arms ready to wrap you up when you need it, and the secure base of a secure attachment figure is like a strong platform underneath your feet as you step out into the world. Being a *safe haven* means being there for your partner to share their vulnerabilities, their worries and their dreams, responding with acceptance and non-judgement, offering comfort and care, providing support, validating their feelings, and helping them to make sense of them. Being a *secure base* means being your partner's number one supporter, holding their dreams in mind even when they lose sight of them, having their back when the world is cruel, reminding them of their strengths, encouraging them when they feel uncertain or their confidence wanes, and supporting their dreams and aspirations. Being intentional about offering these two important functions of a secure attachment figure will vastly improve your bond. All humans need a safe harbour to shelter in when life is stormy and how wonderful that you can give that to each other. See Figure 10.4 for a list of suggestions for intentionally building and maintaining the security in your relationship.

Common pitfalls after resolving an attachment injury

I sincerely hope that you and your partner have been able to work through this book in such a way that the attachment injury now feels mostly healed. I hope that the earlier sections of this chapter have given you some encouragement and tools for maintaining these considerable gains and for the continued growth of the security in your bond. However, there are some

Building Security in Your Bond

Intentional practice to maintain & enhance the security in your relationship

This sheet will help you to think about the many ways that you can enhance trust & strengthen the attachment security in your bond.

Building trust in your relationship

Every time you & your partner can actively engage in the new cycle, you are building your trust in each other to be accessible, responsive & engaged. We know that these are the building blocks of secure attachment.

Ways to build trust:

- Be open to your partner when they raise concerns - this builds your partner's trust in your responses
- Be sensitive in how you raise concerns - this builds their trust in your good intentions
- Try to make your responses predictable & reliable - this creates safety
- Be transparent about your feelings, thoughts & the details of your life - this invites openness
- Share your vulnerabilities with your partner - this shares the risk between you
- Say what you mean & mean what you say - keep your promises - this makes you dependable
- Remember something important that your partner is facing & ask them about it - this shows care
- Give your partner the benefit of the doubt - this shows that you trust in their good intentions
- Accept them as they are & allow there to be differences between you - this allows for authenticity

Building a secure attachment bond

Safe haven

The safe haven of a loving attachment figure is like a big pair of arms ready to wrap you up when you need it.

Being a safe haven means:

- Being there for your partner to share their vulnerabilities, their worries & their dreams
- Responding with acceptance & non-judgement
- Offering comfort & care
- Providing support & reassurance
- Validating their feelings & helping them to make sense of them

Secure base

The secure base of a secure attachment figure is like a strong platform underneath your feet as you step out into the world.

Being a secure base means:

- Being your partner's number one supporter
- Holding their dreams in mind even when they lose sight of them
- Having their back when the world is cruel
- Reminding them of their strengths
- Encouraging them when they feel uncertain or their confidence wanes
- Supporting their dreams and aspirations

Clare Rosoman 2024

Figure 10.4 Building security in your bond.

things that might potentially threaten all this good work, that we would be remiss if we did not consider. When fear runs the relationship, when previous missteps are weaponised, or when partners revert to avoiding painful topics or to hiding things from the other, this can stunt the ongoing healing and even degrade the hard-won recovery from this attachment injury.

One potential threat to the fragile, newly repaired bond is fear. When trust has been betrayed, even after a healing process, fear can still rear its head changing the course of the relationship pattern and creating insecurity in the bond. While fear of being hurt again is completely understandable and reasonable, if hurt partners grapple with intense fear and cannot find soothing by sharing that fear with their partner, it can create an obstacle to closeness. If the fearful partner reverts to attempts to manage their fear on their own, they might become hypervigilant and reactive, rendering the partner helpless to assist. This could manifest as being on the lookout for and overreacting to potential threats, mistrusting the other's good intentions, looking for evidence of hurt, and fruitlessly seeking reassurance. In this way, the fear is now running the show. It dominates the hurt partner's experience and is almost impenetrable. The key to interrupting this process is to notice that it is happening and to reflect on the origins of the fear. It may be that the fear is a well-grounded reaction to something that has been unresolved or something that is happening in the relationship to tweak it. It may be that the fearful partner is struggling to live with the possibility that they could be hurt again in the relationship. Either way, I encourage you both to honestly look at this to see if there is more repair work to be done or if there are things that need changing in the relationship that could soothe or ease the worry. Tackling this together is the antidote to the isolation that can so easily creep in when one is scared and the other feels helpless to assist.

Fear can also show itself by the attachment injury being brought up each time you and your partner get caught in the "old" cycle. When this happens, it can feel as though the one who caused the injury can never be allowed to move on without painful reminders. It can feel like this event is being used as a weapon to punish the other. Of course, this will work against all the progress you made in recovering from the attachment injury and send you back into a negative relational cycle. If this is happening, I suggest returning to Chapters 4 and 5, so that you can identify and exit this negative cycle and access the softer feelings underneath that are evoked by reminders of this injury. Usually, when a past hurt keeps being raised, it means that there is some part of it that needs more healing. It may be that the hurt partner needs more help in how to manage their fear of being hurt again, that there are aspects of their pain that have not been adequately addressed, or that they haven't heard enough from the hurtful partner to assure them that they have learned from this and will not be hurtful again.

The earlier you can identify old patterns creeping back in or fears festering, the better. When in doubt, raise your concerns non-reactively with each other. Regularly check-in on how you are going and on how you each are feeling. Notice if either of you are avoiding certain topics for fear of the outcome. Allowing avoidance to run its course only ever makes the issue being avoided worse. It causes stewing and resentment and leads to missed opportunities for fortifying the new cycle. It permits the old cycle to sneak back in creating distance and threatening your hard-won security. Likewise, if either partner starts to hide things from the other or withhold certain information, they are putting the relationship at risk. Ask yourself what it is that you are hiding and why. Do your best to share this with your partner. Even if an open conversation becomes tough, it is better to be communicating than hiding from each other.

You have worked too hard to let things slide back into old patterns! The good news is that the work you have done to repair the attachment injury to this extent will help you to uncover the source of the stuckness or the block and to work through it in new ways. When partners can process and move beyond an impasse like this, it strengthens their bond further still.

Sex after betrayal

If your relationship was rocked by a sexual betrayal, then rebuilding your trusting bond will have helped your emotional connection immensely. However, rebuilding your sexual bond can present some challenges. For hurt partners, you might find yourself feeling reluctant to connect sexually, maybe wanting the reassurance of physical connection, but fearing exposing your vulnerable core. It is understandable that you want to guard against being hurt or feeling not enough, and the echo of another person's presence might be felt acutely. When the betrayal involved your partner turning to someone else sexually in violation of agreements you had in place, then reconnecting sexually can evoke negative comparisons to the third party, conjuring body insecurities and concern over performance, and killing desire. For hurtful partners, you could be wrestling with ambivalence about reaching out for fear of rejection, you might be plagued with guilt, you might be longing for the reassurance that sex offers, and you might even have some feelings of loss about the other party. With all these concerns swirling around for you both, it's no wonder that this can be a sensitive area to approach. With each partner so tentative, and so much at stake, the context around your sexual relationship becomes fraught.

Thanks to recent research and sex educators dispelling the myth that sexual desire and arousal is usually spontaneous and robust, we now know that sexual desire is actually highly contextual. This means that many factors determine whether we develop into desire and become aroused and the majority of these are unrelated to our bodies. We respond to the context surrounding sex. Certain things will hit your sexual "brakes" and certain things will rev your sexual "accelerator."[1] These contextual factors are usually psychological such as whether you are under stress, whether you feel good in your body, how close you feel to your partner, and whether you trust your partner to respect your boundaries. After a rupture in trust, especially if that betrayal was sexual in nature, the context around sex is bound to be loaded. Even if you had no previous concerns sexually, you might find yourself in extremely uncertain territory now. Each person's desire for sexual contact or lack of desire for it will be infused with attachment meaning leading to questions such as

> do you find me attractive, do you still want me, am I enough for you sexually, am I too much, do you value our sexual relationship, do I have a right to ask for my sexual needs, do I have a right to refuse?

Understandably, this can impact how you feel about sex with your partner and whether you desire it. This context can then create a knock-on effect where sexual function is impacted, making the idea of sex even more fraught and further hitting the brakes on interest.

To reconnect sexually, it is important to be able to talk about the contextual factors that are at play for each of you. This means being able to talk about what your sexual connection means to you both, being able to talk about your fears and needs, and to dispel any myths or assumptions that you could be carrying. Ask yourself what attachment alarms are rung for you by your partner's interest or lack of interest in sex – what does their desire or lack of it say to you about your bond or about your value to them? How do you feel inside and how do you manage this alarm? Do you protest it, and how? Do you shut down, and how? How might your partner interpret your actions when you are triggered in this way? How might that impact the context between you? Do you become caught in a negative interactional cycle that is unique to your sexual connection? Many people do. The difference is that you now have the skills to identify this cycle and to talk about it with your partner, your teammate.

Try to remove as much attachment meaning as you can from the other's sexual interest or function. For instance, try not to assume that if your partner has arousal difficulties, that it is because they aren't attracted to you or that they are in love with someone else. There could be many reasons for their caution, and they need to feel safe enough to share their concerns with you. Furthermore, try not to assume that if sex feels difficult, it means that you are doomed as a couple. Try not to load the sexual connection with too much meaning as you are repairing this fragile attachment bond. Try not to become critical of the other or to hold them responsible for the damage to the sexual connection – this will only put you both back on the battlefield. Instead, get curious about how you impact each other sexually and about the worries and concerns you each hold. The more you can talk openly without scaring each other and by leading with your vulnerability – a skill you have honed by now – the more you will find your way through this together.

Allow yourselves plenty of time to rebuild your sexual connection; there are no rules on how long this might take. If either or both partners are cautious, that is okay, look for other ways to connect and to share the specialness of your bond. Don't rush or hurry your sexual connection – this will just make the context between you, and around sex, fraught and tense. Notice and savour how each person shows their commitment to this relationship in various ways. Relish non-sexual touch and affection. These gestures go a long way to finding your way back to each other physically. Check-in every so often on how you both feel about your sexual relationship and what contextual factors you might need to work on to "rev" your accelerators or to remove the "brakes" on desire for sex. In these gentle and deliberate ways, you are working to create a new sexual cycle.

The aim is for you to both feel secure in your sexual bond. This means that you can clearly signal your needs and boundaries and that you feel safe with each other physically. Secure bonding and satisfying sex go hand in hand – they enhance each other. Emotional connection creates great sex, and great sex creates deeper emotional connection. In this context, sex becomes intimate play, a safe adventure.[2] A secure sexual connection means that you feel emotionally safe and protected, even though you are physically intimate. It means that you feel close to the other but that you are still your own person with your own needs and wants. It means that you can relax and be playful without fearing judgement about your body or your performance, and that you can ask for what you like, knowing that you are accepted. Finally, it means that you can set limits on what doesn't feel comfortable, knowing that your needs will be appreciated and respected.[3] Taken together, these elements form the ingredients for a secure sexual bond. If you can talk about these things and how you can ensure that they are present, this is the beginning of reconnecting sexually. That represents a new sexual cycle where you can be safe for each other and can become a sexual team once more.

Notes

1 Nagoski, E. (2015). *Come as you are: The surprising new science that will transform your sex life*. New York: Simon & Schuster Paperbacks.
2 Johnson, S.M. (2008). *Hold me tight: Seven conversations for a lifetime of love*. New York, NY: Little, Brown.
3 Abrahms-Springs, J. (2020). *After the affair: Healing the pain and rebuilding trust when a partner has been unfaithful* (3rd ed.). New York: Harper.

Chapter 11

When the injury can't be resolved

For some, the outcome of this process may not be so positive. This chapter focuses on loss, grief, and redefining the relationship. I find myself reluctant to write this chapter, because my hope is that you won't need it. However, we must be realistic in acknowledging that for some people, the rupture to trust is just too devastating to repair. Your relational bond might not have had enough stretch in it to withstand this attachment injury, nor each partner the resources left to weave the pieces back together. You might have tried valiantly, but there just was not enough thread to make it whole again. For some partners, particularly the hurt partner, living with the fear of being hurt once more can be too great to stay in the relationship. For others, particularly the hurtful partner, living with the fallout of this injury can feel like an uphill battle – a hill too steep to ever feel that they can come to rest. And in some situations, repair is impossible because, no matter how much one partner wanted it, the other was unable to engage in the resolution process or to bring all the ingredients required to adequately heal this attachment wound. However, you have arrived at this place, it is a very sad situation for you to find yourself in and my heart goes out to you. If you have had to make the painful decision to end your relationship, I am in wholehearted support of the strength it takes to prioritise your need for security and happiness. If you did not choose to end this relationship and your partner has decided to leave, then I imagine the pain is unendurable right now. Not all relationships can be repaired following an attachment injury. It is not a failure if you and your partner cannot heal this rupture.

In this chapter, we name and make room for the huge pain of the loss of an important relationship and look at how you can process your grief and recover, in time. To love another is to leave yourself open to hurt and when we are injured in a relationship *and* lose a loving connection, the pain and grief is visceral and often compounding. We will find a pathway into and through the grief and look at practical strategies for riding the waves of emotion until the storm starts to pass. This chapter will assist

DOI: 10.4324/9781003466499-16

you in processing these painful emotions and in using this suffering as an opportunity for growth.

Losing a precious bond

As humans, we know that separation from an attachment figure is incredibly distressing and disorganising to our emotional world. The loss of our safe haven of comfort and secure base of support is devastating. This loss leaves an aching void, where it can feel like there is no safe other to turn to for co-regulation and no ally to stand shoulder-to-shoulder with you as you face the world. It leaves an awful feeling of isolation. Not only is loss emotionally painful, it also upends our world. Loss can completely alter a person's view of their past and of their future. Suddenly, you might feel that you have no map forwards, you can even find yourself asking who you are, where you are going, whether you are to blame for this loss, and even whether you are fundamentally unlovable. In this way, you are not just grieving the loss of your special person, you are grieving the lost fabric of your life.

I'm sure that the decision to end the relationship won't have come easily. There may be doubts about whether you have made the right decision, guilt about hurting the other, anger directed towards yourself or your ex-partner, and maybe even worry for your ex-partner's well-being. If you feel responsible for the ending of the relationship, then this can be an additionally heavy burden for you to carry, leaving you with guilt and shame and impacting your view of yourself. In this way, you are handling a loss and burdened by responsibility for causing harm to someone you care deeply about. That is a hard place to be. If you did not want to end the relationship, you might be left feeling angry that your partner did not engage in the healing or bring the needed ingredients to the healing process. You might be raging at the destruction caused and the lack of resolution. You might even be so exhausted that you feel relieved to be able to stop trying now that the relationship is over. I want to normalise and acknowledge the various ways you might have arrived at this loss and the range of feelings that might be swirling around for you.

How you respond to the loss of this relationship will be impacted by many factors, such as, the circumstances surrounding the loss, your experience with other losses in life, how committed you were to this relationship, whether the loss was sudden or expected, whether you or your partner ended the relationship, and your own attachment strategies. People's emotional reaction to the loss of a relationship can fluctuate over time between love, sadness, anger, relief, guilt, and shame. Each person's reaction is particular to them and might change daily, especially when the loss is fresh.[1] These responses are all part of the separation and loss process, and we will look at how to ride the waves to recover in time. All in all, grieving lost love is ferocious and relentless, but you will recover. Making room for the facets of your own personal experience is an important part of the work of grief.

Attachment view on loss

As we referenced in Chapter 1, John Bowlby highlighted the importance of early attachment relationships on human well-being. As his thoughts about the importance of human emotional bonds developed, Bowlby was very interested in the impact of separation from an attachment figure. He saw separation anxiety and distress as a natural response to an attachment figure being unaccountably missing. It rings our alarms and propels us to find them. As a result of his research, he observed that humans follow a similar pattern of emotional response when separated from a loved one or when grieving. He went on to map what he called the phases of a separation response, in both children and adults.[2] These phases help us to see the adaptive value of our response to the loss of a loved one.

The first of these four phases is *numbing,* which Bowlby described as a temporary phase of emotional disconnection from the reality of the loss. He noticed that this numbness was often interrupted by outbursts of anger or distress and then numbness would return. It is almost as if the numbness allowed a person to limit how much of the truth of the loss they encountered at a time. He felt that this was self-protective in that it gave a person time to accept the loss in manageable doses.

The second phase is *yearning and searching,* where he noticed that people confronted the reality of the loss. Understandably, this caused heightened distress, including restlessness and preoccupation with thoughts of the other. In this phase, Bowlby found that people were sometimes "seized by an urge" to search for their special other even if they knew this was illogical and futile. He equated the understandable crying and calling out for the lost love with an attempt to call for the missing person, just as a baby cries out for their caregiver. He saw these actions as attempts to recover and restore the connection with the lost attachment figure - a "protest" against the loss.

The third phase is *disorganisation and despair* where the reality of the loss and pointlessness of searching is understood and a grieving person is left feeling intensely sad. This is a time of despair and hopelessness where a person is likely to experience, not only sadness, but a terrible sense of isolation and despondency. This phase is associated with sleep and appetite disturbance, social withdrawal, and extreme depression and loneliness.

The fourth phase as identified by Bowlby is *reorganisation and detachment* where the individual is able to process the loss and let go of or detach from the lost person. This frees them from the searching for the other as the solution to their pain and allows them to reconnect with themselves and others. This is a time of adjustment where the grieving person begins to alter their view of the future without this person in it and to establish other attachment bonds.[3]

Bowlby's phases of separation align with recent developments in the grief and loss field that see the process of grief as involving four key tasks. These four tasks are:

1 Acceptance of the reality of the loss
2 Experiencing the pain of the loss
3 Adjusting to life without the lost love
4 Finding a connection to the past without becoming stuck in it[4]

Grief is not a straightforward process. Humans do not follow a neatly ordered stepwise process as they grieve. It is an emotional and organic process that evolves and shifts and is totally individual. While there are common themes inherent in people's experience of grief, how long they remain in each phase and their movement back and forth between the phases and the tasks of grief will vary greatly. You may experience periods of protesting against the separation and make attempts to contact your ex-partner for resolution, only to sink into despondency at other moments, wanting to hide away from the world. You will have good days where you can get things done and glimpse some hope for the future, and you will have bad days where you are fired up with the injustice of the loss or when you fall into a deep pit of despair and wonder how you will ever go on.

Responding to loss and grief

Bowlby said that the loss of a loved one is one of the most intensely painful experiences any human being can experience, and that to the grieving person, nothing can bring comfort other than the return of the lost person. He also said that there is a tendency to underestimate how intensely distressing and disabling the loss usually is and the length of time it can take to recover.[5] As you can see from Bowlby's four phases of separation and loss, the emotional experience following the end of a relationship is like the grief following the death of a partner. We go through the same processes, however, unlike death, the loss of a relationship is theoretically reversible, which can make the grieving more complicated.[6] Knowing that your partner lives on but doesn't choose you or that they have hurt you terribly can complicate the process of mourning the loss of this relationship. Knowing that you have caused the other pain adds another layer of suffering as you process this loss. Wondering if the relationship is really over or could be repaired can prolong the process indefinitely.

The pain you are likely to be confronting as you take in the loss of this relationship is real and valid and it will take time to heal. This bond matters and you are grieving its loss. Whether your ex-partner will be still in your life in some way or not at all, you are grieving the ending of what you had. It is well documented that the loss of a romantic relationship is associated with emotional distress that can leave people vulnerable to poor mental health outcomes.[7] Your pain honours the love you felt, and indeed may still feel, for this special person. I encourage you to make space for this pain and to be gentle with yourself as you process this loss. It is a huge life-event, one that needs care and attention as you process the fallout.

When recovering from the loss of a relationship, there are two sets of challenges a person faces. The first are *interpersonal*, and they relate to external matters relating to how you negotiate your ongoing relationship with your ex-partner and your life without them. The second are *intrapersonal*, and they concern internal matters, such as how you emotionally manage the grief and loss. In this way, "successful grief" is the ability to adapt to the loss of someone special, emotionally *and* practically, so that you might be able to move on with your life and even to grow from the experience. How people engage in this much-needed process and how they become stuck at certain points is impacted by many things, including their attachment strategies.

We know from research that those with *secure* attachment strategies are more likely to regulate their emotions, to seek support from others, and to move more smoothly through the process of grieving a lost relationship than those who use insecure attachment strategies (anxious, avoidant, or fearful-avoidant). They are usually less concerned about seeing their ex-partner again, report feeling less blame towards their ex-partner, and feeling ready to move on more quickly than people who use insecure attachment strategies.[8] People with secure attachment strategies are also more likely to rely on other relationships, such as their family or friends, to help them in their emotional adjustment to the loss. Alternatively, people who use insecure attachment strategies seem to be more likely to struggle emotionally after a relationship loss. Both anxious and avoidant attachment strategies are related to higher levels of distress during the recovery from a loss than people with secure attachment strategies, and they are more likely to use substances such as drugs or alcohol to cope.[9] Despite these similarities, there are some clear differences between those with anxious attachment strategies and those with avoidant attachment strategies.

Those with *anxious* attachment strategies are more likely to be flooded with emotion, preoccupied with thoughts of their ex-partner, to make attempts to repair or reconcile, and to continue to use their ex-partner as a source of support. As a result, they can find themselves overwhelmed with painful emotion when grieving and can struggle to turn down the heat on their negative emotions, compared to people who don't use anxious attachment strategies.[10] They are more likely to seek-out their ex-partner in the hope that they will respond with care and reassurance,[11] leaving them vulnerable to more upset and rejection if their partner does not respond positively. These factors seem to play a role in slowing the adjustment and acceptance process. While being consumed with painful emotion can serve as an impediment to healing, there is interesting research showing that the more deeply a serious life event impacts you and the more your internal world is turned upside down, the more potential there is for self-reflection and self-growth.[12] This seems to be the case when people can connect with the meaning of the life event and reflect on their contribution.

By contrast, those with *avoidant* attachment strategies tend to display lower levels of distress about the separation than those who use anxious attachment strategies. They are also less likely to engage in contact with their ex-partner or attempt to reconcile and are more likely to use self-reliant coping strategies.[13] This might be because avoidant attachment strategies often involve emotional distancing, which could mean that they are either less emotionally impacted by the loss, or, less aware of the emotional impact of the loss on their emotional world. As a result, they might be more at risk of hurtling through the grieving process, skipping over painful emotion, and not processing the loss to a great enough depth to learn from it.[14] While they might appear to be coping well on the outside, they might not be feeling as resolved on the inside. This could explain reports of poorer post-divorce emotional well-being and adjustment for those with avoidant attachment strategies compared to those with secure attachment strategies. It might be that that some significant losses penetrate through the defences of people who use avoidant attachment strategies.[15]

Finally, if you have *fearful-avoidant* attachment strategies, which incorporate elements of anxious pursuit and avoidant withdrawal, you might experience both anxious distress at this relationship loss and withdrawal from its emotional consequences. Being aware of your coping strategies and how they might fluctuate and flow will be important in your grieving process.

The work of healthy grieving

To cope with a loss as monumental as this, it requires two key undertakings; leaning into the emotional pain to process and learn from it *and* distancing from the emotional pain enough to be able to move forward with your life. This involves two important emotional processes at once, turning up the heat in some areas, and turning down the heat in others. The *emotional* work of grief includes thinking about your lost partner, reflecting on the relationship and how it ended, remembering the good times and the bad times, reflecting on what you've learned from this relationship, and being with the pain of the loss. This work is demanding and needs to be balanced with the other key task of grieving, which is the *practical* work of coping with day-to-day life. This means adjusting the practical aspects of your life to accommodate this loss. This relates to living arrangements, changes to finances, managing co-parenting of any children, changing employment status, or the building of new social connections. This is distinct from the emotional work of grief and does require an element of distancing from overwhelming, painful emotion to be achieved. However, that does not mean that there is not an emotional element to these life decisions and adjustments. Both the emotional and the practical tasks of grieving are equally important to a person's progress in adjusting to the loss of this relationship.

Healthy grief is thought to balance these two tasks and to move flexibly between them so that emotions can be attended to, and life-transitioning can be accomplished. A person's cultural context is also important in governing and supporting their expression of grief and their engagement in practical tasks. Cultural belief systems teach us about how grief is manifested and expressed, and this is an important part of how a person processes their loss. All reactions are welcome and all are important as part of your individual response to the loss of your relationship. Emotions may feel manageable at some times and not at others, your ability to attend to the practicalities of adjusting to this loss may come and go. In whatever way works for you, attending to both tasks, the emotional and practical, is vital to the recovery process.

The model of grief that I am referring to is called the *Dual Process Model of Coping with Bereavement*[16] and it offers a clear way through grief by focusing on the balance between the emotional and the practical work of grieving. This model acknowledges that no one can be deeply processing their emotional experience all the time and still function, and also that it would not be healthy to be exclusively focused on the practicalities of moving on either. This model is realistic in highlighting that we will move into and out of either task, sometimes making adaptive practical decisions, only to be overtaken by painful emotions and side-lined from decision-making. Sometimes we need to emotionally tune out and allow for some distraction from the "heavy-duty work" of grief. Other times we might be able to laugh at happy memories or allow ourselves to cry and mourn for the loss. There can be a comfort in feeling the pain, just as there can in having a break from it and focusing on practical tasks. As I say in my book on relationship loss, so long as you are processing emotion, focusing on practicalities, and allowing yourself to breathe, then no matter how messy and disorganised it might appear, you are doing the work needed to successfully navigate this loss.[17]

Strategies for managing grief

As you enter into the work of grief, I want to help you to keep an eye on *both* the emotional and the practical tasks of grieving so that these important areas are attended to and neither one is neglected. We know that becoming absorbed in painful emotion for long periods of time is going to impact your ability to function in life, and, we know that suppressing or ignoring painful emotions is effortful and wearing.[18] Therefore, managing and processing grief involves self-awareness and attending to both these tasks. If we think of the emotions swirling around following a loss as being full of heat, we need to be able to manage the level of that heat so that we can function in the world, while processing this loss. This means being able to turn up the heat if you notice that you are not attending to the emotions related to this loss and turning down the heat if you are becoming overwhelmed. The same goes for the practical work of adjusting to this loss. If you notice that there are practical considerations that you are avoiding, plan to tackle them gradually, but directly. Alternatively, if you are only focusing on the practical, you might need to turn down the heat in that area and to be more intentional about making time to tune into your emotional world.

When you can observe yourself and hold these two important tasks of grieving in mind, then you are flexibly meeting the challenge of grief. I have earlier referred to this as "Goldilocks flexibility"[19] because it requires a "just right" level of attunement to emotion and a focus on the practical to navigate this tough time. Let's look at how to develop self-awareness, some practical ways to manage the "heat" of your emotions, and how to make the practical adjustments required for the next chapter of your life.

Know your attachment strategies

Your attachment strategies play a role in how you respond to the challenge of grief, and which of these two important tasks comes naturally, and which might feel more difficult. Knowing this can prove invaluable for tailoring your focus as you process this loss. For instance, people with *avoidant* attachment strategies might naturally find themselves managing the practical tasks of adjusting to the loss of their relationship, but they might move away from the emotional tasks required to process the loss. They might need to turn up the heat on their emotional processing and work harder to search for and to listen to their vulnerable feelings to be sure that they are accessed and learned from. Alternatively, someone with *anxious* attachment strategies might naturally do the emotional work of grieving, but, can feel all at sea when it comes to the practical adjustments they need to make to move on from this loss. They might need to work harder to turn down the heat on their emotional reactions and to set aside some time for focusing on the practical arrangements that need to be made to enact the next phase of their life.

Bowlby observed that people struggled in their acceptance of a loss if they either moved too quickly through the phases of grief or if they became arrested in either the protest or despair phase – if they skimmed over the emotional processing or became stuck in it. The challenge for most people when grieving the loss of an attachment bond is to manage the heat of their emotional responses so that they are "just right." For some, they need to access enough of their emotional response to learn from it, without avoiding it and thereby glossing over possibilities for learning and growth. For others, they become lost in their emotion and end up completely overwhelmed. I want to help you to be self-aware so that you can find this balance and can ensure that both the emotional and the practical tasks of grief are attended to.

Emotional processing

Reflecting on the loss and attuning to your emotional experience is vital to grieving, but *how* this reflection happens might be the key to whether it is a healing process or not. We can see that for people with anxious attachment strategies, who tend to experience their emotions more strongly, reflecting on their feelings about a loss can potentially block their recovery, especially if they experience extreme distress, remain stuck in the negative themes, and repeat unhelpful patterns from the past.[20] The potential silver lining in experiencing high levels of distress post-breakup is that it has the potential to exert a transformative effect, but that depends on how the pain is processed. Interestingly, those with avoidant attachment strategies are less at risk of becoming flooded with emotion, but they might miss opportunities for growth that come from the hardship.[21] However, how a person interacts with their post-loss raw feelings can determine whether they become stuck in their negative feelings or whether they move through them to achieve growth.

Taken in balance, we are discovering that spending time with your emotions and reflecting on the pain of a loss can be helpful *if* this contact allows you to process the loss in a productive way that leads to self-awareness and self-development. Spending time with your painful emotions is unhelpful if you experience them as overwhelming, and they keep you stuck in an endless loop of unproductive pain, which leads to unsuccessful attempts to be soothed and repeated rejections from others. Being aware of your own attachment strategies and whether your own emotional processing is helping or hindering your recovery is vital to being able to recover in the most meaningful and efficient way. No one wants to be hurting a moment longer than they need, but not hurting enough can mean that you miss an opportunity for self-knowledge and personal growth. Let's start by looking at how to manage emotions that feel "too much" and then we will look at how to work with experiences that are "not enough" emotionally.

Managing intense emotion

When reflecting on the idea of Goldilocks flexibility, if you find that the intensity of your emotional reaction following this loss is so high that you feel dysregulated and unable to focus on the practical elements of your grief work, then you might need some tools for managing more effectively. We know that processing painful emotions is part of the work of grief. However, if the intensity of your emotion is too high, then this is going to stall your recovery. For the healthy processing of grief, it is important to keep your feelings about this loss within a workable window of toler-ance.[22] This window needs to be wide enough that you can make contact with your painful feelings but not so wide that you become engulfed by them and thrown off balance. The aim is for you to be able to connect with your vulnerable emotions in a loving and open way that honours your pain and taps into the wisdom of your inner world and your own self-compassion. This will allow you to make sense of this loss and to find a new way forward for yourself. That is the best way to ensure that this suffering leads to growth rather than stagnation.

Some suggestions for managing intense emotions are writing down your feelings, such as journaling, or allowing yourself a period of time for rumi-nating on the loss and then distracting yourself with something enjoyable and absorbing to mark the end of that time. Another suggestion is to have a good and honest friend on speed dial to vent to and who can tell you if they see you going down self-destructive pathways or becoming stuck and ruminative. Managing your self-care is important, such as by eating well, getting enough sleep, and having enough regular exercise. These seemingly simple tools will resource you and improve your sense of resilience at this challenging time. Creating a structured plan of action for the next few months and gradually attacking the practical tasks that need addressing can help you feel a little more in charge of your path. Mindfulness and ground-ing techniques are very useful for regulating intense emotion. Being able to attend to your emotions and to observe them from a working distance is a valuable skill for getting the balance between feeling "too much" or "not enough" emotion. As we have explored earlier in this book, attuning to your most vulnerable emotions and teasing out the deeper need embedded within allows you to access the wisdom of your inner experience.

Accessing emotion

Rather than becoming swamped by painful emotion following the loss of this important relationship, you might find yourself feeling eerily unmoved.

Others might note with surprise that you seem to be "fine." You might be nailing the practical tasks of grief but neglecting the emotional tasks. This could be because you grew up using avoidant attachment strategies, such as turning away from or supressing your emotional world, preferring to stay distant from it, coping alone, and being logical and practical. While perfectly adaptive in many situations, this way of managing your inner world can mean that you neglect the emotional processing required to grieve, thereby missing opportunities for growth. This could mean that you turn away from your emotional experiences by not thinking about painful things such as your lost relationship and that you disengage from anything that might stir up feelings for you. The more you push your vulnerable feelings away, the more you can overlook internal lessons that can lead to growth. This is especially the case when a cherished relationship ends. So that you don't repeat past mistakes in future relationships, this is an important time to learn from the ending of this relationship.

After reading this book and learning about attachment, I imagine that you can see that connection with others and attuning to our emotions is important to our well-being as humans. Being able to engage with our own internal world rather than ignoring or denying parts of it is key to finding the meaning in our experience. However, this doesn't mean that we must be in our emotional world at all times; this would not be practical at all! Being able to pay attention to our emotional signals and to process them when we need to are central to emotional regulation.[23] This is a time where processing big emotions is much needed and can be beneficial to your overall growth.

If you have identified that you need to pay more attention to your vulnerable, primary emotions, then that is a great place to start changing the patterns of a lifetime. Simply by acknowledging that you have suffered an important loss, and taking the time to ask yourself how that feels, you are adding a new emotional regulation strategy to your tool kit. By talking about the lost relationship with someone you trust or writing down your thoughts about it, you ensure that you are not neglecting the emotional work of grief. Create time to tune into your emotional world by asking yourself what hurts the most about this loss and your role in it, reflecting on what you will miss, on what you regret, and on what you are grateful for. Spending time reflecting in this way is fundamental for processing your loss. Touching the pain honours your commitment to the relationship, even when it is over. The trickiest part of navigating raw emotions is being *with* our uncomfortable inner experiences. Ask yourself to visit your pain regularly, to stay there for a while – for short periods to build your capacity to touch and hold your painful experiences. This will expand your window of tolerance for being with this aspect of your experience and will allow you to access the learning and wisdom that comes from being with your pain in this open and accepting way. Paradoxically, the more you allow the pain to be there, and you attend to the pain in this new way, the more efficiently you can move into and through it. The more healthily and productively you can process your grief. Give yourself time and allow yourself the space to mourn the loss of this relationship and all it meant to you and still means to you.

Reorganisation and detachment

I am aware that the loss of this relationship is likely to be very new and very raw. You are no-doubt reeling from this loss and grappling with managing the two key tasks of grief – the emotional work and the practical work – as you navigate the inevitable emotional storms that arrive. As you ricochet around Bowlby's four phases of separation and loss, feeling numb and disbelieving, yearning, and searching for your lost love, accepting that it is over and plunging into despair, only to return to numbness, you are probably far from detaching from this relationship.

At some stage in the grieving process, you will need to "undo" the attachment bond with your ex-partner as you redefine or completely sever your bond. This is a sobering reality of the grieving process and the fourth of Bowlby's phases. He said that in order to successfully adjust to the loss of an attachment figure, people need to reorganise their inner world in such a way that they no longer seek out the lost love as a safe haven or secure base.[24] This means that you will need to redefine how you see your ex-partner and to no longer seek them out for your attachment needs. They are no longer your special other and need to be placed further from your heart. They are no longer the first person you will call with good news or who you will turn to when you feel uncertain. This can be extremely painful and can take some time. It is important that you accept that this relationship is forever changed, and that you build other attachment bonds – strengthen your connection to other people who you can turn to in happy times and in sad. Reorganisation requires you to let go of this attachment bond, to build and strengthen other bonds, to be able to soothe yourself, and to map out a path forward without your lost love. What that looks like exactly is as individual as each person reading this book. No matter how it looks, reorganising your view of the other to fit with the new reality of your relationship and redirecting your attachment needs is the final task in the work of grief and loss. It might be too early for you at this stage, but I want to flag that this is the marker of the resolution of this attachment bond. Give yourself time but keep this essential principle in mind.

Notes

1 Sbarra, D.A., & Emery, R.E. (2005). The emotional sequelae of nonmarital relationship dissolution: Analysis of change and intraindividual variability over time. *Personal Relationships*, 12, 213–232.

2 Bowlby, J. (1979). *The making and breaking of affectional bonds*. London: Tavistock.

3 Fraley, R.C., & Shaver, P.R. (1999). Loss and bereavement: Attachment theory and recent controversies concerning "grief work" and the nature of detachment. In J. Cassidy & P.R. Shaver (Eds.). *Handbook of attachment: Theory, research, and clinical applications* (pp. 735–759). New York: Guilford.

4 Worden, W.J. (2018). *Grief counselling and grief therapy, 5th edition: A handbook for the mental health professional*. New York, NY: Springer Publishing Company.

5 Bowlby, J. (1980). *Attachment and loss: Volume 3. loss: Sadness and depression*. New York: Basic Books.

6 Sbarra, D.A., & Emery, R.E. (2005). The emotional sequelae of nonmarital relationship dissolution: Analysis of change and intraindividual variability over time. *Personal Relationships*, 12, 213–232.

7 Sbarra, D.A. (2006). Predicting the onset of emotional recovery following nonmarital relationship dissolution: A survival analyses of sadness and anger. *Personality and Social Psychology Bulletin*, 32, 298–312.

8 Madey, S.F., & Jilek, L. (2012). Attachment style and dissolution of romantic relationships: Breaking up is hard to do, or is it? *Individual Differences Research*, 10(4), 202–210.

9 Davis, D., Shaver, P.R., & Vernon, M.L. (2003). Physical, emotional and behavioural reactions to breaking up: The roles of gender, age, emotional involvement, and attachment style. *Personality & Social Psychology Bulletin*, 29(7), 871–884.

10 Shaver, P.R., & Mikulincer, M. (2016). *Attachment in adulthood: Structure, dynamics and change* (2nd ed.). New York: The Guilford Press.

11 Fagundes, C.P. (2012). Getting over you: Contributions of attachment theory for post-breakup emotional adjustment. *Personal Relationships*, 19, 37–50.

12 Tedeschi, R.G., & Calhoun, L.G. (2004). Posttraumatic growth: Conceptual foundations and empirical evidence. *Psychological Inquiry*, 15(1), 1–18.

13 Davis, D., Shaver, P.R., & Vernon, M.L. (2003). Physical, emotional and behavioural reactions to breaking up: The roles of gender, age, emotional involvement, and attachment style. *Personality & Social Psychology Bulletin*, 29(7), 871–884.

14 Marshall, T.C., Bejanyan, K., & Ferenczi, N. (2013). Attachment styles and personal growth following romantic breakups: The mediating roles of distress, rumination, and tendency to rebound. *PLoS One*, 8(9), e75161.

15 Birnbaum, G.E., Orr, I., Mikulincer, M., & Florian, V. (1997). When marriage breaks up: Does attachment contribute to coping and mental health? *Journal of Social and Personal Relationships*, 14, 643–654.

16 Stroebe, M., & Schut, H. (1999). The dual process model of coping with bereavement: Rationale and description. *Death Studies*, 23, 197–224.

17 Rosoman, C. (2022). *An emotionally focused guide to relationship loss: Life after love*. New York: Routledge.

18 Gross, J.J., & Levenson, R.W. (1997). Hiding feelings: The acute effects of inhibited negative and positive emotion. *Journal of Abnormal Psychology*, 106(1), 95–103.

19 Rosoman, C. (2022). *An emotionally focused guide to relationship loss: Life after love*. New York: Routledge.

20 Nolen-Hoeksema, S., Parker, L.E., & Larson, J. (1994). Ruminative coping with depressed mood following loss. *Journal of Personality and Social Psychology*, 67(1), 92–104.

21 Fagundes, C.P. (2012). Getting over you: Contributions of attachment theory for post-breakup emotional adjustment. *Personal Relationships*, 19, 37–50.
22 Siegel, D.J. (1999). *The developing mind*. New York: Guilford.
23 Shaver, P.R., & Mikulincer, M. (2016). *Attachment in adulthood: Structure, dynamics and change* (2nd ed.). New York: The Guilford Press.
24 Bowlby, J., & Parkes, C.M. (1970). Separation and loss within the family. In E.J. Anthony & C. Koupernik (Eds.). *The child in his family: International yearbook of child psychiatry and allied professionals* (pp. 197–216). New York: Wiley.

Chapter 12

Stronger in the broken place

For those who can restore the security of their bond, this chapter provides a brief opportunity to reflect on the healing process and on each partner's strengths and resilience in working through this painful relational rupture. This allows us to marvel at all you have learned from this harsh life event and all that you contributed to the healing process. We can explore the growth that comes from hardship and what you have discovered because of this attachment injury – about yourself, your partner, and about your bond. In this way, we can use the suffering you have endured for growth. Hardships can become incorporated into the story of the relationship. You become the heroes in the story of your resilient relationship – how you struggled but fought to overcome obstacles to preserve your bond, often against all odds. Your efforts to repair and strengthen your bond are now part of your story together. This injury is part of the relationship "survival narrative."[1] Your bond is stronger in the broken place for having weathered this event. That certainly deserves acknowledgement and celebration! It is a testament to your courage and dedication that your bond has endured and grown beyond this attachment injury. Let's look at all you have achieved and how you can savour and protect these efforts into the future.

Stronger in the broken place

Let your mind wander back for a moment to how it felt at the time of the attachment injury, when you were desperately stuck in a negative cycle that left you bruised and your bond in tatters. Remember how alone you felt with the pain of having your trust broken by or being hurtful to the one you love. Recall how you viewed your partner, the swirl of confusing thoughts and feelings you had about them, and the negative attributions you were making about their motivations and intent. Remember how you viewed yourself and all the faults you would berate yourself over. Recall the bleak lens through which you viewed your relationship. I hope that

DOI: 10.4324/9781003466499-17

you feel differently now. Reflecting on the starting point, the lowest time in your relationship, is a powerful way of observing just how far you have come. I hope that you have felt held in your pain, met in your shame, and that you and your partner have emerged stronger, together, for having endured this body-blow to your attachment bond. To have committed to this work and to have made it to this chapter, you are truly amazing.

Not only have you repaired the damage by attending gently to each other's feelings and rubbing soothing balm on the wounds to be found there, you have committed to a process that has knitted the broken pieces of your attachment bond back together. You have spent time unpacking all the elements of this injury to make sure that it is attended to and repaired. You have explored the surrounding injuries and the negative cycle that might have pre-dated the primary attachment injury to make sure that you have a new, positive cycle in place to help you to navigate any rocky patches moving forward. Now, you have new strategies and new experiences with each other, built through mutual risk and mutual vulnerability. In so doing, you have created a strong and solid base for your relationship, with nothing left lurking in the basement to undermine its security. Importantly, you have strengthened your bond with practice – exercising the muscles of your new cycle until it is honed and strong. With all these listed efforts, you have repaired the broken bone of your bond, and it is now *stronger in the broken place*. This is a remarkable achievement and you both deserve to bask in its glow!

Due to your hard work, your relationship bond is not just surviving, it is thriving. You now have a blueprint for lasting love. Life changes, people change, we face difficulties, life happens. So long as you can meet these challenges with the same steps that you have followed in this book to restore your loving bond, you have all the ingredients needed to hold onto each other for the long term. The concepts we have looked at in this book come from Emotionally Focused therapy and its Attachment Injury Resolution Model and have been proven to reduce relationship distress, to resolve attachment injuries, and to create secure bonds that last for the long haul.[2] When partners commit to a resolution process such as this, they are investing in their relationship and insuring it against future storms. The conversations you have had throughout this work are not easily forgotten, we don't tend to forget moments such as these where we allow our deepest vulnerabilities to be witnessed and soothed by a safe other. These moments change us as people, we grow, we expand. Our relationship grows, and the benefits last over time.[3] Sue Johnson says that conversations where partners are accessible, responsive, and engaged are the language of love. They keep your bond alive and growing.[4]

You now have the secret formula for creating lasting bonds – bonds that can withstand the roughest of terrain and endure into the future.

Reflections on Healing

Take a moment to reflect on the process of healing this attachment injury

Partner 1	Partner 2
What did you bring to the healing process? What did you find most difficult? What are you most proud of yourself for?	What did you bring to the healing process? What did you find most difficult? What are you most proud of yourself for?
What did your partner contribute that was most helpful for you? What have you learned about them? What are you most proud of them for?	What did your partner contribute that was most helpful for you? What have you learned about them? What are you most proud of them for?
What have you learned about yourself from this process? Your strengths? Your needs?	What have you learned about yourself from this process? Your strengths? Your needs?
What have you learned about your partner & your relationship from this process?	What have you learned about your partner & your relationship from this process?

Clare Rosoman 2024

Figure 12.1 Reflection on the healing process.

Let's savour the contributions you have each made and all that you have learned about yourself and your partner. Figure 12.1 will guide to reflect on what you have each brought to and learned from the healing process. Take special note of the particular things that your partner did or said during the repair process that made an impression on you and let them know. Consider what you have learned about yourself, your partner, and your relationship from this process.

Survival narrative

The time-honoured wisdom that good can come from hardship represents the remarkable human capacity to adapt and to thrive. That doesn't mean that working through tough times is simple, but the most important lessons never are. It does promise that humans facing challenges are capable of positive change, of not just surviving a difficult experience and returning to normal functioning, but of growing *beyond* their normal functioning. This is the idea of post-traumatic growth, and it doesn't happen if the lesson doesn't fully seize our attention. In fact, an essential element that determines if a person experiences growth from a trauma is how disorganising it is to their inner world.[5] That is one thing that is for sure about attachment injuries – they certainly grab our attention. When something goes wrong in your life, so wrong that it challenges all your assumptions about the world, about right and wrong, good and bad, about the order of things, about your place in the world, then it is powerful enough to change your view of everything. When the traumatic event you face outstrips your ability to manage, then it truly becomes an opportunity for growth. As awful as it was to face this breach of trust in your attachment bond, the kind of suffering that shatters your core assumptions in this way is more likely to lead to growth than other less agonising life lessons. This is a fundamental part of our human make-up. Pain of this kind makes you question everything. By its nature – because it is so destabilising – it provides an opportunity for transformation. It can be a resource for meaning and growth.

However, it is not enough to have just faced hardship and endured. Transformation happens as result of *how* a person faces that hardship. When people can rise to the challenge of confronting and exploring a trauma such as an attachment injury and can adapt to the changes required of them, then they will grow. That is the process that you have committed to in this book. I am not suggesting you ever need to feel gratitude that this has happened, but I am hoping that all this pain and difficulty has been put to good use as you worked to repair this bond. I hope that you have emerged stronger for this struggle. When people can do this, then they can find meaning in the most disturbing of experiences. Some of the benefits of post-traumatic growth are an increased appreciation of life, a realigning of priorities, closer and more meaningful relationships with others, increased empathy and compassion for others, increased awareness of your own personal strength, tuning into your spirituality, and forging a new direction in life.[6] Now that is awe-inspiring adaptation in action! These positive changes reflect an ongoing life-long process of the development of wisdom. They represent a happy by-product of adversity; not merely surviving, but flourishing.

In light of this, I encourage you to reframe how you view this attachment injury. Instead of seeing it as the darkest time in your relationship and wishing it never happened, tell the story of triumph – of how you struggled and survived. Yes, mistakes were made, yes, you wobbled severely and came close to losing this treasured bond. How mighty is your love to have weathered these toughest of times? Reframe this event as the greatest proof of your commitment to this bond and care for each other. Celebrate your victory! You have toiled for this relationship, you have cried for it, risked for it, put your own needs aside for it, stood your ground and put it all on the line, you have surrendered to the other's care with no guarantee of repair – that means a lot! No one would put their heart on the line unless it mattered greatly. When humans are willing to face extreme hardship for something that matters to them, that is what true grit is made of. You are strong and brave as individuals and even stronger together, united. This is your relationship survival narrative!

Tell the story of your resilient relationship. The story you tell about your relationship is meaningful. As it lays down the wisdom acquired in these hard-won lessons, this narrative becomes a guide for avoiding future troubles. It honours the dedication and commitment from you both and the strength of your bond to survive adversity. In Figure 12.2, I hope that, together, you can write your relationship survival narrative and celebrate your relationship's resilience.

Attachment rituals

The work you have put in to restore the security in your attachment bond is tremendous, and we want this to last a lifetime. An important way that you can maintain and tend to your relationship's bond is by intentionally creating moments to come together to celebrate your relationship. We call these attachment rituals because they are repeated, purposeful actions that recognise the specialness of the connection.[7] These actions are sacred to the two of you and to your relationship. They are the little and the big things that celebrate belonging and that signify your importance to each other. They might be small signals that only you share or understand. A lot can be conveyed in a word, or a phrase, or a touch. Attachment rituals signal love, care, and specialness.

Relationship Survival Narrative

Celebrate your success by telling the story of how you triumphed over adversity to repair this attachment injury & to nurture your precious bond.

How did you struggle & lose your way?

How did you respond to this challenge & triumph?

How have you emerged stronger together for this hardship?

Clare Rosoman 2024

Figure 12.2 Relationship survival narrative.

Paying attention to rituals that might already be there as well as creating new ones can be part of how you maintain your bond. Think for a moment about the small ways and perhaps large ways that you and your partner let each other know that you are special to one another. What are the things that only you share, that you miss doing when you are not in your usual routine, or that others wouldn't understand? Do you have a ritual around hellos and goodbyes or saying good night? How do you celebrate birthdays, anniversaries, successes, or sad times? What little gestures or inside jokes do you share? How does it feel when you share those moments of contact? What we don't tend to can easily drift away. Talking about these rituals together and letting your partner know what their gestures mean to you is a wonderful way to nurture your connection.

To build more attachment rituals, you can pay attention to greetings, partings, and celebrations, making sure that you acknowledge and cherish them. You can offer regular signals of affection or develop a shared understanding about certain gestures that act like codes. One couple I worked with used three hand squeezes as a code for "I love you." This was precious to them and could be signalled at any time without anyone else registering it. You can develop a daily ritual of checking-in with each other, share a cup of tea, or walk the dog. You can set aside longer sections of time to do things together like going for an outing or holiday. These might happen less frequently, but they are planned for as a way to prioritise time together. These seemly small actions can exert a protective function over your relationship by feeding your bond, assuring you of your importance to the other, and creating goodwill. Attachment rituals keep your bond nourished and supple. This means that it has some stretch in it and can better weather minor ruptures, such as small hurts, misunderstandings, or absences. Figure 12.3 will help you to talk about some attachment rituals in your relationship.

Celebration

As a way of appreciating your progress from distress to recovery, in this final chapter you have reflected on the work that went into repairing your bond and what you each brought to this process. You have reflected on all that you have learned and how you have each grown from this hardship. You have observed how your bond has strengthened and deepened for having weathered this injury. Finally, you have savoured your relationship's survival narrative and looked at ways to nurture this growth and tend to your bond into the future with attachment rituals. This progress deserves celebrating!

You have fought for your relationship and, in so doing, have confronted the most difficult and painful places that any of us can visit. Loving is

Attachment Rituals

This sheet will help you to think about attachment rituals you might already have & others you can develop to maintain your attachment security.

What is an attachment ritual?

An attachment ritual is something that you & your partner do to celebrate & acknowledge your connection. They are repeated, purposeful actions that are special to the two of you & to your relationship. They are small signals that only you share or understand. They are the things that denote this relationship's uniqueness to you both & that celebrate belonging. A lot can be conveyed in a word, or a phrase, or a touch. Attachment rituals signal love, care, & specialness. Paying attention to rituals that might already be there as well as creating new ones can be part of how you maintain your bond. What we don't tend to can easily drift away. Talking about these rituals together & letting your partner know what their gestures mean to you is a wonderful way to nurture your connection.

Examples of attachment rituals

Here are some examples of attachment rituals:

- Acknowledging hellos & goodbyes
- Having time together everyday to check-in & see how the other is feeling
- Doing a task together like cooking, walking the dog, having a cup of tea
- Small affectionate touches or gestures
- Having a TV show you watch together
- Learning a new skill together
- Leaving notes for each other or sending messages throughout the day

What are some attachment rituals you already do? Can you let your partner know the things they do that mean a lot to you?

Intentionally adding more attachment rituals

To maintain your bond, are there some more attachment rituals you would like to add? Can you come up with a list together?

Clare Rosoman 2024

Figure 12.3 Attachment rituals.

certainly not for the faint of heart, but we are wired to keep on forming attachment bonds with special others, even if those ties can be perilous. Instead of giving up on love and connection, you have risked for the sake of this bond. After all, nothing worth having is free from risk. I know that you will have grown as a result – together and as individuals. I hope that you are proud of this brave work and the mettle it requires. We build our models of love from an accumulation of interactions with those who are special to us. Through the work you have done in this book and with each other, you have created many more moments of love and connection to be added to your blueprint for what it means to love and be loved. My hope for you is that you can take this growth and the wonderful security that you have cultivated and nurtured forward into a long and happy future together.

Notes

1 Rosoman, C. (2022). *An emotionally focused guide to relationship loss: Life after love.* New York: Routledge.
2 Johnson, S.M., & Talitman, E. (1997). Predictors of success in emotionally focused marital therapy. *Journal of Marital & Family Therapy*, 23, 135–152.
3 Halchuk, R.E., Makinen, J.A., & Johnson, S.M. (2010). Resolving attachment injuries in couples using emotionally focused therapy: A three-year follow-up. *Journal of Couple & Relationship Therapy: Innovations in Clinical and Educational Interventions*, 9, 31–47.
4 Johnson, S.M. (2008). *Hold me tight: Seven conversations for a lifetime of love.* New York, NY: Little, Brown.
5 Tedeschi, R.G., & Calhoun, L.G. (2004). Posttraumatic growth: Conceptual foundations and empirical evidence. *Psychological Inquiry*, 15(1), 1–18.
6 Tedeschi, R.G., & Calhoun, L.G. (2004). Posttraumatic growth: Conceptual foundations and empirical evidence. *Psychological Inquiry*, 15(1), 1–18.
7 Johnson, S.M. (2008). *Hold me tight: Seven conversations for a lifetime of love.* New York, NY: Little, Brown.

Index

For Product Safety Concerns and Information please contact our EU
representative GPSR@taylorandfrancis.com
Taylor & Francis Verlag GmbH, Kaufingerstraße 24, 80331 München, Germany

www.ingramcontent.com/pod-product-compliance
Lightning Source LLC
Chambersburg PA
CBHW052002270326
41929CB00015B/2761